THE MEASUREMENT
OF ABILITIES

The
FACTORIAL ANALYSIS
OF HUMAN ABILITY

by

Godfrey H. Thomson, D.Sc., Ph.D.

The theory of factorial analysis is mathematical in nature, but this book has been written so that it can, it is hoped, be read by those who have no mathematics beyond the most elementary school knowledge. **16/-** NET.

" The book must at once take its place as one of the most important publications of the year in the field of education and psychology." *Nature.*

UNIVERSITY OF LONDON PRESS, LTD.

THE MEASUREMENT
OF ABILITIES

By

PHILIP E. VERNON, M.A., Ph.D.

**Lecturer in Psychology, University of Glasgow
Formerly Head of Department of Psychology,
Jordanhill Training College, Glasgow**

UNIVERSITY OF LONDON PRESS LTD.

10 & 11 WARWICK LANE, LONDON, E.C.4

FIRST PRINTED . . . . *January* 1940

AGENTS OVERSEAS

AUSTRALIA, NEW ZEALAND
AND SOUTH SEA ISLANDS
          W. S. SMART, P.O. Box 120 C.C.,
                              SYDNEY, N.S.W.
CANADA
          CLARKE, IRWIN & Co., Ltd.,
            480–486 University Avenue,
                              TORONTO.
INDIA
          LONGMANS, GREEN & Co., Ltd.,
            BOMBAY : Nicol Road.
            CALCUTTA : 17 Chittaranjan Avenue.
            MADRAS : 36A Mount Road.
SOUTH AFRICA
          H. B. TIMMINS, P.O. Box 94,
                              CAPE TOWN.

Printed in Great Britain for the UNIVERSITY OF LONDON PRESS LTD.,
by HAZELL, WATSON AND VINEY, LTD., London and Aylesbury.

PREFACE

THE present century has seen extensive developments in methods of measuring scientifically the traits and abilities of human beings. Three main influences may be discovered behind this movement. First, there is the tremendous interest which people have always shown in judging one another's qualities. Much of their conversation consists in summing up their acquaintances. Their plans, either for work or play, are very largely guided by their notions regarding the persons with whom they are about to deal. It is obvious that such notions are frequently biased or inaccurate, and yet each one continues to rely, in great affairs or small, chiefly on his own insight into the characters of others. However, it is recognized that in certain spheres of human activity, more accurate and impartial assessments are essential. The examination system, now firmly established in schools, universities, and in many professions, is supposed to measure the achievements and capacities of pupils, of students, and of candidates for various jobs. Although this system is certainly an advance on the earlier system of personal judgments, yet much doubt exists as to its efficiency. A considerable section of this book is therefore devoted to a discussion of the defects of examinations, and of present-day methods of marking pupils' or students' work, and to a study of how these may be improved.

Secondly, mankind is interested, not only in individuals, but also in general problems of human nature and human institutions. Thus another field where accurate measures of human qualities are needed is the scientific investigation of mind, behaviour, and society. Loose thinking and prejudice are extremely prevalent in matters of politics, economics, religion, crime, and the like—as is shown, for

v

example, by Thouless in his book *Straight and Crooked Thinking* (1930). Yet the social sciences, such as psychology and sociology, are endeavouring to study these subjects rationally and impartially, in the same manner as the physicist studies the atom, or the physiologist the workings of the body. Now the data from which a science is built up are very largely numerical and quantitative. The records of a chemical or physical experiment usually consist of measures of weights, times, distances, galvanometer or thermometer readings. Measurement is almost equally important for purposes of precise description and experiment in the social sciences ; and the deduction of sound conclusions from such quantitative data frequently involves the application of statistical treatment. In this connection, then, we shall consider below the nature of measurement in psychology, and the elements of statistical technique, with especial reference to the field of education.

A third source of the mental testing movement lies in the desire for human betterment. Medical science has advanced enormously in its ability to diagnose and treat bodily ills, but psychiatry and psychology are only beginning to learn how to handle mental abnormalities. Yet there are already, in addition to the mental hospitals, numerous clinics where the diagnosis and treatment of emotionally maladjusted patients—adults and children— are carried out. Special schools, and tutorial classes in some ordinary schools, play their part by providing a type of education suited to children who are too greatly handicapped, mentally or physically, to make progress under ordinary school conditions. Industrial schools and the Borstal system aim at re-educating delinquents and budding criminals, so as to turn them into useful members of society. The staffs of all these institutions need accurate methods of measuring the educational and occupational capacities of the ' patients.' Actually many of our most valuable mental tests were first constructed by workers in the fields of educational, emotional, and vocational guidance.

This book is thus intended primarily for three classes of students, namely teachers and examiners, psychologists and others who set out to investigate human phenomena from the scientific standpoint, and doctors and psychologists who wish to make practical use of tests in clinics and schools. It makes no attempt to describe the various mental tests (though a classified list of them is included in Chap. IX), since many good accounts of the main ones are already available, e.g. by Knight (1933), Blackburn (1939), Oakley and Macrae (1937). Most authors, however, seem to have emphasized the value of tests without sufficiently drawing attention to their dangers and difficulties. Thus the main object of this book is to outline the principles of test construction and application or procedure, and the interpretation of the results of tests and examinations, ignorance of which on the part of testers has frequently led to serious errors. Mental measurement undoubtedly needs a high degree of skill, which few of the persons just mentioned have either the time or the opportunity to acquire thoroughly, before they set out to test or examine.

There are also available many excellent textbooks on statistical methods, perhaps the most useful to testers being those of Garrett (1937), Dawson (1933), and Guilford (1936). Yet in the present writer's experience, all of these are too difficult for the majority of students whose psychological training only amounts to between seventy-five and one hundred and fifty hours. This books aims, therefore, to describe the minimum essentials, to show their immediate application to psychological (and especially to educational) problems, and to stress their general significance rather than their technical details.

More advanced students are unlikely to find within much that is original. But, so far as the writer knows, no previous account of the statistics of marking, nor of the construction of new-type examinations, has been published by a British author. The analysis of educational measurement and the discussion of the technique of examining are partly new but owe a great deal to Hamilton's brilliant book, *The Art of Interrogation* (1929). Possibly also some of the practical hints about tests and testing have not been published before.

Lack of space has necessitated some important omissions, such as the whole field of temperament and character assessment, the testing of special (vocational) aptitudes, and of sensory-motor capacities. Actually few of the tests falling under these headings are well standardized, and fewer still can safely be applied by those who are not trained psychologists. The questionnaire, the interview, observational techniques, and the application of scientific methods to educational and social-psychological experiments, are other topics which may, it is hoped, be dealt with in a later volume.

I wish to express my thanks to Mr. B. Babington Smith and to Mr. P. Kemp for reading parts of the manuscript, and for giving valuable suggestions and criticisms. I am also especially indebted to my wife for her advice on points connected with teaching, and for her help in the preparation of the manuscript.

P. E. V.

THE UNIVERSITY,
   GLASGOW,
     July 1939.

CONTENTS

ix

LIST OF FIGURES

LIST OF FIGURES

CHAPTER I

INTRODUCTION TO STATISTICAL METHODS

IT is an unfortunate, yet indubitable, fact that the majority of students of psychology and education find extreme difficulty in grasping and applying the statistical concepts which are an essential prerequisite to sound mental measurement. They take fright at the mere mention of statistics or at the sight of statistical symbols and formulæ. A small minority, on the other hand, find in the manipulations of numbers which we call statistics an intense fascination, closely akin to the musical composer's fascination with interweavings of sounds. Probably statistical ability is as specialized and as rare as is ability in musical composition, and the expert statistician rather easily loses touch with the doubts and difficulties of the beginner. He fails to realize that the statistical way of looking at educational or psychological phenomena, which comes so naturally to him, is at first entirely foreign to the average student. Yet the student's 'phobia' is certainly unnecessary, since the elementary statistics needed for the proper treatment of marks and test scores includes little more than the kind of algebra and arithmetic which he mastered by the age of 14. Statistics means nothing more than numerical data, such as measurements, examination and test results ; and statistical methods are merely the ways of dealing with, or organizing, these data so as to bring out their full significance.

The *raison d'être* of statistical methods is that human beings are apt to differ so widely from one another in any and every measurable characteristic, that results or conclusions which apply to one person or one group of persons (e.g. one school class), do not necessarily apply to another

1

person or group. First, then, we must have efficient techniques of arranging or tabulating the scores and marks obtained from different people, in order to see what is the general run of their scores, and what is the range or extent of the differences. These techniques are described in the present chapter. The ' general run ' and the ' range or extent ' of scores next require more precise definition and measurement ; that is to say, we must know how to work out averages and indices of what is called spread, scatter, dispersion, or variability (Chap. III).

Not only do human beings differ from one another, but also each individual varies in his capacities and characteristics from time to time. The score he achieves to-day may or may not be typical of his usual accomplishments. The same holds true of a class of pupils or students. The extent of this untrustworthiness or *unreliability* (as it is generally termed) of a single measurement or of a set of measurements therefore needs to be determined. Statistical treatment will tell us whether any alteration or variation in scores represents a real and important change—such a change, for example, as we might hope to bring about by means of the teaching given to the individual or to the class —or whether it is merely a matter of chance fluctuations. A further very common and important problem is the reality or significance of a difference between two groups of people. For instance, girls may appear to be better than boys at reading ; but this is not true of all girls and all boys ; so we must have a method of establishing how general and how reliable is the difference (Chap. V).

Still another type of variation requires special techniques of investigation, namely, the variations in people's capacities in different spheres. It is obvious that no one is even all-round in his level of abilities. Yet we are apt to assume that high achievement in one field implies high achievement in other fields. Sometimes also we infer the opposite type of relationship—that if a person is strong in some trait, then he will be lacking in some other trait. The statistical methods of *correlation* enable us to say how far various traits or abilities ' go together ' or are related to one another. They also tell us how far our tests or examinations measure what they are supposed to measure, i.e. how *valid* they are. For example, a Certificate or Matriculation examination at the age of 16–18 may, or may not, validly predict success in a subsequent university career (Chaps. VI–VIII).

Although statistical methods are, then, of undoubted importance, their limitations should also be recognized at this stage in our discussion. They are tools for handling numerical data, but they are not capable of improving data which may be initially inaccurate or biased. When an investigator uses a poor test or examination, or when he observes and records people's behaviour or mental processes wrongly, no amount of statistical treatment of his results can correct such deficiencies. Further, the fundamentally abstract nature of statistical methods needs to be stressed. They are adapted primarily for mass-investigations of measurements obtained from large numbers of persons, and such investigations are apt to lose touch with the concrete individual case. Without them we could not make sound generalizations about human beings, but even with them we cannot usually state whether a generalization applies to a particular human being. The practical handling and understanding of an actual child or adult is still an art rather than a science, though it may be greatly assisted by scientific mental tests and guided by the results of objective psychological experiments and statistical studies.

TABULATION OF MEASURES

Measures and Variables.—By a variable we shall mean an ability or some other characteristic in respect of which human beings vary or differ from one another. Height, age, income, intelligence, examination success, are all variables in this sense. A measure is the numerical expression of a certain standing on, or amount of, a variable. Fifty inches of height, five pounds a week income, and a mark of 6 out of 10 are examples of measures.

Most variables are *continuous* ; that is to say, they can vary by infinitely small gradations. But we only measure them to the nearest convenient unit. For example, heights may be measured to the nearest tenth of an inch. But actually 50·1 inches includes all heights from 50·05 to 50·15 ; 50·2 inches includes from 50·15 to 50·25, and so on. Similarly, a school mark of 6 is usually an approximation representing all degrees of quality from $5\frac{1}{2}$ to $6\frac{1}{2}$. If, however, half-marks are awarded, then 6 represents $5\frac{3}{4}$ to $6\frac{1}{4}$, and $6\frac{1}{2}$ represents $6\frac{1}{4}$ to $6\frac{3}{4}$, and so on. But some variables are *discrete* or discontinuous, since they only vary by units. For instance, if the size of a class of pupils is 40, this does not imply between $39\frac{1}{2}$ and $40\frac{1}{2}$ pupils. The scores for many tests, and some school marks, are of this type, for they represent the exact numbers of questions or test items correctly answered. Thus a pupil would score 6 out of 10 for arithmetic sums even if he had nearly completed a seventh sum. (Such measures are referred to in the next chapter as count or enumeration scores.)

This distinction between continuous and discrete variables needs to be borne in mind when tabulating measures (cf. p. 6).

Tabulation.—Tabulation means arranging a set of measures in an orderly fashion, so as to convey the essential facts about them in convenient and relatively brief form. If we take a class of pupils, and beside each pupil's name write his age, or exam. mark, we get a *list*, but it is not a *table*, since the measures are quite haphazardly arranged. It is very difficult to see from such a list, if it be a long one, what is the general run and range of measures, or whether any particular measure (e.g. John Smith's 6 out of 10) is high, low, or average.

Ranking.—One way of tabulating is to rearrange all the measures in order of size from highest to lowest ; that is, to put them in rank order. The desired information can then be grasped much more readily. But this is a laborious process if the number of pupils is large.

Frequency Distributions.—Under such circumstances it

is better to write in a column each possible measure, in order, and beside it the frequency, *F* ; that is, the number of persons who obtain each measure. The result is called a frequency distribution, since it shows how the various measures are allotted or distributed among the persons.

Ex. 1.—The following is a list of the marks (out of 20) which were awarded to a class of 50 pupils. The table below shows their frequency distribution. Marks : 10, 7, 5, 17, 15, 13, 4, 6, 9, 15, 16, 20, 17, 19, 14, 9, 11, 17, 18, 8, 1, 9, 12, 19, 16, 15, 17, 14, 13, 10, 6, 20, 15, 18, 17, 13, 11, 4, 16, 13, 8, 14, 18, 15, 12, 17, 16, 15, 17, 2.

Measures		F
20	/ /	2
19	/ /	2
18	/ / /	3
17	//// / /	7
16	/ / / /	4
15	//// /	6
14	/ / /	3
13	/ / / /	4
12	/ /	2
11	/ /	2
10	/ /	2
9	/ / /	3
8	/ /	2
7	/	1
6	/ /	2
5	/	1
4	/ /	2
3		0
2	/	1
1	/	1

N = 50

Hints on Drawing Up a Frequency Table.—Do *not* look through the original list and pick out all who got the highest measure, e.g. 20, then all who got the next highest, 19, and so on. This would be a waste of time and would easily lead to mistakes. Instead, go through the measures in the list consecutively, and as each one is reached, put a

2

tally or check mark opposite the appropriate measure in the column. When any one measure recurs for the fifth time, draw a line through the first four tallies. Repeat this on reaching the tenth, fifteenth, etc., tally. Add up the tallies to obtain the F column. Add up the F column itself to make sure that it checks with N, the total number of persons.

Distributions of Classified Measures.—The above procedure is still likely to produce an over-lengthy table, especially when N is large. It would be absurd, for example, to tabulate the heights of all the pupils of a school in this manner. Instead of listing the frequencies of children 40·0, 40·1, 40·2 . . . inches tall, we would give the totals with heights of 40, 41, 42 . . . inches, or the totals with heights of 40 upwards, 42 upwards, 44 upwards, and so on. That is, we would group together sets of contiguous measures under a series of *classes* or categories.

Considerable care is needed in deciding upon what is, or is not, included in a class. When the variable is discrete— for example, test scores ranging from 10 to 93—we may call our classes 10–14, 15–19, 20–24, etc., or else 10 +, 15 +, 20 +, etc. Both of these indicate clearly that all scores of 10, 11, 12, 13, and 14 are included in the first class, and that the size of each class is five units. The same methods may be used for school marks. For instance, 10%–14%, 15%–19% . . . is unambiguous, although, strictly speaking, the first class includes all shades of merit from $9\frac{1}{2}$% to $14\frac{1}{2}$%. But with some continuous variables such as age or height, difficulties often arise because the original measures are themselves only approximations which represent classes of measures (cf. p. 4). Thus if height has been measured to the nearest tenth of an inch, and is tabulated to the nearest inch, we should avoid calling our classes 40, 41, 42 . . ., etc. For 40 might include 39·95 to 40·95, or 39·45 to 40·45, or 39·55 to 40·55. If we write 40 +, 41 +, etc., the first of these is usually intended. With ages, 5 +, 6 + . . . is quite clear, since the 5 + class includes all children who are at, or who have passed, their fifth birthday, but have not yet reached their sixth.

No set rules can be laid down as to the choice of classes, but the following additional hints will apply to most of the tables which teachers or psychologists will need.

(1) The number of different classes is generally somewhere between 6 and 15. Some tables contain more, few less. When the total number of persons, N, is only 50 or less, a small number of classes is generally sufficient ; but if N is nearer 500, a more detailed table with a larger number of classes may be desirable.

(2) Pick out from the original list of measures the highest and the lowest measure to be tabulated, and deduce from them the total range of the distribution. If the range is from 20 to 1, then 7 classes containing 3 different measures each are likely to be appropriate. If the range is from 137 to 65, then 15 classes of 5 are a possibility. In most instances all the classes should contain the same number of different measures, i.e. they should be of the same size.[1]

(3) It is desirable, though not essential, to include an odd number of different measures in each class. The reason for this is that in any subsequent calculations we are going to regard all the measures grouped within any one class as lying at the midpoint of that class. If the classes include, say, 3–7, 8–12, 13–17, 18–22, etc., then we shall count all the 3's, 4's, 5's, 6's, and 7's as 5's, and all from 8 to 12 as 10's. The midpoint of a class is found by taking the average of the highest and lowest measures it can contain ; e.g. $(3 + 7) \div 2 = 5$. The same figure is the midpoint of a class whose true limits are $2\frac{1}{2}$ to $7\frac{1}{2}$. But a class such as 39·95 to 40·95 has the rather inconvenient midpoint of 40·45.

(4) With school marks it is advisable to arrange for any

---

[1] If the distribution is very far from symmetrical, as in the case of incomes, school attendances, and the like, a table with unequal-sized classes may better portray the state of affairs. But no further calculations can be carried out with such a table.

round numbers, such as the 5's and 10's, to fall at the centres of the classes. Teachers are very apt to award these round numbers and to neglect intermediate ones. Hence, if classes of 10–14, 15–19, 20–24 . . . are chosen, most of the frequencies may actually lie at 10, 15, 20 . . ., and it would be illegitimate to regard them as lying at the midpoints of 12, 17, 22. . . . The difficulty will be surmounted if classes of 8–12, 13–17, 18–22 . . . are used instead.

(5) Having chosen the classes and written them out in a column, tabulate the F's by the 'tally' method, as before, and check the total, N.

Ex. 2.—Below is the distribution of the measures already listed in Ex. 1. They have been grouped into classes of 3 marks each.

Classes		F
18–20	⫣⫣⫣ //	7
15–17	⫣⫣⫣ ⫣⫣⫣ ⫣⫣⫣ // . .	17
12–14	⫣⫣⫣ ////	9
9–11	⫣⫣⫣ //	7
6–8	⫣⫣⫣	5
3–5	///	3
0–2	//	2

$$N = 50$$

GRAPHICAL REPRESENTATION OF DISTRIBUTIONS

A distribution may often be portrayed more clearly by means of a graph, either of the type known as a *histogram*, or by a *frequency polygon*.[1] In both of these the frequencies are plotted on the vertical (Y) axis against the measures, or classes of measures, on the horizontal (X) axis. The scale of the graph and the location of the origin (the point of intersection of the axes) are purely matters of convenience. Suppose, for example, that our graph paper

[1] The ogive type of graph, or cumulative frequency curve, will be omitted here. The reader may find accounts of its construction and uses in more advanced textbooks, such as Garrett (1937) or Dawson (1933).

measures 6 inches × 9 inches, each inch being divided into
tenths, and that we wish to plot the distribution given in
Ex. 2.   We might use a scale of 3 persons to the inch on
the Y axis, and one class (3 marks) to the inch on the X
axis. This has been done in Figs. 1–3. Fig. 4 portrays
two distributions of intelligence test scores which have
been grouped into classes 73–77, 78–82 . . . 133–137.

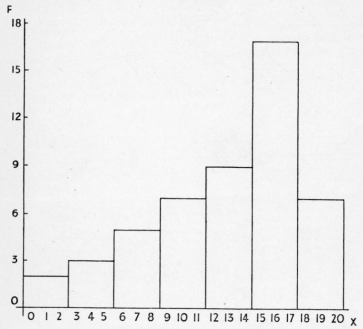

Fig. 1.—Histogram of distribution from Ex. 2.

Each inch on the Y axis represents 5 persons, and each
inch on the X axis includes 2 classes (10 points) of score.

A completed graph generally looks best if its largest
vertical and horizontal dimensions are roughly the same.
Its appearance will be too peaked if the scale of frequencies
is too large, or the scale of measures too small, and too flat
if the converse holds.

The origin is often placed at $X = 0$, but there is no need

for this. Thus in Figs. 2–3, it is at $X = -2$, in order that the Y axis may be drawn at the left-hand edge of the graph paper. And in Fig. 4 it is at $X = 100$, in order that the Y axis may be in the centre of the page.

The Histogram or Column Diagram.—Fig. 1 is a histogram portraying the distribution given in Ex. 2. It con-

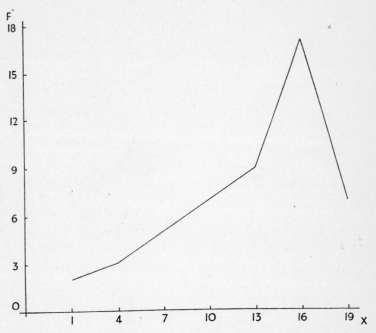

Fig. 2.—Incomplete frequency polygon of distribution from Ex. 2.

sists of a series of pillars or columns drawn side by side. Each pillar represents one measure or, as in this instance, one class of measures, and its height represents the frequency of this measure or class. The marks from 0 to 20 are written along the X axis, but note that each mark is represented by a *space* of $\frac{1}{3}$ of an inch on this axis, not by one of the inch or tenth-inch *lines*. The first class (including 0, 1, and 2 marks) is, therefore, represented by the whole width of the first inch, the second class (3, 4, and 5 marks) by the whole width of the second inch, and so on.

The Frequency Polygon.—All the measures included in a class are here represented by a point on the graph, whose Y co-ordinate is the frequency, and whose X co-ordinate is the midpoint of the class. Thus, in Fig. 2, which represents the same distribution as before, the midpoints are written along the X axis, and this time they are located

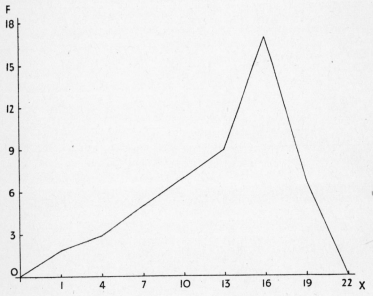

Fig. 3.—Completed frequency polygon of distribution from Ex. 2.

either at an inch or tenth-inch *line*. The points on the graph are connected up by straight lines. This figure is, as it were, suspended in mid-air, hence it is usual to complete it (Fig. 3) by connecting the first and last points with additional points whose Y co-ordinates are zero. The X co-ordinates of these additional points are the midpoints of the classes just below the lowest, and just above the highest classes, in the distribution, i.e. $X = -2$ and $X = 22$.

Ex. 3.—For further illustration there follow the frequency distributions of scores obtained by 136 men and 114 women students on the Cattell Intelligence Test, Scale IIIA. The scores are grouped into classes of 5. The distributions for the two sexes are plotted as frequency polygons on the *same* graph (Fig. 4), and for the sexes combined as a histogram (Fig. 5). Note in the latter that the scale along the Y axis has been halved, since combining the sexes roughly doubles the frequencies to be plotted.

Test Scores		Men	Frequencies Women	Combined
133 +	. .	1		1
128 +	. .	0	1	1
123 +	. .	5	1	6
118 +	. .	8	3	11
113 +	. .	13	9	22
108 +	. .	17	9	26
103 +	. .	21	14	35
98 +	. .	17	30	47
93 +	. .	23	20	43
88 +	. .	14	13	27
83 +	. .	6	12	18
78 +	. .	8	2	10
73 +	. .	3	0	3
	N =	136	114	250

Relative Merits of Frequency Polygons and Histograms.— Frequency polygons possess the advantage over histograms that two or more distributions can be superimposed and compared on one graph, as in Fig. 4. But they are inferior in that the lines connecting successive points give a somewhat inaccurate notion of the distribution, especially when the number of points is small. For instance, in Fig. 4 the connecting line between the two points X = 110 F = 17, and X = 115 F = 13, suggests that 15 men students obtained intermediate scores of $112\frac{1}{2}$, which is quite untrue. In this respect the histogram is unexceptionable, since it gives an exact portrayal of the tabulated data. The total area enclosed within a histogram corresponds accurately to the total number of persons, *N*. The area within a polygon only corresponds approximately. Histograms have a further advantage, namely, that they can be employed when the variable is not a truly quantitative one. For example, examination scripts are often graded, not with numerical, but with letter, marks—A, A—, B +, etc. The frequency distribution of the numbers of examinees who are awarded each letter can be shown by a histogram.

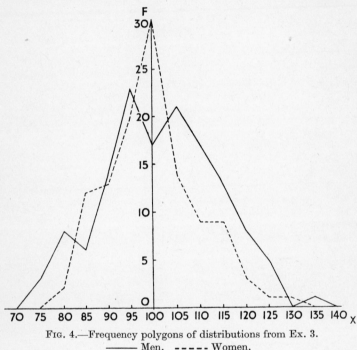

FIG. 4.—Frequency polygons of distributions from Ex. 3.
———— Men.   - - - - - Women.

CHARACTERISTICS OF FREQUENCY DISTRIBUTIONS

Smoothness of Distributions.—Here we must distinguish provisionally between ' objective ' and ' subjective ' measures, and discuss the difference more thoroughly in the next chapter. *Objective measures* are those which are practically independent of the person who makes them, such as heights measured with a ruler, or the scores on a standardized educational or intelligence test. *Subjective measures,* by contrast, depend upon personal evaluations. They include, for example, the marks awarded by a teacher to a series of English compositions, assessments of pupils' characters, and the like.

Now when graphs are drawn of frequency distributions of objective measures, certain characteristic features are very commonly found. First, the graphs are generally very irregular when the frequencies are small, but the

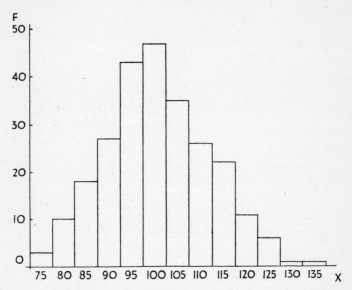

FIG. 5.—Histogram of distribution of men's and women's scores combined, from Ex. 3.

irregularities tend to become ' ironed out ' as the numbers increase. And when *N* reaches a value of several hundreds, the frequency polygon or histogram approximates to a smooth curve. Thus the distribution in Fig. 5 is much more regular in its rise and fall than is the distribution in Fig. 6, which represents the scores of a group of 50 students, selected at random from the previous 250.

Fig. 7, which is a frequency polygon of the heights of 6,194 male adults, gives an almost smooth curve.

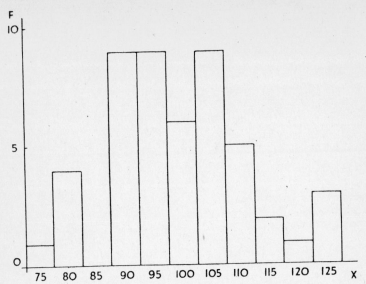

FIG. 6.—Distribution of test scores of a small group.

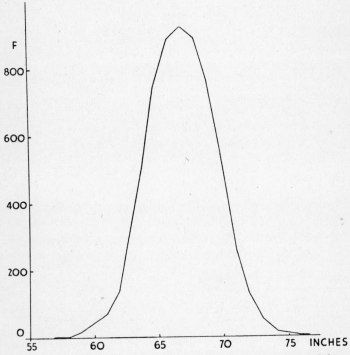

FIG. 7.—Frequency polygon of heights of 6,194 English male adults.

15

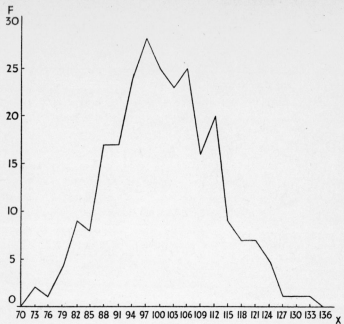

FIG. 8.—Irregular distribution of test scores grouped in small classes.

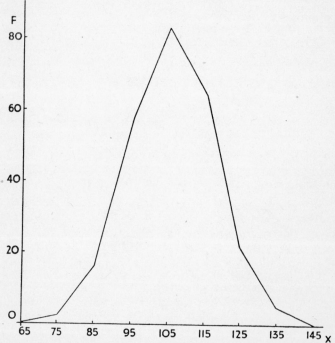

FIG. 9.—More regular distribution of test scores grouped in large classes.

16

Frequencies may be increased not only by increasing the value of N, but also by grouping the measures into larger classes. Figs. 8–9 show frequency polygons for the same set of 250 measures grouped into classes of 3 and 10 respectively. The latter is distinctly smoother than the former.

Types of Distribution Curves.—In actual practice we can never obtain measures of a large enough number of persons for the distribution graphs to become completely smooth curves. Nevertheless, it is customary to represent various types of distributions pictorially by means of curves of appropriate shapes, to which obtained distributions approximate more or less closely. For example, we can say that Fig. 10 represents roughly the type of distribution which might be expected for the incomes of parents of elementary school children. The greatest number would probably lie between £100 and £180 per annum. Very few would obtain less than £80,

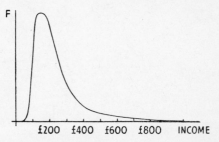

Fig. 10.—Skew curve, illustrating approximate distribution of annual income among parents of elementary school children.

and the frequencies of those at higher income levels would progressively diminish. This particular type of distribution is called a *skew curve*, because of its asymmetry. It is positively skewed towards the upper end, and shows a piling up of cases at the lower end. A bunching at the upper end would give a negatively skewed curve.

Fig. 11 is a *bimodal curve* such as might be obtained if we graphed the intelligence quotients [1] of pupils in two schools, one containing very intelligent children of professional class parents, the other containing inferior children

---

[1] It is assumed that all readers know roughly what is meant by intelligence quotients (I.Q.s). A definition may be found on p. 22, and a more precise account of their meaning on p. 217.

of very poor stock.   Most of the I.Q.s fall either between 110 and 140 or between 70 and 90, but there are a few of even higher or even lower intelligence, and a few (probably drawn from both schools) of intermediate or average intelligence, with I.Q.s of 90 to 110.

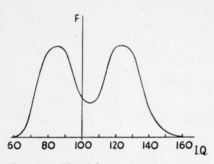

FIG. 11.—Bimodal curve, illustrating intelligence quotients of mixed groups.

The two polygons which appear in Fig. 4 are irregular on account of the small frequencies involved. They approximate, however, to a pair of curves such as those shown in Fig. 12.   Note here that the more highly peaked curve (representing women's scores) does *not* indicate that women obtain, on the whole, higher scores than men, but that women obtain more scores close to the average of 100 points, and fewer extreme scores ; in other words, that men are more dispersed or spread out in their ability.

It should be remembered that the areas enclosed beneath distribution curves are proportional to the total numbers of cases involved.   In Fig. 12

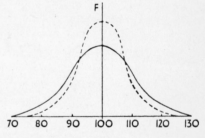

FIG. 12.—Two distributions of intelligence test scores, with different dispersions.

the areas are roughly equal, since the total numbers of the two sexes are about the same.   Fig. 13 shows the curves to which the distributions of scores among Honours and among ordinary degree students approximate.   The latter have, on the whole, somewhat lower scores than, but are four times as numerous as, the former. It is more usual, when groups of such different sizes are being compared, to plot percentage frequencies instead of actual frequencies, since the curves will then possess the same area, and differences in the averages and ranges or dispersions of measures will stand out better.

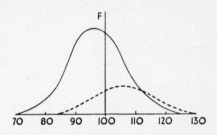

THE NORMAL FRE-QUENCY DISTRIBUTION

FIG. 13.—Distributions of intelligence test scores of two groups, one much larger than the other but of lower average intelligence.

Whenever a large group of human beings is taken at random (i.e. not specially selected like the two schools whose I.Q.s are graphed in Fig. 11), then objective measures of almost any trait or ability they possess—physical or mental—will be found to conform to a certain type of distribution known as the normal curve. This is often referred to as the normal probability curve, the normal curve of error, or the Gaussian curve. It is symmetrical, bell- or cocked-hat-shaped. It indicates that the majority of persons in the group obtain measures round about the average, relatively few obtain extreme measures, and that the frequencies above the average are the same as the frequencies below it. The four curves in Figs. 12–13 belong to this type, and all the graphs from Fig. 4 to Fig. 9 roughly approximate to it, since they represent distributions of scores obtained by unselected groups of persons. Innumerable instances of distributions which tend to this normal shape could be cited : the heights of children in an ordinary school class, the numbers of times they can tap with one finger in a minute, or the numbers of words they can write. Variations in individual performances as well as differences between individuals show the same trend : if a person tries a hundred times to copy a line of a certain length, most of his attempts will be close to his own average, and a few will be considerably too long or too short. Differences between groups are also similar : if all the elementary school classes aged 11 + in a large city are given an objective arithmetic test, and the average mark of each is calculated, then a graph of all these averages may be expected to show a normal distribution.

Conditions which Upset the Tendency to Normality.— There are several factors which may disturb this normal tendency. First, the total frequencies involved may be so small that the irregularities, noted above, may mask it. It is usually apparent, however, even with groups of 50 or less (cf. Fig. 6). Secondly, the group of persons may be selected in such a way as to distort an otherwise normally distributed variable. For example, a school class which has been ' creamed ' will be likely to show a negatively skewed distribution of test scores or examination marks, since there will be a deficiency of pupils of high ability. The police force or the army will not show a normal distribution of heights, since no recruits are accepted below a certain height.

Thirdly, there are a few human characteristics which, although objectively measurable, are known to be abnormally distributed. Accident proneness is one such variable. It is found that a few people are liable to undergo a large number of accidents in any given period of time, whether at home, or in factories, or when driving cars. But the majority have few or no accidents.[1] Thus the distribution takes roughly the form

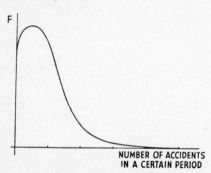

FIG. 14.—Approximate frequency distribution of accident proneness.

NUMBER OF ACCIDENTS IN A CERTAIN PERIOD

[1] Cf. H. M. Vernon (1936).

shown in Fig. 14. Annual income also gives a skew distribution (cf. Fig. 10). There is good evidence that intelligence quotients do not conform precisely to the normal curve. A slight deficiency occurs in the frequencies of I.Q.s of 100–120, and a slight excess in frequencies of I.Q.s around 90 and 130 or over.[1] Nevertheless, the discrepancies are so small that for many practical purposes we may continue to regard the distribution of intelligence, when measured by an adequate test, as normal.

A fourth condition (which is much commoner than the third) is the presence of defects in the method of measuring the variable. We shall see in the next chapter how such defects arise in the testing and examining of abilities, and how they should be dealt with in the light of our knowledge of the characteristics of frequency distributions.

[1] This result was definitely established by the recent Scottish survey of a truly unselected sample of children (cf. Macmeeken, 1939). For a discussion of the grounds for such asymmetry, cf. Burt (1937).

3

CHAPTER II

PRINCIPLES OF MENTAL MEASUREMENT AND MARKING

WE are all accustomed nowadays to regarding a scholastic capacity (e.g. arithmetical ability), like height or weight, as ranging from a very small amount in some people to a very large amount in others, and to assessing these amounts in numerical units such as percentage marks. General intelligence and other aptitudes can similarly be graded as quantitative variables, average intelligence being generally denoted by an Intelligence Quotient or I.Q. of 100, superior or inferior intelligence by larger or smaller numbers. Yet the conception of scaling mental qualities in a manner similar to physical ones is of fairly recent origin—we owe it largely to the work of Sir Francis Galton—and it is still somewhat limited in application and beset with many difficulties. A human ability or trait is far more complex than a length, a weight, or a time ; it can never be completely represented by a single numeral on a scale. Consider, as an example, political opinions—a communist is certainly *more* socialistically inclined than a liberal, and a fascist is *more* reactionary than a conservative. Successful tests have, therefore, been devised which scale these attitudes as a single variable ranging from extreme left-wing to extreme right-wing. But such a scale can hardly do justice to all the various shades of political opinion ; it inevitably involves some over-simplification and artificiality. Particularly in the field of temperament and character does such distortion arise, for here people appear to us to vary from one another, not merely in *amount*, but also in kind or quality.[1] The same is true, though to a

[1] For a fuller discussion of these points, cf. Vernon (1938*b*).

lesser extent, in the field of abilities.   Thus the precise nature of intelligence is an extremely controversial matter, and the common tendency to regard the I.Q. as an accurate measure of some definite and stable mental entity is, as we shall see below, an egregious misinterpretation.

No mental trait or ability can be measured directly by laying some kind of ruler alongside it.   Instead we have to grade it by observing its expression in words or actions. Arithmetical ability, for example, is shown by success at a series of sums ; moral character by certain modes of behaviour.   Indeed, for scientific purposes, we have to regard a trait or ability, not as some power or faculty in the mind, but as a particular class or category of related performances, e.g. of the arithmetical or the moral kind. And special statistical techniques are required for deciding just what performances should be included under one heading, as representative of one ability or trait (cf. Chap. VIII).   Since we cannot, of course, observe and record all the performances which go to make up a mental characteristic, we are forced to take samples of them.   Our procedure, as Binet pointed out, is analogous to that of the mining engineer who cannot examine all the ground in a given locality, but instead takes borings at various points, and from these samples deduces with reasonable accuracy what the district as a whole is like.   Similarly, the psychologist measures intelligence, or the teacher measures achievement in arithmetic, on the basis of the child's success at sample intellectual and arithmetical tasks.   An arithmetic examination sets, perhaps, six questions, the answers to which constitute a sampling of the general field of arithmetical knowledge which the pupil is supposed to have acquired.

How, then, is success at such sample performances expressed in numerical terms ?   The various methods of marking or scoring mental tests and examinations may be classified as follows :

A. Enumeration or count scoring.

B. Ranking.

C. Qualitative grading and classifying.
D. Numerical evaluation.
E. Mixed numerical evaluation and count scoring.

A. ENUMERATION OR COUNT SCORING

This type of marking is the only objective type, in the sense that each person's mark is quite independent of the marker's subjective evaluation of his work. When, for example, a series of simple arithmetic sums is set, the answers to which are all *either* right *or* wrong, or when one mark is deducted for each mistake in a dictation test, then a pupil's total mark is a count or enumeration score. Since this method is applicable only when no doubt can exist as to the correctness or incorrectness of the answers which are counted up, it is largely restricted to very simple kinds of scholastic work. We shall see later, however (Chap. XII), that attainments in more advanced and complex school or university work can be fairly adequately measured by sets of brief, objectively marked questions. The great majority of standardized educational and general intelligence tests follow this method, so as to eliminate the personal element in scoring. Steel and Talman (1936) claim that even English compositions can be marked by counting all the good and bad points of vocabulary, sentence-structure, and sentence-linking which they contain. The scoring is objective also among what are known as performance tests of intelligence or of special aptitudes. The child is set some practical or manipulative task, and a record is obtained, either of the number of pieces successfully put together or of the number of seconds taken.

This type of marking includes two distinct methods of measurement which may be termed the rate method and the power method. A test or examination may contain a number of fairly simple tasks, all of approximately uniform level of difficulty. The score is then the number of these tasks accomplished within a certain time limit. Alternatively, it may contain tasks which are graded in difficulty from quite simple to very hard tasks, such that all persons being tested can answer some of them, and scarcely any or none can manage all of them. Here no time limit is necessary. The score is again based on enumerating the tasks successfully completed, since those whose ability, knowledge, or ' power ' is greater are able to answer tasks of a higher level of difficulty. Greene and Jorgenson (1936) aptly compare these two methods to a hurdle race and a high-jump competition respectively. The table of tests given in Chap. IX lists several examples of both. Thus, Ballard's One-minute Reading and Arithmetic Tests and Burt's Reading Fluency Test belong to the former type. Burt's Graded Vocabulary Tests of Reading and Spelling and the Stanford-Binet Intelligence Test belong to the latter. Most tests and examinations, however, combine the two, i.e. they include easy and difficult items, but also impose a time limit, so that the score depends on power *and* rate of working.

Comparison of Mental Count Scores with Physical Measures.—We must ask now whether such count scores can legitimately be regarded as measures of mental abilities, analogous, say, to measures of height and weight or of physical abilities such as rate of running, power of muscular contraction, and the like. Actually the numbers in terms of which abilities are expressed show several important differences from numbers such as inches on a ruler or pounds on a weighing machine. The latter, physical, units are all equal to one another at any point on the scale. E.g. the difference between 50 and 49 inches is precisely the same as the difference between 40 and 39 inches. Moreover, they always have a zero point : e.g. 0 lb. means no weight at all. Mental ability units often lack these features, and this fact precludes us from adding, averaging, or otherwise treating them as if they were true numbers.

For example, a one-year-old child might fail to pass any of the Stanford-Binet Intelligence Tests, but his zero score shows, not that he possesses zero intelligence, but that the tests are an inadequate measuring instrument for this purpose. Again, a child with an I.Q. of 120 cannot be considered twice as intelligent as one with an I.Q. of 60, because we do not know what is the zero point of the I.Q. scale. Even in a rate test of, say, reading speed, a child who reads 50 simple words in a minute, and so scores twice as much as one who reads 25 words in the same time, cannot properly be said to be twice as good at reading.

It is obvious that the units in a rate test, such as words read, can never be precisely uniform in difficulty. Similarly, the various errors in a dictation test may vary considerably in seriousness. It should be noted also that two children who obtain the same score on a rate test do not necessarily accomplish precisely the same items, since one may fail on, or omit, certain items which the other passes ; and they may each make the same number of mistakes in the spelling of a certain passage, many of which are different. Our tests, then, might be compared to a weighing machine with a large number of pound weights, some of which are slightly heavier, some slightly lighter, than a pound. When using the machine to weigh children we do not always pick out precisely the same set of weights. Now, in spite of these defects in the weights, we can claim that two children, both found to be 70 lb., are very nearly the same weight, provided that the irregularities among the pounds are small. And if four children are found to weigh 90, 80, 70, and 60 lb., we can claim that the difference between the first two is likely to be nearly equivalent to the difference between the last two. Thus this analogy indicates that when the number of items in a mental test is large, and irregularities are small, the mental units may be regarded as approximately equivalent.

In tests of the pure power, or combined rate and power, types, the items are not intended to be equal in difficulty. Instead, each item should exceed the previous one in difficulty by approximately the same amount. For example, each test in the Stanford-Binet Scale (from Year VI to Average Adult level) is supposed to represent an

increment of two months of mental age.[1] But it is generally admitted nowadays that mental age units are not
equivalent, and that the difference between a child of
M.A. 13½ and one of 13 is probably much smaller
than the difference between children of 6½ and 6.
Here, then, it is as if we ran out of (nominal) pound
weights after a certain point, and had to use further
weights which progressively increased in heaviness. Obviously this leads to grave difficulties in the mental age
method of scoring (cf. Chap. IV). Several group intelligence tests, however, do manage to maintain approximately equal increments throughout.

The units of measurement of many physical skills present
similar problems, as Blackburn (1936) has pointed out.
That equal increments of score do not necessarily represent
equal increments of skill can be seen from the example of
golf scores. It is decidedly easier for a player who requires
140 strokes for a round to improve to 130, than it is for a
player who takes 70 to improve to 60 (or even—if we could
assume golf scores to follow a geometrical rather than an
arithmetical progression—to 65). Here, also, it is impossible to establish a zero point of ability, or to calculate
ratios between abilities.

Special techniques have been devised by Thorndike,
Thurstone, and others for the production of measuring
scales with equal units, and for determining the zero points
on such scales. They are too complex for description here.
But they depend in the main upon the principle of normal
distribution of objective measures, which was enunciated
in Chap. I. Well-constructed tests always tend to yield a
normal frequency distribution ; hence we are entitled to
regard departures from normality as indicative of bad
construction or bad scoring. For example, a mental test
which contains plenty of easy and moderately difficult
items, but whose later items increase too rapidly in difficulty to allow sufficient headroom, will give a negatively
skewed distribution. The analogy with a weighing

[1] For a definition and discussion of mental age, cf. pp. 82–87.

machine would be as follows : suppose that the available weights beyond the seventieth became progressively bigger than 1 lb., and that a large group of children were measured whose true weights averaged about 70 lb., and ranged from 50 to 90 lb. The distribution would then be distorted from normal to negative skew type, as in Fig. 15. Conversely, a test which contains insufficient easy items, so that it only differentiates effectively among the better pupils, is likely to show a positively skewed distribution.

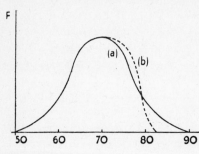

FIG. 15.—Normal distribution (*a*) altered to negative skew curve, (*b*) by increasing the size of the higher units.

Application to School Marks and Examinations.—It is difficult to apply this principle to school marks, since the groups are usually so small (less than 50) that great irregularities in distribution are sure to arise. The following table, however, gives the marks obtained by two 11 + classes in an ordinary school on an objective arithmetic test. Owing to the deficiency in difficult questions, many pupils at the top got full marks (80), and the real extent of their ability was not tested at all.

Ex. 4.—An abnormal frequency distribution of arithmetic marks.

Mark				F
80	.	.	.	. 15
70 +	.	.	.	. 6
60 +	.	.	.	. 6
50 +	.	.	.	. 14
40 +	.	.	.	. 17
30 +	.	.	.	. 8
20 +	.	.	.	. 4
10 +	.	.	.	. 5
0 +	.	.	.	. 3

N = 78

Further problems occur in the interpretation of count scores. Physical measures, such as 60 inches or 15 seconds, always represent definite amounts. No doubt exists as to their largeness or smallness, because an inch or a second has an absolute, standard size. Laymen and teachers often wrongly suppose that the same is true of mental measures, such as the mark awarded to a pupil's work. They talk of 15/20 or 60% as if these numbers implied the same level of achievement whenever, or by whomsoever, they are awarded. Yet it is surely obvious that such scores, by themselves, tell us nothing at all about the goodness or poorness of achievement. Such statements as : " Johnny is doing well at arithmetic. He got 8 sums out of 10 correct," or " His dictation is terrible ; he made 15 mistakes "—are quite meaningless unless we also know the difficulty of the sums and of the passage dictated. Johnny may be the poorest arithmetician in his class, and yet score 8/10 if sufficiently simple sums are set. Or he may be the best speller in his class, and yet make 15 mistakes if the passage happens to be taken, say, from a textbook of organic chemistry. The speaker is, of course, implying that the tasks are of a level of difficulty such that most of the class score less than 8 and − 15. In other words, the marks possess only a relative, not an absolute, significance. Again, when an inspector or head teacher complains that the average examination mark of a class is ' too low,' he is presumably comparing the mark and the difficulty of the examination with subjective recollections of the achievements of other similar classes. Undoubtedly there is a great deal of loose thinking about these matters, and much can be learnt from the more systematic procedure of the scientific mental tester.

The tester realizes that the goodness or poorness of a child's test performance can be interpreted only by comparing it with the performances of other similar children. Hence he applies his test to large numbers of children, similar as to age and other relevant circumstances, scores their performances all in the same way, and can then state definitely whether a certain performance is superior or inferior, and how *much* better or poorer it is than the average. This procedure is called the establishment of norms or standards for the test. A discussion of the main types of test norms is given in Chap. IV, where it is also shown how the adoption of analogous methods may greatly help in the interpretation of school and examination marks.

B. Ranking

Ranking means listing a group of pupils or students in order of their attainment, 1st, 2nd, etc., down to bottom. This method may be applied to any form of scholastic work, including composition, handwriting, and the like, which are scarcely amenable to count scoring. It is actually the soundest of all forms of marking, in spite of its many limitations, because these limitations are so obvious and so easily recognized. The first drawback is that the number of persons who can be ranked is rather small. Even the arrangement of twenty in order involves a good deal of uncertainty, especially near the middle of the list. Those at the extremes are usually more readily discriminated from one another. Next, it is clear that these ranks do not provide a true numerical scale, since the numbers 1, 2, 3, etc., are by no means equally spaced. Usually the differences between the attainments of Nos. 1 and 2, 2 and 3, 18 and 19, 19 and 20 (out of 20) are greater than the differences between Nos. 9 and 10, 10 and 11—hence the difficulty, just mentioned, in ranking the medium pupils. The frequency distribution is rectangular (Fig. 16), and is

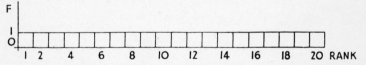

Fig. 16.—Rectangular frequency distribution given by a rank order.

entirely unlike the normal curve. These numbers, therefore, may give quite false impressions if they are added, averaged, or otherwise manipulated. For example, a pupil who is first in one examination and third in another should be regarded as better than, not as equal to, a pupil who is second in both (cf. p. 70).[1]

A third main drawback is that these numbers are always relative to the particular set of persons who have been ranked. Thirtieth place is not an unequivocal number like 30° on a thermometer. For 30th out of 32 is much poorer than 30th out of 50. Moreover, if any one person higher on the list should happen to be absent, the 30th rank would change to 29th. It is not even analogous to, say, 30 mistakes in a dictation test, since such a test can be applied to large numbers of children, and norms can be collected which will tell us how low is the level of ability to which 30 mistakes corresponds. In contrast, a rank position can never be so interpreted with reference to outside standards.

C. Qualitative Grading and Classifying

Examination scripts, essays, etc., are often merely classified into some three to ten grades which are distinguished by letters (A, A −, B +, etc. ; α, β, etc.) or by names (Credit, Pass, Fail ; 1st class, 2nd class, etc. ; Excellent, Very Good, Good, etc.). This is a more primitive type of grading than numerical evaluation (e.g. on a 0 to 10, or a percentage, scale), though it is of course often applied to scripts which have already been awarded percentage marks. For instance, examinees whose mark is 80% or more are informed that they have obtained First Class or Credit, and so on.

Since these grades make no pretence of being numerical measures, we need not cavil at the eccentricity of their frequency distributions. They are, however, liable to another, still more serious, defect which is not found among count scores or ranks, namely that different

---

[1] The numbers can, however, be converted into a normally distributed set of scores (cf. Garrett's or Guilford's books). And it is possible, without any conversion, to correlate one rank order with another, e.g. to compare a teacher's ranking of school work with the pupils' results on a group intelligence test (cf. Chap. VI).

teachers or examiners often employ widely different scales or standards of grading. Although they are supposed to represent absolute evaluations of achievement, they are actually found by experimental investigation to involve such gross discrepancies that neither pupils, parents, nor teachers can hope to interpret their significance correctly. For example, Hartog and Rhodes (1935) arranged for 48 School Certificate French scripts to be graded independently by six experienced examiners. One of the examiners awarded 46 credits, 2 passes, and 0 failures. Another gave 17 credits, 12 passes, and 19 failures. The remaining four were intermediate. Similarly, Boyd (1924) had 26 essays by 11 + children graded by 271 teachers as either Excellent, VG +, VG, G +, G, Moderate, or Unsatisfactory. Some of the teachers awarded one or other of the two highest grades to as many as 15 of the essays, others to none of them. Some also awarded one or other of the two lowest grades to 17 of the essays, others to none of them. In view of such results, it is clear that there is no agreed meaning as to the absolute amount of ability which these gradings should signify. A mark of Excellent may represent a high level of ability if it is awarded by a teacher who very seldom gives Excellents. It may mean little better than average ability if it is awarded by a teacher who habitually grades nearly half his papers as Excellent. In other words, this type of marking is actually a relative one, like ranking. A mark of G +, or β −, or Pass, etc., only achieves any meaning if we know what proportions of candidates obtained better or poorer marks, in just the same way as a rank position of 30th can only be interpreted if we know how many candidates were ranked lower than 30th.

Qualitative grading should then be regarded as a form of ranking where, instead of there being as many different ranks as there are pupils or examinees, there are only some 3 to 10 ranks, any one of which may be awarded to several pupils whose work is of approximately equal merit. Its grave defect is that any one script is not usually compared directly with the scripts of a particular group of pupils before receiving its grade ; it is merely compared with the marker's more or less vague recollections of the scripts which he has marked in the past. The only possible rational meaning for Excellent or First Class is that the script which receives this grade seems to him to rank higher, or to be relatively better, than almost all the scripts produced by similar pupils which he has come across. The other grades are similarly referred to rough subjective standards which he has set up during his previous marking experience. And since his experience naturally differs from all other markers' experiences, so will his standards differ, unless he has taken the trouble to discuss and compare them with others, and to try to adjust them accordingly.

Finally, as in the case of rank orders, there is no possibility of exact comparison of such grades with external standards or norms, and they cannot be added or averaged in any satisfactory way.[1]

D. Numerical Evaluation
and
E. Mixed Numerical Evaluation and Count Scoring

Numerical evaluation consists, nominally, in assigning absolute numerical grades to pupils' abilities, school work, or examination scripts, either on a 0–10, 0–20, percentage, or some other scale. It exhibits all the ambiguities of the qualitative grading just described, and possesses several additional defects of its own. In other words, although it is the most commonly used, it is quite the worst type of marking. Unfortunately, since it involves numbers, it is frequently confused with the count scores obtained from objective marking (Type A). Teachers assume that the label of, say, 15/20 which they award to an English composition is equivalent to a score of 15 correct arithmetic sums out of 20. Often the two become inextricably mixed.

[1] When the group of pupils is a large one, their grades can be converted into rational scores ; cf. Dawson (1933), pp. 91–3.

For instance, partial credits involving subjective judgments of merit may be awarded to partially right sums. Or an examination in history, science, languages, etc., may include, say, five questions each of which is marked subjectively out of 20, the marks then being added as if they were count scores to yield percentage totals. Or some analytic plan of marking may be adopted whereby one mark is *counted* for each correct fact or idea, and so many are added for *subjective* impressions of style or general merit.

Distributions of such marks are sometimes smooth and symmetrical, but are often wildly irregular or skewed. In an examination where a pass mark of, say, 50 % has been fixed, it is common to find very large numbers of 50's, 51's, and 52's, but no 45's to 49's. Some teachers show peculiar idiosyncrasies, such as avoiding certain marks altogether. For instance, they may award 9, 8, 6, 5, or 3 out of 10 very often, but scarcely ever give 10, 7, 4, 2, or 1. Two illustrations may be given of distributions among students or pupils who also took an examination which was objectively scored.

Ex. 5.—Distributions of (Subjective) Marks for Reading and (Objective) Marks for Geography.

Mark	Reading F	Geography F
10	24	2
9	25	3
8	13	8
7	6	10
6	4	11
5	2	9
4	0	9
3	0	7
2	0	10
1	0	4
0	0	1
	74	74

The reading marks in Ex. 5 are fairly typical of the distribution adopted by teachers in evaluating this subject, or composition, or handwriting. Note that this teacher was not, as she supposed, marking out of 10, but out of 6, since she only used 6 different grades. The fact that about one-third of the class get 10 implies that the work of all these children was equally good, which is certainly not true. The geography marks awarded by the same teacher were derived from a new-type test paper, and so give a roughly normal distribution. It is surely obvious that 5/10 for geography does not have the same significance, nor represent the same achievement, as 5/10 for reading. In the one it means approximately the average for the class, in the other it means right at the bottom of the class. But the children themselves and their parents are likely to assume that 5/10 always means the same thing.

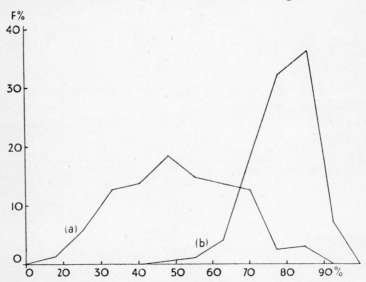

FIG. 17.—Distributions of percentage marks from (a) an objective examination, and (b) a subjectively marked examination.

Fig. 17 compares the distributions of percentage marks obtained by a large group of students on a new-type examination and on an ordinary examination of the essay-type. The former, though somewhat irregular, tends towards the normal, symmetrical shape, and includes marks ranging from 19% to 86%. The latter is skewed, and it ignores the bottom half of the available scale of marks, since it ranges only from 50% to 90%.

Education authorities would surely distrust a school doctor the weights on whose weighing machine varied, say, from $\frac{3}{4}$ lb. to $1\frac{1}{4}$ lb. each. Yet the units implied by the distributions which many of their teachers employ are probably quite as variable as this, unless some scheme of rationalization is applied (cf. Chap. IV). It is notorious also that some faculties in a university use quite different scales of marks, or are much more lenient than other faculties.

It must be obvious that such marks are not true measurements. 60% does not represent $\frac{60}{100}$ of anything whatsoever. True, it lies a certain distance between 0 and 100, but as nobody can define what is meant either by zero or perfect ability, that fact does not help much. Like the qualitative grades of Type C, they are merely labels whose precise size is fixed more or less vaguely by convention. Naturally the convention varies in different institutions. For example, the pass standard in degree examinations is called 60% at some universities, 40%, 20%, or even 10% at others.

Numerical grading, like qualitative grading, actually consists of ranking the scripts in relation to the marker's subjective past experience. It differs merely in that number labels are substituted for verbal ones, and that most numerical scales contain a larger number of different labels than do qualitative scales. This latter feature leads to still another common defect. When an essay or a single examination answer has to be marked on a percentage basis, the implication is that the marker can distinguish, and keep in mind, a hundred different grades of ability (or 51 different grades if he confines himself to a range of 40% to 90%). Actually it has been proved by experiment that people cannot consistently discriminate more than about 10 grades, and some would say only 5.

The Reformation of Marking

The would-be reformer of marks meets with many objections and criticisms. Most of them either rest upon ignorance of elementary statistical principles, or else ' boil down ' to the view that the systems in vogue at present are firmly established, generally understood by all concerned, and work too well and smoothly to be upset. While such a reactionary attitude is entirely unwarranted, yet there are admittedly many occasions in school marking where the rationality of the scales employed matters little, or where an eccentric distribution may be an actual advantage.

Some important examinations do not aim at measuring the abilities of all the pupils, but purely at selecting a certain proportion of them. For instance, the English Special Place Examination attempts to pick out the best 10 % or so of candidates for secondary school scholarships. The Scottish Qualifying Examination has roughly the opposite purpose, namely to eliminate the poorest pupils who are unfit for secondary or advanced work. Mowat (1938) points out that the most appropriate examinations or tests in these two instances will be ones which will spread out, or discriminate between, candidates whose marks are close to the respective borderlines. The former then should yield a positively skewed distribution and give plenty of headroom, while the latter should yield a negatively skewed distribution and give plenty of footroom. The marks of the bottom three-quarters of candidates in the former, and of the top three-quarters in the latter, scarcely matter. Hence, it would be a waste of time to construct an examination which would spread them all out in the proper normal fashion.

Next we can distinguish examinations which are constantly set in schools for such pedagogic purposes as ensuring that all, or practically all, the pupils have successfully accomplished a certain stage in their work, or that they have learnt, say, some French grammar, chemical formulæ,

4

or history notes, set to them for preparation.   Other exercises are needed, notably in mathematical subjects, for practice in the operations which the pupils are in process of acquiring.   In these instances we may expect distributions to show a strong negative skew.   The tests will naturally be designed so that the majority can get full or nearly full marks.   The weaklings will be somewhat more spread out, but even the poorest may be able to attain half marks.   Doubtless it is because these abnormal distributions have become habitual in classwork that most teachers are so blind to the defects in their examination marking. Such tests which are used as pedagogic aids should be kept quite distinct from tests or examinations designed for purposes of measuring abilities.   When the object is to compare different pupils or to find how able a pupil may be in different subjects, then they should certainly be constructed and marked according to the principles outlined below.   Further, when a standardized (published) test of intelligence or attainment is to be given to a class or to a group of students, it should always be chosen so as to yield a proper frequency distribution (cf. pp. 210–11).

Rationalization of Marking.—Marking will probably never become scientific so long as it is confused with value judgments.   Thus the first point to realize is that *marking is a process of differentiating between the various levels of ability existent among the scripts which are being marked.*   Either it is a process of arranging them in rank order or of assigning them to one of a limited number of qualitative or numerical grades.   But it is *not* a process of deciding whether all, or some, of the scripts are ' good ' or ' bad,' whether the pupils ' ought to have done better ' or ' have tried hard,' whether they ' pass ' or ' fail.'   All such decisions should be postponed until the actual marking is completed.

Often it is desirable that the examination should be of the new- or objective-type.   The reasons for this advice appear in a later chapter, but one of the main ones is that marking is greatly simplified and rendered far fairer.   In such examinations difficulties arise, not in the scoring (which is purely of the count type), but in the setting. They should be of such a length, and contain questions of sufficient ease and difficulty, to differentiate among both the poorest and the best pupils, and to yield an approximately normal distribution. Ideally the average pupil in the class, or the average examinee, should get as near as possible to half marks, the poorest pupil little better than zero, and the best pupil little less than full marks. For if no examinee scores less than, say, 40%, then it is obvious that the easy questions at the beginning are a waste of everybody's time. And if no one scores more than, say, 70%, the most difficult questions at the end are also wasted.

Humanitarian Objections.—An immediate, and quite pardonable, objection will be raised against this ideal, namely, that if marks range from nearly 0% to nearly 100%, the poorer pupils will become greatly discouraged when they habitually obtain marks of around 10% to 20%, and their parents will become bitterly resentful. Some teachers are so conscious of the stimulating effects of success and the depressing effects of failure, that they deliberately distort marks, giving the duller pupils who have tried hard more than their work deserves, and the brighter ones who have not done so well as they might less than they deserve. It may be that this kindheartedness of teachers towards the dullards has been partly responsible for forcing up their distributions of marks into the absurd shapes typified by Ex. 5 above. Perhaps equally potent has been their fear of the criticisms of head teachers and inspectors if they admitted their failure to teach the almost ineducable pupils by marking their work on its true merits. Worthy as such humanitarian objections may be, they do not constitute an excuse for bad test construction or bad marking. But the solution is not difficult. We shall see in Chap. IV that the actual average, and range, or the scale of marks, employed do not matter in the slightest, provided that everyone agrees to use the same scale. Either, then, the test may contain sufficient (useless) questions

which are easy enough to encourage the poor pupils ; or
the test may be rationally constructed, as indicated above,
so as to yield a range of, say, 4 to 26 out of 30, or 10 to 70
out of 80 ; and when the marking is complete the marks
can readily be converted into some more acceptable and
conventional scale, such as 40 % to 90 %, by the methods
described in Chap. IV. A third alternative is to withhold
all numerical grades from pupils and parents, since they
are so liable to misinterpretation, and instead, once the
scientific marking is done and is recorded for administra-
tive purposes, to reconsider the scripts and attach any
verbal or letter labels to them that appear suitable for
pupil and parental consumption.

Grading of Complex Educational Products.—Certain
types of work such as English composition and handwriting
usually have to be graded on the basis of total subjective
impression. The same is true of many examination scripts
when the answers consist of a series of historical, scientific,
or other essays. Here all the answers to any one question
should invariably be marked before the examiner proceeds
to another question. Whenever there are about twenty or
more such essays (or other educational products) to be
dealt with, resort should be made to the quality or product
scale method (cf. p. 179). The marker should first skim
through a fair number of the scripts until he has gained a
rough impression of their average level and of their extreme
range of attainment. No account whatever should be
taken of his feelings that this level is laudably good or
deplorably bad. What is needed is the actual average of
these particular scripts. Next he should look through
them more carefully and pick out one which typifies the
average, set it aside, and call it 5. Next the two should
be taken which appear to be the best and worst of the
bunch ; these should be called either 9 and 1, or 8 and 2.
Finally, others should be selected which seem to represent
levels intermediate between 9 (or 8) and 5, and between
5 and 1 (or 2). These should be numbered (8), 7, 6, 4, 3,
(2). A good deal of revision of first impressions may be

required before a final decision is reached as to these nine (or seven) samples. Once they are chosen the marking is straightforward. The rest of the scripts are simply compared one by one with the samples and each is awarded the mark of the sample which it most closely resembles in merit. Should one or two turn up which are superior to No. 9 or inferior to No. 1, they may be given 10 or 0.

One obvious advantage of this plan is that it enables the marker to be self-consistent and to maintain the same standards throughout. Another is that it does not demand impossibly fine discriminations. The number of samples can be reduced to five, or extended to eleven, if desired, or some scripts may be given a mark midway between two samples, e.g. $6\frac{1}{2}$. But usually seven or nine grades are sufficient. Most important, however, is the fact that the final distribution will be fairly smooth and symmetrical if the number of scripts is large and the samples have been well chosen. Even if their number is small there should be a majority of 6's, 5's, and 4's, and a minority of 9's, 8's, 2's, and 1's ; and there should be about as many above as below 5. The precise marks given to the samples do not matter. They may, for example, equally well be called 90%, 85%, 80% . . . 55% 50%, so long as the marker resolutely avoids all temptations to withhold 90% on the irrelevant grounds that the best scripts in the bunch do not seem to him to be ' up to 90% standard.' It is, however, probably better to do the marking of each question on a 0–10 scale. Such marks for several questions in an examination can legitimately be added. The final totals can then be converted into any desired conventional scale, just as can the scores from an objective test.

Other Types of Marking.—It is more difficult to give definite recommendations as to the marking of work of mixed type, where only part of the merit or demerit resides in points which can be counted. In foreign language examinations, history, science, etc., both correct or incorrect facts, and general style, or originality and the like, may need assessment. Sometimes these quantitative and qualitative features can be graded separately and later combined in due proportions. It might be better if, as is suggested in Chap. XIV, such papers were not set ; either they should be definitely new-type, or definitely of the qualitative essay-type. Nevertheless, the main requisites of good marking should always be attainable, namely a similar distribution and similar average level of marks in all subjects, or in all the questions set in any one subject, and an approximation of this distribution to normality.

Still more difficult are the problems of the marker who has only a few scripts with which to deal, e.g. a university external examiner who is called in to assess half a dozen degree candidates. Even if the papers consisted of perfectly constructed new-type tests, they would inevitably yield extremely irregular and variable distributions. The examiner is, therefore, forced to employ subjective recollections of the merits of similar candidates whom he has marked in the past. Nevertheless, he should keep the normal curve in mind, for in the long run all the scripts that he meets are likely to be normally distributed. He should try, therefore, to build up definite mental specifications of his 9, 8, 7 . . . 2, 1 levels, and attempt, by thorough discussion with the internal examiners, to decide where on this scale the First Class, Pass, or other standards fall.

Some additional points bearing on these plans, and the answers to some of the possible criticisms, will be discussed when we have studied, in the next chapter, the statistical conceptions of percentiles, averages, and standard deviations.

CHAPTER III

STATISTICAL METHODS FOR HANDLING FREQUENCY DISTRIBUTIONS

Numerical Description of Distributions.—So far we have dealt with various types of distributions of measures almost wholly in verbal terms, and have compared one distribution with another mainly ' by eye.' More exact study of them necessitates quantitative description and definition. We need first a numerical expression for the ' general run ' of the measures, and, secondly, some index of the range or spread of measures. For instance, if we want to know how intelligent Johnny Smith is, and ask a psychologist, he will tell us Johnny's score on an intelligence test and, in order to enable us to interpret this score, he will add that the normal score for children of Johnny's age is so and so, and that Johnny's score falls at such and such a level in the distribution. Again, if we ask a teacher what are the heights of the children in her class, she might in reply show us a complete table of the distribution of heights, or she might tell us with greater precision that the average was 50 inches and the range from 42 to 57 inches.

Actually the range is not a good index of the way the measures are spread out above and below the average, since it depends on only two of the measures, those obtained by the extreme pupils who were measured. For example, although this class contains children ranging from 42 to 57 inches, all the rest might lie between 46 and 54 inches, and we would hardly get a fair picture of the spread if we were only told that the total range is 15 inches. A much better index is called the Standard Deviation—often abbreviated to S.D. or σ, which will be described below.

A distribution of measures can then generally be defined

43

numerically by means of its average and standard deviation. But we shall describe first an alternative system which possesses certain practical advantages. This is based on what are known as the median, quartiles, and deciles or percentiles. These terms all refer to certain levels or fixed points in a distribution. Suppose the measures to be tabulated or arranged in order, then the median is the middle measure, i.e. the measure half-way up counting from the bottom, or half-way down counting from the top. The lower and upper quartiles, usually referred to as Q_1 and Q_3, are the measures one-quarter and three-quarters way up. The decile measures are one-tenth, two-tenths, etc., and the percentiles one-hundredth, two-hundredths, etc., of the way up. Stated in a different way, the Xth percentile is the measure below which X% of all the measures fall.

Determining the Median.—Ex. 6.—Consider the following distribution of only five measures. Clearly the median is 15, that is the third measure up from the bottom or down from the top.

$$19$$
$$17$$
$$15$$
$$13$$
$$11$$

From this example it may be seen that the median is the $\dfrac{N + 1}{2}$th measure, not the $\dfrac{N}{2}$th.

Ex. 7.—In the following distributions, N = 8, hence $\dfrac{N + 1}{2} = 4\frac{1}{2}$.

9	10	19
8	9	17
8	8	14
7	7	12
7	6	9
6	5	5
6	4	4
5	3	1

Thus the median is half-way between the fourth and fifth measures from the bottom. In the first distribution the fourth and fifth measures are both 7, hence the median is 7. In the second, the fourth and fifth measures are 6 and 7, hence we have to take $6\frac{1}{2}$ as the median. In the third distribution the data are too sparse for an accurate median to be determined. The best we can do is to interpolate and call it $10\frac{1}{2}$.

Determining the Quartiles and Percentiles.—The quartiles are similarly obtained by counting the measures which are $\dfrac{N+1}{4}$ and $\dfrac{3(N+1)}{4}$ from the bottom. For the distribution given in Ex. 1 (p. 5), $N = 50$, hence the required measures are $12\frac{3}{4}$ and $38\frac{1}{4}$ up the list. The 11th, 12th, and 13th measures are 9, the 37th to 43rd measures are all 17, hence $Q_1 = 9$, $Q_3 = 17$.

Of the percentiles, the most useful are the 100th or 99th, 90th, 75th, 50th, 25th, 10th, 1st, or 0th. The 100th and 0th are, of course, the top and bottom measures in the distribution, respectively. The 75th and 25th are the quartiles, the 50th is the median. The 90th percentile or 9th decile is the measure which is $\dfrac{9(N+1)}{10}$ from the bottom.

Determining Percentiles from Tabulated Data.—When dealing with measures which have been grouped into classes, these various levels are likely to fall somewhere in the middle of a class. For instance, in Ex. 3 (p. 12), the median of 250 measures is the $125\frac{1}{2}$th, which lies somewhere within the class 98–102. Its position is found by interpolation, and the following formula may be used.[1]

$$X_P = L + \frac{C}{F}\left(\frac{PN}{100} - S\right)$$

$P =$ the percentile.

$X_P =$ the measure falling at this percentile level, which we wish to find.

---

[1] The formula should not be used for finding the 100th or the 0th percentiles. These are the highest and lowest measures, respectively, in the original list.

L = the lower limit of the class, somewhere within which
  X_p lies.

S = the sum of all the frequencies up to, but not including, this class.

F = the frequency within this class.

N = the total of all the frequencies.

C = the size of the class.

Ex. 8.—To find the median of the distribution given in Ex. 3, substitute in this formula :

P = 50.   L, the lower limit, = 98.   S = 3 + 10 + 18 + 27 + 43 = 101.

F = 47.   N = 250.   C = 5.

$$X_p = 98 + \frac{5}{47}\left(\frac{50 \times 250}{100} - 101\right) = 100 \cdot 5 \text{ (to the first place of}$$
  decimals).

By applying the same formula, we find the 99th, 90th, 75th, 25th, 10th, and 1st percentiles to be 128, 117, 109, 94, 86, and 77, respectively (omitting decimals).

Comparison of Median and Average.—If the distribution is a perfectly smooth and normal one, the median is identical with the average. In any fairly regular and symmetrical distribution they will be quite close to one another. Thus in Ex. 8, where the median is 100·5, the average happens to be 100·68. For rough work the median is often used as an approximation to the average, since its computation is far easier.[1] Sometimes, indeed, it gives a better notion of the ' general run ' of the measures than does the average. For example, the average age of a school class may be unduly raised because the class includes two or three pupils much older than all the rest. They cannot very well be omitted in calculating the average, but if the median is found, they no longer exert a disproportionate effect upon the result. Similarly, if a

---

[1] The main disadvantage of medians, and also of percentiles, is that they cannot readily be manipulated statistically. For instance, given the medians of distributions A and B, we cannot determine from them the median of the combined distribution, A + B ; whereas the averages of A and of B will give us the average of A + B.

free word association test is applied to a child at a psychological clinic, most of the child's responses may be given within two to three seconds, but some of them may take much longer, and a few words may evoke no response at all. In such a case the average cannot be determined, and the median is the only possible measure of the child's speed of response.

Here is another instance where the median may be very useful. Suppose an investigator wishes to find the approximate average speed with which a group of pupils or students can perform a certain task, such as handwriting. There is no need for him to time each person separately, nor to count the number of words each one has written in a certain time, and then add up and average the results. Instead, he may set the whole class writing a standard passage, and tell them to hold up their hands directly they finish. Then he may count the hands raised, and stop the test as soon as the median person raises his hand, noting the time at which this occurs. The median speed of writing for a class of, say, 41 persons can be calculated from the time taken by the 21st quickest person.

When a distribution is strongly skewed, the median differs appreciably from the average, being larger if the skew is negative, smaller if it is positive. In Ex. 1 (p. 15), the median is 14, the average 12·86. This difference is often used as a measure of skewness (the formula can be found in more advanced textbooks).

Uses of Percentiles.—The percentile levels in a distribution clearly provide us with as complete a numerical description of that distribution as we may need. For example, the figures quote above for the distribution of students' scores on the Cattell Intelligence Test (the 99th, 90th, 75th, 50th, 25th, 10th, and 1st percentiles) give a reasonably full answer to the question—how did the students do on the test ? Knowing these levels, we can begin to interpret the significance of any one person's score, since we can tell how he stands relative to this group of students. Thus a score of 92 on the Cattell test would not be a very good one for a training college student. It falls at about the 20th percentile, which means that 80% of the students did better at the test, only 20% did worse. But when we are told that the same score falls at the 94th percentile for normal adults (not students), we realize that it does represent quite high ability. The applications of percentiles to the interpretation of school marks and to test norms will be considered later.

Inter-quartile Range.—The range of scores from the 25th to the 75th percentiles (Q_1 to Q_3) is often called the inter-quartile range. It tells us what the middle 50% of the group accomplished. Half of this range is often referred to as Q, the semi-interquartile range, and this is used as a measure of the degree of spread or dispersion of the distribution. When the distribution is smooth and normal, Q is usually equal to about one-eighth of the total range of measures. In Ex. 3 (p. 12) the total range is 61, and $Q = \dfrac{109 - 94}{2} = 7 \cdot 5$, which is one-eighth of 60.

CALCULATING THE AVERAGE OR MEAN

More accurate statistical treatment of distributions demands the use of the average and standard deviation in place of the median and Q. Everyone knows how to calculate an average or arithmetic mean—often referred to as ' the mean '—but most people use an unnecessarily complex method, which is very liable to lead to mistakes. We will therefore outline this and the shorter alternative methods.

(1) The ordinary method consists in adding up all the measures and dividing by the number of cases. Expressed as an algebraic formula, $M = \dfrac{\Sigma X}{N}$. M = the mean or average, X = any one measure, and Σ = the sum of all the . . . , hence ΣX signifies the sum of all the separate measures. As a rough general rule, this method may be used when N does not amount to more than about 20.

With larger numbers it becomes very inefficient, unless an adding machine is available.

(2) Often it is quicker to tabulate the measures, to multiply each X by its F, and then to sum.   The formula now becomes $M = \dfrac{\Sigma\,(FX)}{N}$.

Ex. 9.—The method is here applied to the distribution already given in Ex. 1.

X	F	FX
20	2	40
19	2	38
18	3	54
17	7	119
16	4	64
15	6	90
14	3	42
13	4	52
12	2	24
11	2	22
10	2	20
9	3	27
8	2	16
7	1	7
6	2	12
5	1	5
4	2	8
3	0	0
2	1	2
1	1	1
N = 50		643

$$M = \frac{643}{50} = 12 \cdot 86$$

(3) The process is shortened still further if the measures are tabulated in classes. If x is the midpoint of each class, then $M = \dfrac{\Sigma\,(Fx)}{N}$.

Ex. 10.—The method is here applied to the distribution given in Ex. 2.

X		x	F	Fx
18–20	.	. 19	7	133
15–17	.	. 16	17	272
12–14	.	. 13	9	117
9–11	.	. 10	7	70
6–8	.	. 7	5	35
3–5	.	. 4	3	12
0–2	.	. 1	2	2
			N = 50	641

$$\varsigma \ (Fx) = 641$$

$$M = \frac{641}{50} = 12\cdot82$$

Note that this value of M, 12·82, is not precisely identical with that obtained by the previous method, 12·86, though the discrepancy is only 0·3%. The reason is, of course, that the figures are somewhat distorted by being grouped into classes. We are regarding the 20's and the 18's as 19's, the 17's and 15's as 16's, and so on. In the long run these distortions tend to cancel one another out, and therefore have very little effect upon the final result. They only become serious if the grouping is too coarse, i.e. if the number of classes in the table is too small.

(4) The amount of computation, when large numbers are involved, may be much reduced by applying the device of the *arbitrary* or *guessed mean*. The following illustration may explain it. Suppose we wish to find the average height of a class of children, we could first of all measure each child's height from the ground to the top of his head, add up the figures and divide by N. An alternative plan, which would do equally well, would be to place each child by a 3-foot table, and measure the height from this to the top of his head. We would average the measures as before, but would add 36 inches to our final result. Again, we might take a still higher table, say 50 inches, and measure from this up to the tops of the heads of the larger children, down to the heads of the smaller ones. If we added together the former, subtracted the latter, divided

by N, and finally added 50 inches, we should, of course, get exactly the same result as before. But the figures with which we should be dealing would be far smaller than in the first instance. We would be averaging, e.g. $+ 6, + 1, - 2, + 3, - 5$, etc., instead of 56, 51, 48, 53, 45, etc.

The method consists, then, in making a rough guess at the mean, listing the amounts by which each measure deviates from (is greater or less than) this arbitrary mean, averaging the deviations, and finally adding the average to the arbitrary mean.

$$M = \frac{\Sigma(FD)}{N} + A.$$ A is the arbitrary or guessed mean, and D the difference between each X and A.

Ex. 11.—

X			D	F	FD
20	.	.	$+ 7$	2	14
19	.	.	$+ 6$	2	12
18	.	.	$+ 5$	3	15
17	.	.	$+ 4$	7	28
16	.	.	$+ 3$	4	12
15	.	.	$+ 2$	6	12
14	.	.	$+ 1$	3	3
13	.	.	0	4	$+ 96$
12	.	.	$- 1$	2	2
11	.	.	$- 2$	2	4
10	.	.	$- 3$	2	6
9	.	.	$- 4$	3	12
8	.	.	$- 5$	2	10
7	.	.	$- 6$	1	6
6	.	.	$- 7$	2	14
5	.	.	$- 8$	1	8
4	.	.	$- 9$	2	18
3	.	.	$- 10$	0	0
2	.	.	$- 11$	1	11
1	.	.	$- 12$	1	12
					$- 103$

$A = 13$ $M = \dfrac{+ 96 - 103}{50} + 13 = - 0 \cdot 14 + 13 = 12 \cdot 86$

The method is here applied to the distribution given in Ex. 9 (p. 49), and it yields precisely the same result for M as was obtained by the ordinary method of averaging. Note that in this example $\dfrac{\Sigma(FD)}{N}$ is a minus quantity, and is therefore subtracted from A. If we had chosen $A = 12$, $\dfrac{\Sigma(FD)}{N}$ would have been a plus quantity, namely $+ 0.86$.

(5) By far the most efficient method when N is large, say 100 or more, is to average, not the actual amounts, but the numbers of classes, by which the tabulated measures exceed or fall short of A. For instance, suppose we have a table of the distribution of ages of all the inhabitants of a town, grouped into classes of ten years, with midpoints of the classes at 5, 15, 25, etc., years. Wishing to calculate the average age we take 35 as our arbitrary mean. Obviously there is no need to sum the numbers who are 10, 20, 30, . . . years more or less than this A. We might just as well sum those who are 1, 2, 3, . . . decades more or less. Then, when we have calculated the average deviation from A in *decades*, we must multiply it by 10 to turn it back into *years*, before adding it to, or subtracting it from, A.

The formula for this method is $M = \dfrac{\Sigma(Fd) \times c}{N} + A$,

where d is the number of the class above or below that class of which A is the midpoint, and c is the size of each class.

Ex. 12.—The method is here applied to the distribution given in Ex. 3 (p. 12).

X			d	F	Fd
133–137	.	.	$+ 6$	1	6
128–132	.	.	$+ 5$	1	5
123–127	.	.	$+ 4$	6	24
118–122	.	.	$+ 3$	11	33
113–117	.	.	$+ 2$	22	44
108–112	.	.	$+ 1$	26	26
103–107	.	.	0	35	$+ 138$

X		d	F	Fd
98–102	. .	− 1	47	47
93–97	. .	− 2	43	86
88–92	. .	− 3	27	81
83–87	. .	− 4	18	72
78–82	. .	− 5	10	50
73–77	. .	− 6	3	18
			250	− 354

The arbitrary mean is taken as the midpoint of the 103–107 class, i.e. as 105. Classes above and below this are numbered consecutively.

$$\frac{\Sigma(Fd)}{N} = \frac{+ 138 - 354}{250} = - 0\cdot 864$$

This is the average number of *classes* by which M differs from A. We must multiply by 5 to get the average deviation in *years*, since $c = 5$.

$$M = 105 - 5 \times 0\cdot 864 = 100\cdot 68$$

Once the student is accustomed to this method he will find it far quicker and more accurate than any other. If in this example he had used one of the first three methods, he would have been involved in a sum totalling about 25,000. Points which require special caution are : (i) Making sure what measures are included in a class, and what is the size of c ; (ii) determining A correctly ; (iii) multiplying $\frac{\Sigma(Fd)}{N}$ by c before adding it to A ; (iv) making sure of the sign of this quantity before adding it to, or subtracting it from, A.

THE MEAN VARIATION

The Mean Variation or Average Deviation (M.V. or A.D.) is occasionally employed as an index of the extent to which the measures are spread out on either side of the mean. As its name indicates, it is the average of all the differences between each measure and the mean (or sometimes the median), regardless of whether these differences are plus or minus.

5

Ex. 13.—In this very brief distribution, the mean is 5·6. The D column lists the deviations. M.V. $= \dfrac{\Sigma D}{N} = 2·08$. If the data were in the form of a frequency distribution table, the same method would apply, but the formula would be M.V. $= \dfrac{\Sigma(FD)}{N}$.

X	D
9	3·4
7	1·4
6	0·4
4	1·6
2	3·6
	——
N = 5	10·4
M = 5·6	

Clearly the M.V. will be larger the more widely dispersed or spread out the measures. Its value is a little greater than that of Q, being generally about one-seventh of the total range of measures. (This does not hold in Ex. 13 owing to the shortness and irregularity of the distribution.) The M.V. happens to be of very little use for purposes of further statistical treatment, hence it is usually passed over in favour of the Standard Deviation.

THE STANDARD DEVIATION

The S.D. is also a kind of average of all the deviations from the mean, but it differs from the M.V. in that the deviations are squared before they are summed, and the square root of their average is taken.

$$\text{S.D. or } \sigma = \sqrt{\frac{\Sigma D^2}{N}}$$

Ex. 14.—The working is here shown for the same short distribution as in Ex. 13.

X	D	D²
9	3·4	11·56
7	1·4	1·96
6	0·4	0·16
4	1·6	2·56
2	3·6	12·96
		——
N = 5		29·20
M = 5·6		

$$\frac{\Sigma D^2}{N} = \frac{29·20}{5} = 5·84$$

$$\sigma = 2·42$$

As the mean is seldom a whole number, the squaring of deviations from it is troublesome.   Generally it is simpler to list the deviations from some arbitrary mean which is a whole number, and then to apply a correction according to the following formula :

$$\sigma = \sqrt{\frac{\Sigma D^2}{N} - (M - A)^2}$$

Note that the correction is invariably subtracted, whether its sign before squaring is positive or negative.

Ex. 15.—In the same distribution, let $A = 6$, i.e. the nearest whole number to M.

X	D	D²
9	3	9
7	1	1
6	0	0
4	2	4
2	4	16
		—
		30

$\dfrac{D^2}{N} = \dfrac{30}{5} = 6\cdot0$

$(M - A)^2 = (5\cdot6 - 6)^2 = 0\cdot16$

$\sigma^2 = 6\cdot0 - 0\cdot16 = 5\cdot84$

$\sigma = 2\cdot42$

The same formula may be extended to several different types of distributions.

(a) When the distribution is a short one, and all the measures are whole numbers, A may be chosen at zero. The D's will then be the original X's, so that :

$$\sigma = \sqrt{\frac{\Sigma X^2}{N} - M^2}$$

Ex. 16.

X	X²
9	81
7	49
6	36
4	16
2	4
	—
	186

$\dfrac{\Sigma X^2}{N} = \dfrac{186}{5} = 37\cdot2$ $M^2 = 31\cdot36$

$\sigma^2 = 37\cdot2 - 31\cdot36 = 5\cdot84$

$\sigma = 2\cdot42$

(b) Often the mean is not known, but is calculated at

the same time as the S.D. Now $M = \dfrac{\Sigma D}{N} + A$. Hence an alternative version of the same formula is :

$$\sigma = \sqrt{\dfrac{\Sigma D^2}{N} - \left(\dfrac{\Sigma D}{N}\right)^2}$$

(c) When the measures are grouped into classes, the formula becomes :

$$\sigma = c\sqrt{\dfrac{\Sigma(Fd^2)}{N} - \left(\dfrac{\Sigma(Fd)}{N}\right)^2}$$

Here c is the size of each class, and d the deviation of each measure from an arbitrary or guessed mean in terms of number of classes.

Ex. 17.—The formula is here applied to the distribution whose mean was calculated in Ex. 12. It was found there that $\dfrac{\Sigma(Fd)}{N} = -0.864$. Hence the correction $\left(\dfrac{\Sigma(Fd)}{N}\right)^2 = 0.746$.

X	F	d	d^2	Fd^2
133 +	1	+ 6	36	36
128 +	1	+ 5	25	25
123 +	6	+ 4	16	96
118 +	11	+ 3	9	99
113 +	22	+ 2	4	88
108 +	26	+ 1	1	26
103 +	35	0	0	0
98 +	47	− 1	1	47
93 +	43	− 2	4	172
88 +	27	− 3	9	243
83 +	18	− 4	16	288
78 +	10	− 5	25	250
73 +	3	− 6	36	108
	250			1,478

$$\dfrac{\Sigma(Fd^2)}{N} = \dfrac{1478}{250} = 5.912$$

$$\sigma = 5\sqrt{5.912 - 0.746} = 11.36$$

One more instance will be given, to illustrate the calculation of the mean and S.D. in one operation.

Ex. 18.—The following distribution of school marks is grouped into classes of two.   Take A at the 11–12 class, i.e. at 11·5.

X	F	d	Fd	Fd^2
19–20	2	$+ 4$	8	32
17–18	5	$+ 3$	15	45
15–16	4	$+ 2$	8	16
13–14	4	$+ 1$	4	4
11–12	3	0	$+ 35$	0
9–10	7	$- 1$	7	7
7–8	4	$- 2$	8	16
5–6	4	$- 3$	12	36
3–4	2	$- 4$	8	32
1–2	1	$- 5$	5	25
N = 36			$- 40$	213

$$\frac{\Sigma(Fd)}{N} = \frac{-5}{36} = -0{\cdot}139.$$

This is in terms of classes.   In terms of marks,

$$\frac{\Sigma(FD)}{N} = -0{\cdot}278$$

Thus M $= 11{\cdot}5 - 0{\cdot}278 = 11{\cdot}22.$

$$\frac{\Sigma(Fd)^2}{N} = \frac{213}{36} = 5{\cdot}917 \qquad \left(\frac{\Sigma(Fd)}{N}\right)^2 = 0{\cdot}019$$

$$\sigma = 2\sqrt{5{\cdot}917 - 0{\cdot}019} = 4{\cdot}858$$

These calculations are quite quickly and easily accomplished with a little practice, though some care is needed in checking the arithmetic.   For example, the whole of the above calculation, using 4-figure logarithms and checking by slide-rule, occupied the writer less than four minutes.

The S.D. is always greater than Q or the M.V.   This is to be expected, since any big deviations from the mean receive much greater weight in the S.D. than in the M.V. by being squared before they are averaged.   It generally amounts to one-fifth or one-sixth of the total range, or sometimes more if the distribution is irregular, as in Ex. 18. This rule enables us to apply a rough check to our result. If in Ex. 18 we had obtained $\sigma = 2$ or $\sigma = 10$, we should have known that there had been some mistake in the computation.

The Significance of the S.D.—Before we go further with this description of statistical methods, it would be well to adopt a more uniform notation or set of symbols. For reasons which will appear later, it is often preferable to deal not with original measures (which are denoted by the symbol X), but with measures expressed as deviations from their own mean. The latter will be denoted by x. Thus when $X = 80$ points of **I.Q.**, and the mean **I.Q.** $= 100$, $x = -20$. Again, actual frequencies (which are denoted by F) are often replaced by proportionate frequencies, that is, the actual frequencies divided by N. And since frequencies are always plotted graphically along the Y axis, they will be denoted by y. For example, in Exs. 12 and 17, 26 students obtained test scores of 108 to 112. The mean was 100·68, and N was 250. The x and y values for such students are therefore :

$$x = 110 - 100 \cdot 68 = + 9 \cdot 32 \qquad y = \frac{26}{250} = 0 \cdot 104$$

Now, it is well known that many graphs, such as the straight line and the parabola, can be represented by certain algebraic equations. For instance, $y = kx$ gives a straight line, running through the origin, whose slope depends on the size of k. In the same way a normal distribution curve is represented by an equation which involves x, y, σ, and certain constants.[1] This is a most important fact, since it signifies that any normal distribution can be completely defined or numerically described if we know the mean and S.D. alone. It will be remembered that the alternative, percentile, system of defining distributions required the citation of some half-dozen percentile

[1]
$$y = \frac{e^{\frac{-x^2}{2\sigma^2}}}{\sigma \sqrt{2\pi}}$$

No attempt will be made to deal here with the theory of probability from which this equation is derived, nor with certain other (less common) types of distribution curves for which other equations are available. Cf. Dawson (1933), Kelley (1924).

levels in order to provide a reasonably complete numerical description. This system, based on the mean and S.D., is therefore much more efficient. But it is restricted to normal, or practically normal, distributions, whereas the percentile system will apply to any shape of distribution.

If, then, we know the S.D. we can deduce y for every value of x, that is the frequency of every possible measure. For instance, although we cannot measure the intelligence quotients of the whole population of Great Britain, yet, if we may assume that the I.Q. is a variable which is normally distributed, with a mean of 100 and a S.D. of $16\frac{1}{2}$, we can state at once just what proportions of the population have I.Q.s of 100, 101, . . . etc., or what proportion lies below 67 I.Q., or between 120 and 130 I.Q., and so on.

Furthermore, there are available in most statistical text-books tables which will tell us the value of y corresponding to each value of $\dfrac{x}{\sigma}$, regardless of what the variable may be (I.Q., height, handwriting speed, etc.). These are known as 'probability integral' tables. The graph given in Fig. 18 is based on such tables, but is probably easier to use, and is accurate to two or three significant places.

Against $\dfrac{x}{\sigma}$ is plotted, not y—the actual proportion of measures which deviate from the mean by this amount— but *the proportion which deviate by this amount or more.* Taking the lowest curve, it can be seen that nearly 0·16 or 16% of measures in any normal distribution differ from the mean of the distribution by $1 \times \sigma$ or more. For example, if the S.D. of I.Q.s is $16\frac{1}{2}$, then about 16% of the population have I.Q.s of $116\frac{1}{2}$ or more, and, equally, about 16% of the population have I.Q.s of $83\frac{1}{2}$ or less. The upper curves are for dealing more accurately with larger values of $\dfrac{x}{\sigma}$ and smaller values of y. Each curve is, as it were, a 10 times magnification of a section of the curve below. For instance, we can read off from the first curve that about

0·023 or 2·3% of the population differ from the mean by 2σ or more, but the second curve allows a more accurate reading, namely 0·0228.

Ex. 18.—In a school population of 25,000, how many children may be expected to have I.Q.s of 120 to 130 ? And what will be the highest I.Q. among the least intelligent 1,000 of these children ?

Intelligence is something which varies continuously ; that is to say, every possible value of I.Q. in between 119 and 120 can occur, although we usually calculate it only to the nearest whole number. Strictly speaking, then, we want to know how many children have I.Q.s between 119·50 and 130·50, and to exclude those whose I.Q.s are 119·49 or less (who would count as 119's), also those whose I.Q.s are 130·51 or more (who would count as 131's). Now 119·5 and 130·5 differ from the mean by 19·5 and 30·5, that is by 1·18σ and 1·85σ, taking σ as 16½. Reading off from Fig. 18, the corresponding proportions are 0·119 and 0·0322. Hence the proportion of the population within the given limits is 0·119 − 0·0322 = 0·0868 = 8·68%. 8·68% of 25,000 is 2,170, the answer to our first question.

In the second question, 1,000 out of 25,000 is a proportion of 0·040. From Fig. 18, 0·04 corresponds to an x value of 1·75σ. 1·75 × 16½ = 28·875. The lowest thousand therefore have I.Q.s of 100 − 28·875, or less. Hence the answer, to the nearest whole number of I.Q., is 71.

Ex. 19.—Does the distribution of intelligence test scores given in Ex. 17 (p. 56) conform to a normal distribution ? In other words, are the obtained frequencies similar to the frequencies which would be expected for a truly normal distribution with the same mean (100·68) and the same S.D. (11·36) ?

These test scores, unlike I.Q.s, are discrete. Nobody could score 107½, however carefully his score was computed. If he nearly, but not quite, completed 108 items, his score would still be 107. Thus in order to find what proportion may be expected (according to the normal curve) to fall within the 103–107 class, we must determine the proportion with scores of 103 or more and subtract from it the proportion with scores of 108 or more, *not* the proportions lying between 102·5 and 107·5. The calculations for all classes are given in the following table. For example, 103 is a deviation of + 2·32 from the mean, or + 0·20σ ; 108 deviates + 7·32 or + 0·65σ from the mean. From Fig. 18 we find the proportions lying at or beyond these two limits to be 0·421 and 0·258 respectively. Hence the proportion to be expected within the 103–107 class is 0·421 −

0·258 = 0·163. N is 250, and 0·163 × 250 = 41. The penultimate column lists the expected frequencies (omitting decimals), and the last column gives the frequencies actually obtained. The two columns agree fairly closely, but there are some discrepancies. At present we lack a method for telling whether these discrepancies should be regarded as appreciable or important, but such a method will be described later (pp. 102–3). The full answer to this question will therefore be postponed.

X	x	$\dfrac{x}{\sigma}$	Proportions lying at or beyond these values of x/σ	Proportions expected in each class	F expected in each class	F actually obtained
133 +	+ 32·32 +	+ 2·85	0·00219	0·00219	1	1
128 +	+ 27·32 +	+ 2·41	0·0078	0·00561	1	1
123 +	+ 22·32 +	+ 1·97	0·025	0·0172	4	6
118 +	+ 17·32 +	+ 1·53	0·062	0·037	9	11
113 +	+ 12·32 +	+ 1·09	0·138	0·076	19	22
108 +	+ 7·32 +	+ 0·65	0·258	0·120	30	26
103 +	+ 2·32 +	+ 0·20	0·421	0·163	41	35
98 +	− 2·68 +	− 0·24	0·404	0·175	44	47
93 +	− 7·68 +	− 0·68	0 246	0·158	40	43
88 +	− 12·68 +	− 1·12	0·133	0·113	28	27
83 +	− 17·68 +	− 1·56	0·059	0·074	18	18
78 +	− 22·68 +	− 2·00	0·023	0·036	9	10
73 +	− 27·68 +	− 2·44	0·0073	0·0157	4	3
68 +	− 32·68 +	− 2·88	0·00195	0·0073	2	0
			1·00000		250	250

On examining Fig. 18, we see that the proportions whose scores deviate by 2·5σ or more are very small, less than 1 in 100, and that those who deviate by 3σ or more only number about 1 in 1,000. Here, then, we have the reason for a statement made earlier, namely that the S.D. usually amounts to one-fifth or one-sixth of the total range of a distribution. For when N is about 100, and the distribution is a regular one, we shall ordinarily find the measures ranging from + 2·5σ to − 2·5σ, i.e. a total of 5σ. And when N approaches 1,000 we may find scores running from + 3σ to − 3σ, a total of 6σ.

There is yet another way of interpreting normal distributions, which will be useful to us later, that is in terms of probabilities. Since 0·159 of persons may be expected to obtain measures 1σ or more above the mean, the probability that any one person will measure this much or more is $0\cdot159$. The probability that he will measure less is $0\cdot841$. In other words, the odds are 841 to 159, or about $5\frac{1}{2}$ to 1 against his measure being as high as or higher than this. Similarly the probability of a measure as high as $+3\sigma$ or more is $0\cdot00135$, and the chances against it are 740 to 1. This means, for example, that we should probably find only one child in an ordinary elementary school of about 740 pupils with an I.Q. of 150 or more, if we assume the I.Q.s of school children to be normally distributed with a σ of $16\frac{1}{2}$, since 150 is just over $100 + 3 \times 16\frac{1}{2}$. Actually the σ of I.Q.s among elementary school children is usually much lower, which makes the odds against high I.Q.s much greater. If σ is $12\frac{1}{2}$, then 150 is 4σ above the mean, and we can deduce from Fig. 18 that only about 1 in 31,000 reaches this level.

CHAPTER IV

INTERPRETATION OF SCHOOL MARKS AND TEST SCORES

Combining or Comparing Distributions of Marks.—In Chap. II we found that the marks awarded to school work or examinations are often so erratically distributed that it is impossible to interpret them, as they stand, correctly. The first stages in the interpretation of marks involve combining and comparing them. For instance, the marks for different questions in one examination, or different examinations in one subject, need to be combined to give a total score. Often the marks on several subjects are combined to yield a general view of the pupil's or student's all-round ability. Comparison enters when we wish to know whether a pupil or student is better on one subject than on some other subject (subjects which may have been marked either by the same, or by different, examiners or teachers). In large-scale examinations where several examiners each deal with a proportion of the scripts it is, of course, essential that their markings should be comparable. Sometimes, also, age allowances must be made ; the marks of younger and older pupils need to be rendered comparable by the elimination of differences due to age.[1]

Now, none of these processes can be carried out directly unless the marks to be combined or compared occur in closely similar frequency distributions. This is a fundamental statistical principle, very elementary in nature, yet very widely neglected. But with the aid of the statistical tools described in Chap. III, we are now in a position to determine whether such distributions are sufficiently

---

[1] Davies and Jones (1936) discuss this point and describe a simple method of making age allowances.

similar, and if they are not, to adjust them in such a way as to make them so. These tools will further assist in interpretation, since they provide a scientific definition of those exceedingly vague conceptions—the goodness or badness of a mark or test score, and the ease or difficulty of an examination question or test item.

Distributions may be dissimilar from one another in three respects : (1) differences in their averages arise, for example, when one examiner is far more lenient than another ; (2) differences in their dispersions may arise when one examiner spreads out his marks far more widely above and below the average than another ; (3) differences occur in their shapes, e.g. normal, skew, rectangular, etc. For the time being we will consider only the most important shape, the approximately normal. We may then state that marks can be directly combined or compared only if drawn from distributions with the same mean and the same S.D.

The Importance of Equivalent Standard Deviations.— Identity of S.D.s is the more important of these two requirements, though it is less often recognized. In many instances of combination of marks, the averages do not matter in the slightest.

Ex. 20.—Suppose that the final marks of a group of pupils or students depend on their results in three subjects, A, B, and C, and that the distributions are as follows :

Subject	Mean	Range	S.D.
A	60	40–80	7
B	50	30–70	7
C	80	60–100	7

Now, a pupil who is average on all three subjects obtains a total of 190/300, and another who is average on two subjects but top on the third scores 210/300 *whatever the subject.*

Ex. 21.—In contrast to Ex. 20, let us now combine the following sets of marks, whose S.D.s differ.

Subject	Mean	Range	S.D.
A	60	40–80	7
B	50	10–90	14
C	80	70–90	$3\frac{1}{2}$

A pupil who is average all round again scores 190. But now a pupil who is average in two subjects and top in a third obtains 210, 230, and 200 according as the third subject is A, B, or C, respectively. The fact of doing well in subject B (which has the lowest average) actually raises the score the most because B has the biggest S.D. And doing well in C has the least effect in raising the final total (although it has the highest average), because it has the smallest SD. Similarly if we compare the performances of three pupils who are at the lower quartile on one subject but average on the other two, we find their respective marks to be 185, 181, and 188. Doing badly on B has a big effect, but doing badly on C has little effect.

The general principle, illustrated by these examples, is that when several sets of marks are combined, their relative ' weights,' i.e. their respective degrees of influence upon the final total, are proportional not to their averages but to their S.D.s. If in a final mark we wish to give more weight to one subject than to another, e.g. twice as much weight to written as to mental arithmetic, we shall accomplish it, not by making the average mark on the former twice the average on the latter, but by making the range and S.D. of the former twice as large. The usual procedure in such weighting is to multiply the former set of marks by two. This may produce the desired effect, not because it doubles the average, but because it doubles the S.D. The same effect would follow if the average remained unchanged while the deviation of each pupil's mark from this average was doubled. When the marks derived from several questions in a single examination are to be combined in certain proportions, this same technique of adjusting the S.D.s rather than the averages for the questions should be adopted.

In order to combine or compare two sets of marks whose distributions are dissimilar, we should then express each set in the form of deviations from their own means, and multiply one set by a figure which will raise or lower its S.D. to the same level as that of the other set. For instance, in the two sets B and C in Ex. 21, the ratio of S.D.s is 14 to $3\frac{1}{2}$, or 4 to 1. The deviations in C will therefore become equivalent to those in B if multiplied by 4. Alternatively, each mark may be expressed in $\dfrac{x}{\sigma}$ form. The top marks on A, B, and C thus become $\dfrac{80-60}{7}$, $\dfrac{90-50}{14}$, and $\dfrac{90-80}{3\frac{1}{2}}$. All of these equal $+2\cdot86$. When so converted, they are all equivalent.

The Importance of Equivalent Means.—Naturally the averages of distributions are important under some circumstances. If marks on several questions or several subjects are to be combined, and alternatives are allowed, so that each pupil's final mark is derived from a selected number of questions or subjects, then it is extremely essential to ensure equivalent means. Thus in Exs. 20 and 21, if pupils took either A and B, or A and C, those who were at the average level would total 110 on the former combination, 140 on the latter. Again, when scores are to be, not combined, but compared, it is obvious that differences in means will entirely upset the comparisons. The adjustment of discrepancies in means is easy—merely add or subtract so much from all the marks in one subject or question until its average is the same as that for the other subject or question. More often than not, however, discrepancies in means are accompanied by discrepancies in S.D.s. In that case resort must be made to the technique already described, according to which each mark is expressed as $\dfrac{x}{\sigma}$, or to some modification of this technique (cf. pp. 71–3).

EQUATING OF MARKS BY THE PERCENTILE TECHNIQUE

Although the statistical treatment of distributions in terms of means and S.D.s is far from difficult, it may admittedly lie outside the scope of the ordinary teacher or examiner. Further, it cannot be used when the distributions bear no resemblance to normality. For instance, if a headmaster, to whom were submitted the marks listed in Ex. 5 (p. 34) wished to compare the pupils' standings on reading and geography, he could not use this technique. The alternative, percentile, system would, however, be quite suitable for making such a comparison, and it is probably simpler for the uninitiated to comprehend. (It does not even involve looking up squares and square roots, as does a technique based on the S.D.)

Percentiles will provide a uniform scale in terms of which comparisons may be made between any sets of marks. Whatever the test or examination which a group of pupils or students takes, a certain percentile level always means the same level of achievement (relative to that group of people). For instance, on looking at Ex. 5 we might be inclined to suppose that 8 marks for reading represents a better achievement than 3 marks for geography ; certainly the pupils themselves would infer that this was so. But actually they are precisely equivalent, since both marks fall at the 25th percentile, Q_1. The teacher may, of course, assert that the general standard of reading in that class is good and the geography poor. This is an objection which will frequently be raised by critics of this chapter, and we will show later why we believe it to be baseless.

Percentile Graphs.—One of the best ways of comparing two sets of marks is by a 7-point percentile graph, which is illustrated in the following example.

Mark			Frequencies	
			English	Arithmetic
90 +	.	.	1	5
80 +	.	.	10	11
70 +	.	.	15	13
60 +	.	.	17	15
50 +	.	.	8	10
40 +	.	.	5	2
30 +	.	.	1	0
20 +	.	.	0	1
			—	—
			57	57

Ex. 22.—The table shows the marks of 57 pupils, aged 12 +, in a Scottish school on final examinations in English and arith-

metic. Though the tabulation is coarse, it indicates that the two distributions differ in their means and S.D.s, and that, while the first is roughly normal, the second is negatively skewed. The procedure is, first, to determine the 99th, 90th, 75th, 50th, 25th, 10th, and 1st percentiles for each set of marks. From the original lists these are found to be 90, 84, 77, 67, 59, 49, 39, and 97, 89, 81, 71, 60, 53, 35, respectively. Draw a graph, as shown in Fig. 19, where English marks are plotted along the Y axis against arithmetic marks on the X axis. Plot these

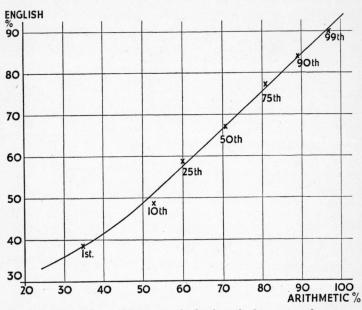

FIG. 19.—Comparison of two sets of school marks by means of a seven-point graph.

seven points (X = 97, Y = 90 ; X = 89, Y = 84 ; etc.), and connect them up by a straight line or smooth curve which runs as nearly as possible through them all. This line may be extended at both ends so as to cover the total ranges of marks. From it we can now read off the mark on the English scale which corresponds to each mark on the arithmetic scale, and vice versa. Thus 41 in English is equivalent to 39 in arithmetic, 80 in English to 85 in arithmetic.

Often it is not necessary to determine as many points as seven in order to fix the graph. Three points, preferably the 90th, 50th, and 10th percentiles, may give sufficient accuracy. Note that just the same procedure could have been used even if the distributions had differed widely in range and dispersion, e.g. if one subject had been marked out of 40, the other out of 200.

Interpretation of Marks by Means of Percentile Levels.— It would be a great step forward if examiners at universities or training centres, and even at secondary schools, were required to publish with their mark lists a table of the median, quartiles, and some of the other percentiles for the marks which they had actually awarded.[1] Lecturers and students would soon learn the significance of these terms, and would then be able to see what standards of marking their various examiners were adopting. And each student could interpret the excellence or poorness of his own marks in various subjects. The subject in which he was best would not necessarily be the one in which he obtained the highest examination mark, but the one in which his percentile level was highest. Similarly, if he obtained the same mark in two subjects, this would not show that his ability at the two was the same (as he often supposes at present), unless it happened that their percentile levels were the same.

Defects of Percentiles.—It has sometimes been suggested that teachers and examiners should not publish their pupils' or students' marks at all, but only their percentile levels. This would, indeed, be much fairer than most present systems. The 50th percentile would always represent average achievement ; percentiles approaching 100 and 0 would always represent the same very high and very low achievements. But such a plan is defective in that it might not be intelligible to interested persons, e.g. to children or to most of their parents. They would probably fail to realize that percentiles make no pretence of providing an absolute evaluation of achievements, as do ordinary sets

---

[1] This scheme would not, however, be feasible in an examination taken by a very small number, say less than twenty students (cf. p. 79).

6

of marks (albeit the pretence is false). Percentiles only indicate achievement relative to the particular group or groups of pupils who have been marked. In fact, they are the same as rank orders, except that they always run from 100 to 1, whereas rank positions run from 1 to N.

A more important defect is that percentiles, although invaluable for purposes of comparing distributions, may be very misleading if used for combining distributions. The reason is that percentile units are very far from equivalent to one another, since they are far closer together at or near the median than they are at or near the extremes. It can be seen from the 'probability integral' graph (Fig. 18) that a percentile level of 90, i.e. the measure above which only 10% of the measures lie, corresponds to an $\frac{x}{\sigma}$ score of +1·28. The 80th similarly corresponds to + 0·84, the 60th and 50th to + 0·25 and 0·00. Thus the difference between the first two of these, 0·44, is decidedly greater than that between the second pair, 0·25. Actually the 99th, 94th, 78th, 50th, 22nd, 6th, and 1st percentiles are all aproximately equally spaced, in the sense that a child who is at the 99th percentile is as superior to one at the 94th, as the 94th is to the 78th, or the 78th to the 50th. The consequence of this inequality of units is that, although we may, if we wish, average or otherwise combine a person's percentiles on different tests, we shall obtain thereby quite different results from those obtained by averaging his scores.

Ex. 23.—Pupil A's marks on two examinations lie at the 98th and 54th percentiles; Pupil B's marks on both examinations lie at the 85th percentile. A's average percentile of 76 is distinctly poorer than B's 85. But if these figures are converted into $\frac{x}{\sigma}$ scores, i.e. into units which really are equivalent, it will be found that A is actually slightly better than B. For the $\frac{x}{\sigma}$ values of the 98th and 54th percentiles are + 2·054 and + 0·100, average + 1·077; whereas the $\frac{x}{\sigma}$ value of the 85th percentile is only + 1·036.

It is advisable, therefore, never to use percentiles for combining marks. The same is true of rank orders (cf. p. 30).

Adoption of a Standard Scale for All School or Examination Marks.—The following solution to this difficulty may be recommended. Each chief examiner, headmaster, or other authority who is concerned with combining, comparing, and interpreting sets of marks awarded by subexaminers, class teachers, etc., should adopt an arbitrary standard scale. He might, for instance, choose a percentage scale ranging roughly from 30% to 90%, with a mean of 60% and a S.D. of 10. Now, on such a scale the 7 percentile points mentioned above fall at 83, 73, 67, 60, 53, 47, and 37 respectively. Each set of marks submitted by a teacher or examiner should be converted into this scale by the graphical method already described. If this is done all the marks from all the markers will be strictly comparable with one another, and they will be expressed in units which are (sufficiently closely for all practical purposes) equivalent to one another, so that they can be combined or averaged at will. And there is the further advantage that the scale corresponds well to the present conventional conception of high and low percentages. Naturally any other standard scale can be chosen if preferred, and its percentile points determined from the probability integral graph.[1] Fig. 20 shows the graphs for transforming the two distributions of Ex. 22 into the suggested scale. 97 for arithmetic and 90 for English are plotted against 83 (the 99th percentile point) on the standard scale, and so on. The standard mark for any other mark can be read off. Thus 81% in arithmetic becomes 67% standard, and 81% in English becomes 71% standard.

Another way of achieving the same result is as follows. With the aid of the probability integral graph a table should be drawn up showing the proportionate frequency

[1] The $\frac{x}{\sigma}$ values of the 99th and 1st percentiles are $+$ and $-$ 2·326 respectively, of the 90th and 10th they are $+$ and $-$ 1·282, of the 75th and 25th they are $+$ and $-$ 0·675.

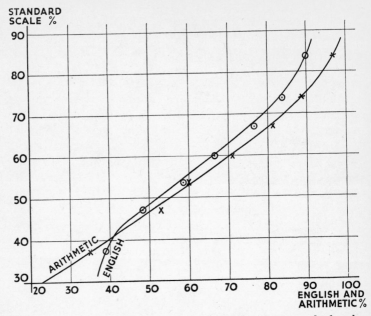

Fig. 20.—Conversion of two sets of school marks into a standard scale.

of each mark on the desired standard scale, using the same method as that described in Ex. 19, p. 60.

Ex. 24.—The following table shows the proportions to be expected within successive classes of 5 marks, when the mean is 60, the S.D. 10.

Mark	F%
88–92	0 or $\frac{1}{2}$
83–87	1
78–82	3
73–77	$6\frac{1}{2}$
68–72	12
63–67	17
58–62	20
53–57	17
48–52	12
43–47	$6\frac{1}{2}$
38–42	3
33–37	1
28–32	0 or $\frac{1}{2}$
	100

Teachers or sub-examiners may be given such a table and instructed to award marks to their pupils roughly in accordance with the frequencies there shown (precise conformity is not necessary). Or, alternatively, the chief examiner or head teacher may take each of the distributions of unscaled marks, award a scaled mark between 88 and 92 to the top 0 or $\frac{1}{2}\%$ of the examinees, marks between 83 and 87 to the next 1% of them, and so on. Only very exceptionally good or poor candidates—those better or worse than 999 in 1,000 of the ordinary run—should be given marks of over 90% or under 30%. For in a normal distribution only a proportion of 0·135% is expected to score more than $+ 3\frac{x}{\sigma}$, or less than $- 3\frac{x}{\sigma}$.

Ex. 25.—

Mark	Frequency (a)	Frequency (b)
20		
19		
18	Exceptional cases only	
17		
16		
15	1	
14	3	} 1
13	6	3
12	12	5
11	18	7
10	20	8
9	18	7
8	12	5
7	6	3
6	3	
5	1	} 1
4		
3		
2	Exceptional cases only	
1		
0		
	100	40

Burt (1917) recommends an alternative standard scale of marks, based on a similar plan, but with an average of 10

and a maximum range of 0–20. The scale is given here
with the frequencies to be expected when (*a*) 100 and (*b*) 40
pupils are marked according to it. Here also exact adherence
should not be demanded. Any one set of marks for 40 pupils
may depart from it fairly widely. But in the long run all the
marks awarded by any one teacher or examiner should show
the same mean, S.D., and tendency to normality as does this
standard scale.

Objections to Rationalized Marking

There is no doubt that many teachers and examiners will
object strongly to the principle upon which this chapter is
based, that the average and the dispersion of sets of marks
should always be the same in any one institution. Faculties in a university which consistently award high marks
sometimes try to justify themselves by claiming that they
get a ' better run ' of students than do those which consistently award low marks. Examiners regard it as only
natural to award different average marks to the answers to
different questions in one paper, since some questions are
' done better ' than others. Teachers similarly regard
their classes as ' better at ' some subjects than at others,
and so deserving of higher marks. Again, the class they
have this year may seem to them an exceptionally ' good '
or ' bad ' one, and the compositions written by the class
may be ' better or poorer than usual.' Finally, those
mathematical lecturers and teachers who are particularly
prone to award very widely dispersed marks state that
their students exhibit a ' wider range of accomplishment '
than do students of other subjects.

*Justification for Equalizing the Average in All Sets of
Marks.*—Many of these claims are extremely dubious.
Thus it is more likely that the university departments
which award high marks will attract a poorer, rather than
a better, run of students, and that the subjects which are
marked more strictly will be pursued chiefly by the better
students who care more for the subjects than for marks.
Again, one is justified in suspecting teachers' judgments
about the merits of their classes, since some teachers

appear, year after year, to be blessed with good classes, and others to be cursed with bad ones. According to what is popularly known as ' the law of averages,' one would expect the number of good pupils to be balanced in the long run by an equal number of bad ones. As a matter of fact, the statistical techniques outlined in Chap. V give us a method of predicting just how much classes are likely to vary from year to year, or English compositions from week to week, owing to so-called fluctuations of sampling. Here is one instance. A class of 45 pupils averages 60% in their general scholastic work on a scale of marks running roughly from 30% to 90%. From these data it may be stated that there is an even chance that the average level of next year's class will lie between 59% and 61%, and that it is extremely improbable that next year's will differ from this year's by more than 3% or 4%, up or down. Consider also the marking of English compositions, or of half a dozen or more separate questions in an examination paper. If the scale of marks employed ranges roughly from 4 to 20 (S.D. 3), then we can predict that the maximum variation likely to occur in the average marks for different compositions or questions is 3 marks, provided that there are at least 36 scripts, and only 2 marks if there are 81 scripts. An individual pupil may certainly range very widely in his level of performance on different questions, but the average level of a group of pupils is far more stable than is commonly supposed. The apparent variations in the goodness of answers are due much less to variations in the pupils than to irregularities in the suitability of the questions or of the topics for compositions. But if an examiner sets a bad question which is beyond the scope of the majority of examinees, or which does not allow them to express their fullest capacities, there is no justification for giving low marks. It is, therefore, much fairer to give the same average mark to the actual average script in all cases, as was suggested in Chap. II.

It is a different matter when a group of pupils or students is known, from objective evidence, to be selected in such a way as to be, on the average, superior or inferior to the mean of some larger group. A special class for scholarship candidates and one for backward pupils will naturally show generally good and poor attainments respectively. But in most cases the teacher or examiner who claims to have a specially good or poor set of pupils or scripts is judging purely on the basis of subjective recollections of what he regards as average level. When a test or examination is applied to all the pupils of a certain age in a school, or in several schools, then the whole group should be marked according to the principles already outlined, and the marks for separate classes within this wider group may be picked out and averaged. Such averages will then quite justifiably show a certain range of variation. But when a test or examination is given only to a single class, it is far safer not to trust the marker's subjective view of the class's general level, but to award an average mark to the average script actually obtained from this class. Similarly the averages for different school subjects should be the same, regardless of whether a class *appears* to be better at one subject than at another, except when objective evidence (derived from the application of the same tests or examinations to other, larger, groups of pupils) *proves* that the class's attainments are uneven.

The ' Goodness ' or ' Badness ' of a Mark.—We still have to face the wider question : what do teachers and examiners mean when they say that a pupil's work is good or bad, or an examination paper easy or difficult? For endless objections of the type discussed above will be raised until this is settled. Most persons who have marking to do obviously believe that they possess in their minds some absolute standard of goodness and badness by means of which they can evaluate a pupil's or a class's achievement. But numerous experiments have proved that such subjective judgments of merit or difficulty, when obtained from several different persons, are often widely discrepant. It was for this reason that we were forced to conclude, in Chap. II, that all marking consists primarily in ranking a set of performances in order, and that it is a matter of relative comparison, not of absolute placement. The goodness of a child's performance at some task can therefore mean only that he ranks high when his performance is directly compared with the performances of other children at the same task, under similar circumstances. An achievement is good if only very few people can do as well or better, and it is poor if only very few people do it as badly or worse. Similarly, the rational definition of the difficulty of a task is the fewness of people who can accomplish this task.

' Fewness of people,' in statistical terminology, connotes either percentile level or, preferably, $\frac{x}{\sigma}$ value. A mark is not necessarily a good one because it happens to be 80% or 9/10 and the like. But it is good relative to the marks of some particular group of persons if it falls at the 95th percentile, or is 2σ above the mean mark obtained by these persons, or if it stands high on a standard scale whose mean and S.D. are known. Such designations of goodness or badness are entirely unequivocal.

The Ease or Difficulty of Questions.—By approaching marking from this standpoint we obtain a rational scale, not only of the goodness or badness of pupils' work, but also of the ease or difficulty of questions or test items. If, for example, five items are answered correctly by 16%, $22\frac{1}{2}$%, 31%, 40%, and 50% of a large group of persons, then we can state that (for these persons) the items are all equally spaced in difficulty. For these proportions correspond to $\frac{x}{\sigma}$ values of $+ 1 \cdot 0$, $+ 0 \cdot 75$, $+ 0 \cdot 50$, $+ 0 \cdot 25$, and $0 \cdot 0$ respectively. Similarly some questions which are below average difficulty will be equally spaced if answered by, say, 91%, $93\frac{1}{2}$%, and 96% of pupils, for here the proportions of incorrect answers, namely 9%, 6%, and 4%, correspond to $\frac{x}{\sigma}$ values of $- 1 \cdot 35$, $- 1 \cdot 55$, and $- 1 \cdot 75$, respectively.

Justification for Equalizing the Dispersion in all sets of Marks.—The claim that mathematical accomplishments vary more widely than do accomplishments in other subjects requires some further consideration. It is true that it is usually easier to discriminate between different levels of mathematical than of, say, English composition, ability, because tests in the former can generally be marked more objectively and accurately. Thus in the work of an ordinary school class it may be impossible to distinguish more than about ten different levels of essay writing, whereas perhaps a hundred levels of mathematical skill may be distinguished. Although there is some justification for attaching greater weight to marks obtained by the more efficient measuring instrument, yet this greater efficiency is no criterion of the range of ability, as the following analogy shows. In a school quarter-mile race, one referee may time the boys with a seconds' hand watch, and find that some take 50, others 51, 52, . . . 60 seconds. Another referee may possess a tenth-of-a-second stopwatch and find that some boys take 50·0, others 50·1, 50·2 . . . 59·9, 60·0 seconds. But the range of ability is the same in both cases.

There is only one way in which the claim might be scientifically substantiated. All the pupils of a certain age attending both the best, the medium, and the poorest schools in a district should be given tests, preferably of the objective type, in arithmetic and English, and their scores should be tabulated. On studying the scores in any one school it would doubtless be found that the ranges and S.D.s on both tests were somewhat smaller than they were among the whole group of pupils, because the pupils in one school are always more homogeneous in their abilities than are the population at large. If the increase in homogeneity (i.e. the decrease in S.D.) turned out to be greater for English than for arithmetic, then the claim would be proved. But, so far as the present writer is aware, no experiment of this type has ever indicated a tendency for the range of mathematical abilities in a group of pupils or students to be more diverse or spread out—relative to the range in the population at large—than the range of English or other abilities. Probably then the claim is based (*a*) on the greater efficiency of the instruments for measuring mathematical ability, (*b*) on the assumption that there exists an absolute criterion of high and low ability. The former point is, as we have seen, irrelevant, and the latter fallacious.[1]

The Marking of Small Groups.—Peculiar difficulties still remain in applying the principles and techniques of this chapter to the marking of small groups. The mean and the S.D. of marks among, say, half a dozen Honours students may vary far more from year to year than they do among 40 or 100 students. If the average is taken as 60% this year, the odds are even that it will lie somewhere between 57 and 63 next year, but it may drop as low as about 50%, or rise as high as 70%. And if there is only one candidate who is awarded 60% this year, a single candidate next year may deserve anywhere from 30% to 90%. Until such time as objective tests are available, standardized on Honours students from many universities, or over several years, the examiner can only employ subjective marking scales, as indicated in Chap. II (p. 42).

TEST NORMS

Test norms are tables of the scores of large groups of children or adults by reference to which it is possible to interpret the significance of the score obtained by any person, or group of persons, to whom the test is applied. The mental tester fully admits that a test performance, as such, tells us nothing as to its goodness or badness, and that it must be compared with the performances of other similar persons tested under the same conditions. Thus some tests are standardized, and norms are obtained, by being applied to large groups of typical 11-year English elementary school children, or to Scottish qualifying examination candidates; others are given to school

---

[1] It is only fair to mention, however, that Thomson (1939) believes that greater variability would be found in mathematical than in other abilities, if it were possible to measure variability absolutely.

leavers aged 14 to 15, or to central school pupils ; others
to normal adults, or to university students, and so forth.
American testers often publish grade norms, i.e. the
standards obtained by successive school classes in their
elementary and high schools. But they realize that the
standards in different schools cannot possibly be uniform.
In this country the variations are so great that the system
has scarcely ever been adopted.

A mere statement of the average or median scores of
such groups is, of course, insufficient. Often the deciles
are quoted, so that it is possible to state that a person's performance is, say, as good as that of the best 20% of the
group upon which the test was standardized. A system
based on $\dfrac{x}{\sigma}$ values of the various scores would be better
because, as was shown above, percentile units are so unequal to one another. Such a system has seldom been used,
presumably because it demands more statistical knowledge
than most untrained testers possess. Often, however, the
mean and the S.D. of the scores obtained by the standardization group are available, so that the tester can readily
determine how many times σ above or below the mean
are the scores of his testees, and so can interpret the goodness or badness of their scores.

It should by now be obvious that the usefulness of such
norms is strictly limited by the nature of the standardization group. Norms are purely and simply a summary of
the test performances of a particular group of testees, and
must be interpreted with reference to that group. For
example, if an American educational test is given to a
British child and his score falls at the 70th percentile
according to the norms published with the test, this means
that he did better than 70% of the American children who
took the test, but does not necessarily show that he is
above the British median or average. In point of fact
American educational tests are almost useless in this
country because their standards differ so greatly from ours
(cf. McGregor, 1934), and, of course, because their content

and wording are often unsuitable.   Probably the same is
true of group intelligence tests, but not of the Stanford-
Binet test (cf. Chap. IX).   Even between England and
Scotland the differences are so big that few tests which have
been standardized in the one country can be used in the
other, unless fresh norms have been collected there.   The
appalling efficiency of Scottish teaching methods raises the
performance of Scottish elementary school children on
tests of the 3 R's by anything from 10% to 50% over the
English level.   Such evidence as we possess, however,
points to no appreciable differences on tests of general
intelligence.

Many tests have been adequately standardized in London
or Glasgow, but are not appropriate for use in the provinces
or in rural areas where the educational level, and possibly
also the intelligence level, are likely to be different.   Probably it would be better to provide more than one set of
norms for such different types of school, so that a child's
test performance could be referred to the most suitable set.
Apparently even the size of school has some effect upon
educational level (cf. Mowat, 1938).   Perhaps still more
potent is socio-economic status, since this is known to have
a marked effect upon educational and intellectual levels.[1]
Thus if a test has been standardized by being applied only
to children in a rather poor area, its norms will not be
appropriate for schools in a relatively superior area.
Adequate norms for, say, children aged 11+ would be
obtained only if all types of schools containing pupils of
this age were adequately represented in the standardization
group.   Norms derived only from one type of school may
still be of some use, but the tester must then remember to
interpret his testees' results with reference to this type.

The origin and the adequacy of many of the published

[1] Cf. Burt (1937).   The reasons for this effect are probably partly
environmental and partly hereditary.   Poor surroundings and upbringing undoubtedly have many adverse influences upon education.
But in addition there is indisputable evidence of a connection, albeit
a small one, between intelligence and social class, quite apart from
environmental influences.

test norms are so dubious that we would advise testers in schools to treat them all with caution, and when possible to do without them. Once a whole school class, or all the children of a certain age in the school, have been tested, each child's standing relative to the rest of this group will be known, and will provide most of the information needed for educational diagnosis and prognosis, without reference to any outside standards. And if the same tests can be applied in a school for several years, an extremely useful set of ' local ' norms could quite easily be collected, either in terms of percentiles or of σ scores.

Age Norms

Age norms may be defined as follows. A child who obtains a Mental Age or M.A. (on an intelligence test), or an Educational Age or E.A. (on an educational test) of x years is one whose performance is as good as that of the average child of Chronological Age or C.A. of x years. For example, a child aged 10·0 may do as well in an intelligence test as an average 11·0 year old, but only score up to the level of a 9·0 year old on tests of reading and arithmetic. He is then said to possess C.A. 10·0, M.A. 11·0, Reading and Arithmetic Ages of 9·0. At first sight this system of expressing test results is far simpler than the percentile or $\frac{x}{\sigma}$ systems. It provides a uniform scale of units by means of which a child's relative performances on any number of tests can be compared. His strong or weak points in different school subjects, or even in particular aspects of school subjects (e.g. the main arithmetical skills), and his superiority or inferiority on verbal and non-verbal intelligence tests, etc., can be seen at a glance from a table or graph of his various E.A.s and M.A.s. Nevertheless, there are many serious weaknesses in this type of norm, which we shall have to describe in detail.

Difficulties in Establishing Age Norms.—First there are almost insuperable difficulties in collecting standardization groups which will be truly representative of all the children of a certain age. Between 6 and 11 years the elementary schools will provide groups whose average scores are probably close to the averages in the total population. Any one age group will, of course, be scattered through a large number of different school classes. But the range of ability in elementary schools is restricted, since some of the brightest and dullest sections of the population attend private and special schools, respectively. And, as we have seen, the range or dispersion of a distribution is quite as important as its average. Beyond 11 to 12 years, when elementary school pupils proceed to various types of schools, it becomes increasingly difficult to secure samples whose averages, let alone ranges, are likely to be typical. In a very few instances results have been obtained from practically all the children in a given district,[1] or from all the children born on certain dates.[2] But often the best that can be done is to control the socio-economic factor. Suppose that a district contains a hundred schools, and that a tester wishes to standardize a test on pupils in ten of them, he should see that the schools he selects cover the whole range of socio-economic level, in due proportion. An extension of this method was used by Cattell (1934) in establishing adult norms for an intelligence test. His testees were classified according to their occupations, and the numbers at each main occupational level were compared with the corresponding numbers in the total population. Since he had an unduly high proportion of professionals, and too low a proportion of labourers, he reduced the weight of the former and increased that of the latter group, before calculating the mean and the S.D. of test scores for his combined groups.

The same difficulty in obtaining representative samples hinders us from tracing accurately the course of intellectual and educational growth from childhood, through adoles-

---

[1] Cf. Fraser Roberts, *et al.* (1935).
[2] Cf. Scottish Council for Research in Education (1933), also the more recent survey of intelligence of 873 Scottish children, carried out by the Research Council (Macmeeken, 1939).

cence, to adulthood. The available evidence, however, shows fairly definitely that this growth is not entirely regular, which means that M.A. and E.A. units are not equivalent throughout. The year by year increase of intelligence in an average person seems to be reasonably constant from about 3 to 10 years, after which the rate of increase diminishes, and the M.A. units become progressively smaller, until a constant level is reached somewhere in the neighbourhood of 15 years. Probably this upper limit is reached at different ages on different tests, e.g. an average adolescent may show no further improvement after about 12 on a simple performance test, but continue to advance slightly on complex group verbal tests even up to 17 or 18. The upper limit for a very dull child is, of course, far lower ; he may never surpass the performance of an average 10 year old on any test. It is not yet certain whether he reaches this limit at the same C.A. as an average child reaches his, or somewhat earlier. A very bright child, on the other hand, naturally improves well above the normal 15-year level, and so we express his intelligence as M.A. 16, 17, . . . up to 22 or even higher. But these units are entirely artificial. A 20-year M.A. does not mean that a testee's performance is equal to that of an average person aged 20, but only that his performance is a good deal better than the performance of average persons aged anything from 15 years upwards. We must conclude, then, that M.A. units are so complex, and likely to be so uneven above about 12 years, that it would be far better to discard them altogether at such levels.

Lack of Equivalence of M.A. and E.A. Units.—Still less is known about E.A. units. Possibly the increase is fairly steady from about 6 to 11 years, but then there is a strong tendency in most schools to force children unduly, in order that they may pass the special place or qualifying examinations. Thereafter some relaxation is allowed. Hence the 11 to 12-year unit is likely to be exceptionally large and the 12 to 13-year unit exceptionally small. The units may then tail off among those who receive no higher education, but among secondary school pupils and university students there is likely to be progress well into adulthood. Clearly then E.A. and M.A. units do not provide comparable scales much above 10 years. A child of 13 with an M.A. and an E.A. of 14 is not equally superior in intelligence and in education, since 14 minus 13 is a bigger quantity in the latter than in the former. Nor, of course, is this superiority of 1 year equivalent to the superiority of a child of 7 whose M.A. and E.A. are 8 years.

Not long after Binet put forward the M.A. system of scaling intelligence, the discovery was made that a child's relative advancement or retardation do not remain constant, but increase as his age increases. Burt (1917) proved that the same was true of E.A. A child of 5 with an M.A. or E.A. of 6 will usually show an M.A. or E.A. of 12, not of 11, when he reaches C.A. 10. In other words, a superiority of a year in a young child is much greater than the same superiority in an older child. But the ratio of M.A. to C.A., or E.A. to C.A., does seem to remain approximately constant, hence the I.Q. and E.Q. have been very widely adopted as measures of intellectual and educational advancement and retardation.

Ambiguity in I.Q. Units.—There is yet another flaw both in M.A. and I.Q. and in the corresponding educational units, namely that the range and S.D. of scores expressed in these units are wider for some tests than for others. For example, the application of educational tests to a class of 9 year olds might show that their average E.A. was 9, and that 20% of them had E.A.s of 10 or more. But the application of a group intelligence test to the same pupils might show an average M.A. of 9 and as many as 30% with M.A.s of 10 or more. If this was so, then clearly an advancement of 1 year, or an I.Q. or E.Q. of 111 (i.e. $\frac{10}{9} \times 100$) does not mean the same thing on different tests.

Some intelligence tests yield I.Q.s with a S.D. of 15 or even less, others yield I.Q.s with a S.D. as high as 25 or more. Probably educational tests show similar irregularities.

7

The S.D. of Stanford-Binet I.Q.s seems to be established now as $16\frac{1}{2}$, though for long it was regarded as 15. An ordinary school class, tested with this test, will commonly obtain a range of I.Q.s from $+ 2\sigma$ to $- 2\sigma$, i.e. from 133 to 67. But the same class tested with a group test whose S.D. is 25 will range in I.Q. from 150 to 50. To take another example : a class of very bright children may have an average I.Q. of $116\frac{1}{2}$ according to the Binet test. The same class tested with a group test may have an average I.Q. of 125. The following table illustrates the same phenomenon ; it shows the proportions to be expected in the total population with I.Q.s of 125 or more, or 75 or less, on tests with various S.D.s.

S.D.				% I.Q. > 125 or < 75
15	.	.	.	5
$16\frac{1}{2}$	.	.	.	$6\frac{1}{2}$
20	.	.	.	11
25	.	.	.	16

Unfortunately it is impossible to assert that any particular value of the S.D. of I.Q.s is the ' right ' one, and that the other values are too large or too small. The value depends on certain features of the test which are still somewhat obscure, and are too complex for discussion here.[1] The figure 15 is implied when we talk of 70 as the borderline for mental deficiency, since most of the testing of borderline cases has been carried out with the Binet test whose S.D. was believed to be 15. And because this figure has been so widely accepted, some group intelligence tests have been constructed in such a way that their I.Q.s yield this same S.D.[2] But there is only one really satisfactory

[1] Certain explanations are put forward by the writer elsewhere, cf. Vernon (1937*b*). But it seems likely that the main factor, not mentioned in that article, is the degree of heterogeneity among the items or sub-tests. The more homogeneous the test material, the higher will be the S.D. of the test I.Q.s. Hence the Binet test and most ' omnibus ' group tests seem to have lower S.D.s than tests which are composed only of a few separate sub-tests.

[2] Namely the Moray House Tests. Cf. Thomson (1932).

solution to this problem, and that is for testers and others to give up using I.Q.s in the present loose fashion, as though they represent a standard scale of measurement which is independent of the particular test employed. Actually, like all other test scores, they can only be correctly interpreted if their S.D. is known, in addition to their average of 100.   As we shall see in Chap. X, I.Q.s are open to numerous additional misunderstandings.

To conclude : the measurement of abilities in age units and quotients is simple and convenient, but liable to great inaccuracies beyond the age of 11 years.   A far better system would be to establish the mean test scores of successive age groups, and then to express superiority or inferiority to the means not in terms of M.A. or E.A. but by σ scores.   Real accuracy would be obtained if we could say that a child of 10 was 1σ superior to average 10 year olds on the Binet test, $\frac{1}{2}\sigma$ on performance tests, $1\frac{1}{2}\sigma$ on reading tests, and so on.[1]   This system, moreover, would be applicable at all ages.   Its only disadvantage is that testers would have to have some statistical insight in order to understand and use it.

[1] Possibly a scale ranging from $+ 2\cdot5$ to $- 2\cdot5$ (or $+ 3$ to $- 3$) is a little inconvenient.   Hence American testers often transfer such scores into a scale with a mean of 50 and a S.D. of 10 or 20.

CHAPTER V

RELIABILITY AND THE THEORY OF SAMPLING

Untrustworthiness of Results obtained from Small Numbers of Persons.—This chapter is likely, we must admit, to cause considerable difficulty to readers unfamiliar with statistical concepts. It introduces a point of view with regard to educational measurements and experiments which may at first seem very complex and involved, yet which is absolutely essential to a proper understanding of scientific education and psychology.[1]

The scientific investigator naturally wishes to arrive at results which are true for people in general. He wants to prove that a certain method of teaching gives superior results with *all* children, that the correlation [2] between intelligence tests or school examinations and subsequent scholastic achievement *always* reaches a certain figure, or he wants to know the average test score of *all* persons brought up in a particular environment, e.g. of rural as contrasted with urban children, or Scottish as contrasted with English, and so on. But he can seldom, if ever, measure all the persons to whom his conclusions are supposed to apply. He is forced to work with, as it were, a sample of the population, and he is therefore entitled to regard his result—whether it be an average, or a difference between two averages, or a correlation coefficient, etc.—only as a sample result, which might alter to some extent if he repeated the work on another sample of the population.

He must, of course, take precautions in the first place to

[1] A particularly clear explanation has been given by Thouless (1939*b*).

[2] The reader who is unfamiliar with the conception of correlation may be advised to study pp. 105–8 of the next chapter before continuing with this chapter.

see that his sample is not what we call a biased one. Supposing his problem is the securing of norms for a group intelligence test, and he wishes to find the average and the dispersion of scores among children aged 11 +, he must, as we saw in the previous chapter, avoid choosing only slum schools or only private schools. But even when such bias in selection is eliminated, he would still have to content himself with a limited sample of the children aged 11 + in the country as a whole, and the average of this sample might differ to some extent from the true average. Similarly if his problem was the comparison of the intelligence of slum and private school children, he could not measure all the schools of these types. Thus the difference which he obtained would only be an approximation to the difference that might result from much more complete investigations. Here are two concrete instances.

Ex. 26.—Twelve of the writer's training college students were given an American objective test of reading ability, namely the Nelson-Denny test, which measures knowledge of word meanings and comprehension of paragraphs. Their scores, arranged in order, were : 140, 136, 135, 133, 126, 120, 109, 108, 98, 89, 87, 82.

Now, most of these scores are well above the average for American college students, namely 96. Their average, 113·6, falls at the 78th American percentile. But obviously the scores are very variable. The question is, then, are we or are we not justified in deducing from them that Scottish training college students possess higher reading ability than American college students ? Obviously no such deduction could be made from the score of only a single student, but does the average of a sample of 12 provide a much surer basis ? The 12 were picked at random from among the writer's 264 students. Thus he was careful to avoid selecting only those, or a preponderance of those, who had an Honours degree in English. And men and women were equally represented, since it was conceivable that a sample composed only of women or only of men would be biased. Yet it is quite possible that he unintentionally picked an undue number of clever students, and that if he picked another dozen, their scores might be mostly below 100, and their average no higher, or even lower, than the American figure. How liable then is such an average of twelve measures to vary ?

The question can be answered in this instance, since the same test was given to 21 other sets of 12 students, also chosen at random. The 22 averages range from 103·6 to 126·8, their distribution being shown in the following table. As we suspected, the averages are rather variable, though less so than the separate scores, which range all the way from 62 to 160. And though our first average of 113·6 happens to be fairly close to the grand average of 114·9, yet we might, in the luck of the draw, have obtained an average as much as 10 points above or below this figure.

Average Mark		Frequency
124 + .	.	1
121 + .	.	3
118 + .	.	2
115 + .	.	3
112 + .	.	8
109 + .	.	2
106 + .	.	2
103 + .	.	1
		—
		22

Ex. 27.—The correlation coefficient was calculated between the marks of 25 students on an examination given near the beginning of the year, and their marks on another paper at the end of the year. The coefficient was + 0·53. But 25 students is only a very small sample, and similar results calculated for 13 other similar samples varied widely, as shown in the following table.

Correlation Coefficients		F
+ 0·60 to + 0·69 .	.	1
+ 0·50 to + 0·59 .	.	1
+ 0·40 to + 0·49 .	.	2
+ 0·30 to + 0·39 .	.	5
+ 0·20 to + 0·29 .	.	2
+ 0·10 to + 0·19 .	.	1
0·00 to + 0·09 .	.	1
— 0·10 to — 0·01 .	.	1
		—
		14

Thus the original figure is far from trustworthy, and even the average coefficient of + 0·315, for 350 students, though probably much more reliable, might also alter to some extent if the same examinations were compared among other similar large groups of students.

The Scientific Standpoint.—The scientific investigator, therefore, always looks on any numerical result as a sample one which may deviate more or less from the truth. Even when he has excluded errors of selection such as would make the persons he is measuring in any way unrepresentative, he has to consider the probable extent of these so-called chance errors of sampling. He therefore goes on to imagine that it is theoretically, though perhaps not practically, possible to obtain a very large number of other such samples. The two tables given above are instances on a small scale. They both bring out a vital step in our argument, namely that such additional samples tend to conform to normal distributions. The numbers involved are small, hence these distributions are irregular, but there exists ample evidence to show that larger numbers would eventually yield smooth normal curves.

Let us take a fresh instance, where only a single sample result is available, in order to illustrate the further stages of the argument.

Ex. 28.—The average scores for 136 men and 114 women students on the Cattell Intelligence Test III (cf. Ex. 3, p. 12) were 101·55 and 99·65 respectively. Thus the men were 1·90 points superior.

Can we deduce that men students, of the type tested, are in general better than women, or would we, if we applied the same tests to many other similar groups, find the difference to be larger in some cases, negligibly small in other cases, or even reversed in others ? This difference, which we shall call d, is only a sample one, which should be regarded as falling at some point on the distribution of a large number of possible alternative d's. Clearly the best possible estimate of the true difference between men and women would be a grand average of all these hypothetical d's. This quantity—the mean of the distribution of d's— we shall call D. The particular d which we know is a more or less inaccurate approximation to D.

A formula has been worked out by means of which it is possible to predict, from the actual data available, what would be σ_D, that is the S.D. of this distribution of d's. The formula will be given later. In the present instance it yields $\sigma_D = 1 \cdot 41$. As the distribution is a normal one, this figure will enable us to define its limits. We can state that about one-third of the d's must fall between D and $D + 1 \cdot 41$, another third between D and $D - 1 \cdot 41$, and that about one-sixth of them must deviate more widely from D. Scarcely any of them, or only $0 \cdot 135\%$, will be as large as $D + 4 \cdot 23$ (i.e. 3σ), and only $0 \cdot 135\%$ will be as small as $D - 4 \cdot 23$. Hence $99 \cdot 73\%$ (i.e. $100 - 2 \times 0 \cdot 135$) of the d's lie within the limits $D \pm 4 \cdot 23$, and the odds against any d lying outside these limits are $99 \cdot 73$ to $0 \cdot 27$, or 370 to 1. As a general rule, the probability is 370 to 1 that any d which deviates from D purely on account of chance errors of sampling will not do so by more than $3\sigma_D$.

Certain other probabilities have been deduced from the probability integral graph (Fig. 18), and are listed in the following table :

Limits	Frequencies of d's falling outside these limits	Odds against d's falling outside these limits
$\pm 4\sigma_D$	$2 \times 0 \cdot 0032\%$	15,600 to 1
$\pm 3\sigma_D$	$2 \times 0 \cdot 135\%$	370 to 1
$\pm 2\sigma_D$	$2 \times 2 \cdot 28\%$	21 to 1
$\pm 1\sigma_D$	$2 \times 15 \cdot 9\%$	2 to 1
$\pm 0 \cdot 6745\sigma_D$	$2 \times 25 \cdot 0\%$	1 to 1

Now these predictions must apply to the particular d which we happen to know, whose value is $1 \cdot 90$. The odds are very much against its deviating as much as $3\sigma_D$ from D, but it might quite possibly deviate as much as, say, $2\sigma_D$, since the odds against this are much lower. We can therefore, as it were, reverse the argument, and state with practical certainty that D must lie between $1 \cdot 90 \pm 3\sigma_D$, i.e. between $+ 6 \cdot 13$ and $- 2 \cdot 33$. We do not, of course, know what is the value of D, but if it was greater than $+ 6 \cdot 13$, or less than $- 2 \cdot 33$, our d would be more than $3\sigma_D$ removed from it, which is highly improbable. Similarly we can state that the chances are 21 to 1 that D is not greater than $+ 4\cdot72$, nor less than $- 0\cdot92$ (i.e. $1\cdot90$ $\pm 2 \times 1\cdot41$).

The Standard Error as an Index of the Trustworthiness of a Result.—It may be seen then that σ_{D} provides us with an index of the margin of uncertainty in our d. It tells us that the difference of $1\cdot90$ in favour of men students is by no means trustworthy, since the true value of D may be considerably larger or smaller. There are $2\cdot28$ chances in a hundred that it may be as high as $+ 4\cdot72$, and $2\cdot28$ chances that women may actually be better than men by $0\cdot92$.

This is the manner in which the scientific investigator always thinks of the results of psychological or educational experiments. His obtained result, being only a sample based on a limited number of cases, is likely to deviate more or less from the true result which he would obtain if he could experiment on a very much larger set of people. He can, however, work out the σ_{D}, often referred to as the Standard Error or S.E. of his result, which tells him, not precisely how much his result is in error, but *what is the probability that his result is in error by various amounts.* There is a 2 to 1 chance that the error may be no bigger than the S.E., and the odds against the occurrence of a larger error rise very rapidly, so that it is extremely unlikely to be greater than three times the S.E.

The Probable Error.—The figures at the foot of the table, above, show that there is an even chance of D lying within, or lying outside, the limits $\pm 0\cdot6745\sigma_{\text{D}}$. This particular fraction of the S.E. is known as the Probable Error or P.E. The name is not a very good one, but in a sense it is the most probable error, since the odds against either larger or smaller errors than this are higher than $1 : 1$. In our example, the P.E. $= 0\cdot6745 \times 1\cdot41 = 0\cdot95$. This means that D is just as likely to lie between $1\cdot90 + 0\cdot95$ and $1\cdot90 - 0\cdot95$ as it is to lie outside these limits.

The P.E. is frequently used as an index of the unreliability or margin of uncertainty, in preference to the S.E. Instead of saying that the odds against D deviating from d

by $3 \times$ S.E. are 370 to 1, we can say that a deviation of $4\frac{1}{2} \times$ P.E. possesses this degree of unlikelihood, since $4\frac{1}{2} \times 0.6745 \times$ S.E. is approximately equal to $3 \times$ S.E. Or if $\pm 2 \times$ S.E. are regarded as the limits within which D may reasonably be expected to lie, we can alternatively denote these limits as $\pm 3 \times$ P.E. Often a numerical result such as our d of $+ 1.90$ is stated in the form : 1.90 ± 0.95, where the second figure is the P.E. of the first.

While both the S.E. and the P.E. indicate the likely amount of error in some numerical result, the S.E. is, as we have seen, primarily a measure of the dispersion of all the possible sample results. The same is true of the P.E. In the hypothetical distribution of sample d's, the limits $D +$ P.E. to $D -$ P.E. enclose 50% of these d's, and 25% of them are greater than $D +$ P.E., 25% less than $D -$ P.E. Note therefore that the P.E. is identical with Q, the semi-interquartile range, of this distribution. For the limits Q_1 to Q_3 also mark off the middle 50% of measures in a normal distribution.

The Statistical Significance of a Difference.—Many experiments have shown that the scores of comparable groups of men and women on intelligence tests are practically identical, or that any differences found are not reliable. Since, in our example, the odds are only 21 to 1 against D being greater than 4.72 or less than $- 0.92$, it seems quite possible that here too the d is not reliable, and that the true value of D is zero. If this be so, then it is easy to determine from the probability integral graph the chances that a sample might show a d of $+ 1.90$, merely through errors of sampling. 1.90 is 1.35×1.41, or $1.35\sigma_D$. Consulting the graph (Fig. 18), we see that 9% of measures in a normal distribution lie at or beyond 1.35σ from the mean. Hence when D is zero, 9% of the sample d's amount to $+ 1.90$ or more, 41% lie between 0 and $+ 1.90$, and 50% are below zero. Thus the odds against a d of 1.90 being due to errors of sampling are only 91 to 9, or about 10 to 1. In other words, it might occur as a matter of chance once in ten testings of similar samples of students. Such odds are too low for us to put any trust in the conclusion that men students are better than women at this test. Had d been $+ 4·23$, or even $+ 2·82$ (3 or $2 \times \sigma_D$), we might have felt more certain, since the odds against such deviations from a D of zero would have been 99·865 to 0·135, or 740 to 1, and 97·72 to 2·28, or 43 to 1, respectively.

A difference between the average scores of two groups divided by its S.E. is often referred to as a *critical ratio*, or indicated by the symbol t. In this example t is only 1·35. It is customary to place very little reliance in a difference when its t is less than 2, or preferably 3 ; in other words, to regard such a d as lacking in *statistical significance*. Alternatively, a d is regarded as reliable, and statistically significant, if it exceeds 3, or preferably $4\frac{1}{2}$, times its P.E.

We should note that, even if d had been large enough in the above example (relative to its S.E. or P.E.) to be accepted as significant, the conclusion that men are somewhat superior at the test would have applied only to the type of students tested, namely Scottish university graduates who had chosen the teaching career.. It could not be extended to English training-college students, nor to other university students, far less to men and women in general, since the persons actually tested could not be regarded as typical or representative of these wider groups. Again it would be safer not to claim that such a difference was a difference in intelligence, but only in the ability which is measured by this particular group intelligence test. The statistical treatment which has been applied to the distributions of scores only informs us how sound and reliable are the results in respect of other similar testees, i.e. it takes care of sampling errors, but it does not eliminate errors or bias in selection. As mentioned in Chap. I, statistical methods cannot improve data which are in any way inaccurate or defective ; they merely bring out the significance (or lack of significance) of the data actually obtained.

FORMULÆ FOR THE STANDARD AND PROBABLE ERRORS OF NUMERICAL RESULTS

Common sense tells us that a numerical result such as an average, or a correlation, or a difference between two averages, will always be more reliable the greater the number of cases on which it is based. In Ex. 26 (p. 89) it was shown that the averages obtained by sets of twelve students on a test of reading ability were exceedingly variable. Obviously twelve is far too small a sample upon which to base conclusions. In order to make a trustworthy comparison between the performance of Scottish and American students at this test, we should need much larger numbers. Hence most of the formulæ for reliability involve the quantity $\dfrac{1}{\sqrt{N}}$, which means that by quadrupling the size of a sample, we can halve the variability of any result computed from this sample, or double its reliability. Another important factor which governs the reliability of a result is the variability among the original measures. Suppose that, in Ex. 28, all the men students had scored 101 or 102 (average 101·55), and all the women had scored 99 or 100 (average 99·65), we should certainly have been entitled to claim that men students do better at the test than women. But it is because the men's scores range all the way from 73 to 134, and the women from 78 to 129, that we felt suspicious of the difference in averages, and applied statistical treatment to it. There was so much overlapping that about 42% of the women obtained higher scores than the average man, and about 42% of the men scored lower than the average woman. Hence the reliability formulæ also involve some measure of the dispersion or extent of variation of the original measures.

The S.E. of a Difference.—This S.E. is given by the formula :

$$\sigma_{\mathrm{D}} = \sqrt{\frac{\sigma_1{}^2}{N_1} + \frac{\sigma_2{}^2}{N_2}}$$

Here σ_1 and σ_2 are the S.D.'s of the scores in the two groups, N_1 and N_2 are their numbers. The P.E. of a difference is $0 \cdot 6745$ times this quantity.

Ex. 29.—As a fresh illustration, let us compare the scores on the Nelson-Denny reading test of students having Honours degrees in Arts with the scores of students having Honours in Science or ordinary degrees. The essential data are as follows :

	N	M	σ
Honours Arts students .	66	129·47	16·42
Other students . .	198	109·97	18·90

The difference between the two averages is 19·50.

$$\sigma_D = \sqrt{\frac{16 \cdot 42^2}{66} + \frac{18 \cdot 90^2}{198}} = \sqrt{4 \cdot 088 + 1 \cdot 804} = 2 \cdot 427$$

Here the critical ratio is $\dfrac{19 \cdot 5}{2 \cdot 427}$, or approximately 8. Such a difference could not possibly occur through chance errors of sampling. Hence we may conclude that Honours Arts students, of the type tested, are definitely superior to other graduate students at this test.

S.E. of a Difference between Averages of Scores which are Inter-correlated.—When one group of persons takes two tests, or if they repeat a test, and we wish to examine the statistical significance of the difference between their two average scores, we must use a modified formula. This applies whenever there exists a correlation, r, between the two sets of scores.[1]

$$\sigma_D = \sqrt{\frac{1}{N}(\sigma_1{}^2 + \sigma_2{}^2 - 2r\sigma_1\sigma_2)}$$

Ex. 30.—Marks in English and arithmetic were awarded to a class of 57 children. These are tabulated in Ex. 22, p. 67. Apparently the arithmetic marks run higher than the English ones. Is the difference significant ? The figures are as follows :

	Mean	Difference	σ	N
English . .	67·615		12·94	
		2·895		57
Arithmetic . .	70·510		14·64	

[1] An alternative version of the same formula is :

$\sigma_D = \sqrt{\sigma_1{}^2 + \sigma_2{}^2 - 2r\sigma_1\sigma_2}$, where σ_1 and σ_2 are not the S.D.s of the original measures, but the S.E.s of the means of these measures (cf. the following paragraph).

The correlation between the two sets of marks is indicated by a coefficient of $+ 0\cdot542$.

$$\sigma_D = \sqrt{\tfrac{1}{57}(12\cdot94^2 + 14\cdot64^2 - 2 \times 0\cdot542 \times 12\cdot94 \times 14\cdot64)} = 1\cdot761$$

The difference of $2\cdot895$ is only $1\cdot64$ times its S.E., hence it is not significant.

S.E. of a Mean.—An average is, as we have seen in Ex. 26, quite as likely to vary through errors of sampling as a difference between averages. Hence it is very useful to know how near to the true average of a very large group is likely to be the average obtained from a group of limited size. The S.E. of the mean is often symbolized by σ_M, and is given by the formula : $\sigma_M = \dfrac{\sigma}{\sqrt{N}}$. Here σ is, of course, the S.D. of the original scores, whose average has been computed.

Ex. 31.—The twelve scores on the Nelson-Denny test, listed in Ex. 26, have a mean of $113\cdot58$ and S.D. of $20\cdot07$.

$$\sigma_M = \frac{20\cdot07}{\sqrt{12}} = 5\cdot794.$$

The P.E. of M is $0\cdot6745 \times$ S.E. $= 3\cdot908$.

Thus the true mean for students of the type tested may just as well lie outside the limits $113\cdot58 \pm 3\cdot91$ (i.e. $117\cdot49$ to $109\cdot67$) as within them. It may be as much as $3\sigma_M$ away from $113\cdot58$, i.e. as high as $130\cdot96$ or as low as $96\cdot20$, but is unlikely to exceed these limits. Obviously the figure is extremely unreliable.

By contrast the mean for 264 students was $114\cdot9$ and the S.D. $20\cdot15$. Here $\sigma_M = \dfrac{20\cdot15}{\sqrt{264}} = 1\cdot24$. The sample is 22 times as large, hence σ_M is $\dfrac{1}{\sqrt{22}}$ its previous value. The P.E.$_M = 0\cdot836$.

From these figures it follows that there is an even chance of the true mean lying between $115\cdot7$ and $114\cdot1$, and that it almost certainly does not lie outside the limits $118\cdot6$ and $111\cdot2$.

S.E. of a Standard Deviation and of a Difference between S.D.s.—Not only the mean but also the S.D. of a set of measures may be affected by errors of sampling. The formula for the S.E. of a S.D. is :

$$\sigma_\sigma = \frac{\sigma}{\sqrt{2N}}$$

The S.E. of a difference between two S.D.s is given by :

$$\sqrt{\frac{\sigma_1{}^2}{2N_1} + \frac{\sigma_2{}^2}{2N_2}}$$

Ex. 32.—The S.D.s of the intelligence test scores of men and women students were 12·36 and 9·95 respectively, indicating that the dispersion of ability was greater among the men. The S.E. of the difference of 2·41 between these two figures is :

$$\sqrt{\frac{12·36^2}{2 \times 136} + \frac{9·95^2}{2 \times 114}} = 0·998$$

The difference is 2·42 times its S.E., and this shows a fair degree of statistical significance. The odds against such a difference occurring through chance errors are 99·23 to 0·77, or 129 to 1. The result therefore allows a reasonably strong presumption that men students of the type tested are in general more spread out in their ability at an intelligence test than are women students.

S.E. of a Percentage and of a Difference between Percentages.—Often it is not possible to measure the amounts of some quality in a group of persons, but only to state what percentage of the persons possess or do not possess it. Suppose that in several schools 60% of the boys and 65% of the girls regularly take milk, does this indicate a reliable sex difference ? Again the trustworthiness of the result depends on the number of cases. If p is the percentage, and $q = 100 - p$, then the S.E. of p is $\sqrt{\dfrac{pq}{N}}$, and the S.E. of a difference between two percentages is :

$$\sqrt{\frac{p_1 q_1}{N_1} + \frac{p_2 q_2}{N_2}}$$

Ex. 33.—From how many children would it be necessary to obtain milk-drinking records in order to be practically certain that the difference of 65% − 60% is reliable ?

This example is posed in the reverse form from Exs. 29–32,

but the same method is employed. If a difference of 5% is reliable, it must be three times its S.E. That is, the S.E. must not be greater than $\frac{5}{3} = 1\cdot667$. Let the number of both boys and girls in the schools where records are obtained be N. Then :

$$1\cdot667 = \sqrt{\frac{60 \times 40}{N} + \frac{65 \times 35}{N}} \qquad N = 1{,}683$$

The answer is, then, that the sex difference of 5% would be significant if based on some 1,600 odd boys and an equal number of girls, but that it would not be so if the numbers were much smaller.

One of the commonest faults in writings about educational topics is the quotation of percentage results without any indication of the reliability of these results, often without even any mention of the actual numbers of cases from which the P.E.s could be calculated.

It should be noted that all the formulæ quoted above for the S.E. of a difference (between means, between S.D.s, and between percentages) are derived from one and the same formula :

$$\sigma_D = \sqrt{\sigma_1{}^2 + \sigma_2{}^2 - 2r\sigma_1\sigma_2}$$

where σ_1 and σ_2 are the S.E.s of the means, S.D.s, and percentages, respectively (not the S.D.s of the original scores). The third term, $2r\sigma_1\sigma_2$, applies whenever there is any correlation between the original measures from which the means, S.D.s, or percentages are derived. But when, as in most of our examples above, there is no such correlation, the term vanishes.

Statistical Treatment of Small Samples.—It has been shown by Fisher (1930) and others that numerical results obtained from very small samples are even less reliable than the statistical treatment described above would lead us to expect. Under such circumstances it is better to calculate a S.E. by substituting $N - 1$ for N in the denominator. Special tables or graphs are available,[1] which show the probability of various values of t. However, this modified treatment makes very little difference until N falls below about 15. And as the enormous majority of

[1] Cf. Fisher (1930), Dawson (1933).

educational experiments are carried out on much larger numbers than this, we will not give any further details here.

S.E. and P.E. of a Correlation Coefficient.[1]—The correlation between two sets of measures is likely to be very unreliable if the number of persons is small, as was shown in Ex. 27 (p. 90). The S.E. or P.E. of a correlation coefficient tells us how widely this coefficient may be expected to deviate from the true value, i.e. the value which would be obtained from an unlimited number of persons. The formulæ for these errors will be given in Chap. VI.

S.E. and P.E. of an Individual Test Score or Examination Mark.—If some pupils or students take a test or examination two or more times, or answer two or more supposedly parallel tests in the same subject, they will not obtain precisely identical scores on each occasion. Hence any score or mark derived from only a single test is to some extent unreliable. It may deviate more or less from the score which would be obtained with far more thorough testing. In other words, the single test only gives us a limited sample of the pupils' or students' capabilities. Here, too, then the conception of the S.E. has valuable applications. But the reliability of a score depends, not on the number of persons who take the test, nor on the wideness of dispersion of scores, but on the thoroughness of the test itself, or the number of items of which it is composed, and on the amount of variability in pupils' answers to these items. The methods of calculation are described in Chap. VII.

Finally, when a test or examination is employed for predicting a pupil's success or lack of success during his subsequent educational or vocational career, it is obvious that the estimate obtained from the test score will deviate more or less from the truth. The reliability of such predictions naturally depends mainly upon the adequacy or

[1] It seems to be the convention in psychological literature to employ the S.E. in the statistical treatment of averages and the like, and the P.E. in the treatment of correlations and individual scores. There is no logical reason for the convention, but we shall usually adhere to it in this book.

8

validity of the test. It, too, can be expressed in terms of a S.E. or P.E., and the appropriate methods will be given below.

Goodness of Fit

A somewhat different type of problem, to which the theory of sampling also applies, is known as testing for goodness of fit. One instance which frequently occurs in educational psychology is the investigation of whether or not a distribution may be regarded as normal. We have seen that distributions of small numbers of measures may depart considerably from the smooth normal shape, and that by increasing N the irregularities tend to become ironed out. Here also, therefore, the result obtained from a limited sample (the result being an irregular distribution) can deviate considerably from the result which a much larger sample would yield (a regular distribution), purely through errors of sampling. The test for goodness of fit tells us whether such a departure from normality is a chance one, or whether it is so great that the distribution cannot be accepted as an approximation to the normal shape.

Ex. 34.—The following results were obtained in Ex. 19 (p. 60).

F	F_e	$F - F_e$	$\dfrac{(F - F_e)^2}{F}$
1	1 ⎫		
1	1 ⎬	$+ 2$	0·6667
6	4 ⎭		
11	9	$+ 2$	0·4444
22	19	$+ 3$	0·4737
26	30	$- 4$	0·5333
35	41	$- 6$	0·8780
47	44	$+ 3$	0·2045
43	40	$+ 3$	0·2250
27	28	$- 1$	0·0356
18	18	0	0·0000
10	9	$+ 1$	0·1111
3	4 ⎫	$- 3$	1·5000
0	2 ⎭		
250	250		5·0723

They show in the F column the actual frequencies of scores obtained by students on the Cattell test, and in the F_e column the frequencies which would be expected if the distribution of scores was a truly normal one.

The method is to tabulate the differences between each actual and expected frequency. The smallest frequencies, at the head and foot of the column, are usually grouped together, as shown here. The differences are squared and divided by their respective F_e's. The sum of these quantities is called chi squared (χ^2). Tables are available showing the probability of any value of chi squared for any number of classes. In this instance the probability is 0·75.[1] That is, we might expect as great, or greater, deviations of the distribution from normality in three cases out of four by pure chance. The approximation to normality is quite satisfactory.

The same method can be used to determine whether or not a set of frequencies conforms to any other expected distribution.

Ex. 35.—At the time of a Scottish university Rectorial election, 32 women students informed the present writer as to their votes for the four candidates. These votes are listed in the F column below. Now the voting for the candidates among the student body as a whole was 38%, 26%, 20%, and 16% respectively. If, then, the 32 students were a representative sample of the student body, i.e. if they had cast their votes in the same proportions as the rest, the figures would be approximately as shown in the F_e column. Clearly the F and F_e

Candidate	F	F_e	$F - F_e$	$\dfrac{(F - F_e)^2}{F_e}$
Pacifist	18	12	$+6$	3·000
Nationalist	4	$8\frac{1}{2}$	$-4\frac{1}{2}$	2·382
Unionist	5	$6\frac{1}{2}$	$-1\frac{1}{2}$	0·346
Socialist	5	5	0	0·000
	32	32		5·728

columns are decidedly different, but before we can conclude that these 32 were not a typical sample of the student body, we must examine the probability of such divergences occurring through mere errors of sampling. The procedure is the same

[1] We have not the space here to explain the use of chi squared tables. Those who have need of them should study the concept of ' degrees of freedom ' in Dawson's, Fisher's, or other textbooks.

as before. The value of chi squared which is obtained, 5·728, is found from the tables to possess a probability of 0·125. That is, it might occur by chance 1 in 8 times. Hence the difference between the two distributions is not reliable.

Suppose, however, that there had been a hundred students instead of 32, voting in the same proportions as these 32. Chi squared would then have been $\frac{100}{32}$ times as big, and its probability would have sunk to approximately 0·001. From this larger sample we could certainly have deduced that the women students were more pacifistic, less nationalistic, than the other students, but such a deduction from the small sample would have been very untrustworthy.

CHAPTER VI

MEASUREMENT OF CORRELATION

A VERY wide range of problems in educational, and other branches of, psychology depends on the study of relationships between variables. For example, examinations are set at the end of the primary school career, partly in order to test the work that the children have done, but also partly because achievement in English and arithmetic is supposed to be related to, or predictive of, future achievement in more advanced work. The main object of applying intelligence, or other aptitude, tests is to show probable ability in various fields which are related to the test performances. In many secondary schools the pupils are allotted to different classes for general work, for mathematics, and for foreign languages, since it is believed (with much justification) that abilities in these three types of study are not very closely related, that some may be good in general work, poor at mathematics, medium at languages, and so on.

Several different methods, applicable to different kinds of data, are available for determining the extent of relationship between two variables. Almost all of them yield indices ranging from 0 (no correlation) to $+1\cdot0$ (perfect correlation). By far the most frequently used are the product-moment correlation coefficient and the rank-order correlation coefficient. We will point out later the limitations of these two methods, and mention briefly some of the alternatives.

Ex. 36.—The following marks were obtained by a class of 36 children on examinations in history and geography. A glance will show that there is some correspondence ; that those who obtain high marks in one tend to get high marks in the other,

Name	X_1 History	X_2 Geography	X_1	X_2	X_1	X_2
Allan	16	12	10	5	8	6
Helen	19	15	14	18	20	12
John	17	11	8	6	17	11
....	10	17	6	4	12	8
....	18	14	18	20	7	2
	18	16	14	8	17	16
	15	4	12	4	14	11
	17	13	18	14	14	9
	12	12	16	10	12	3
	16	8	6	4	16	1
	11	10	18	14	20	15
	14	9	12	11	17	6

and that low marks in one tend to go with low marks in the
other ; but that there are many exceptions to this trend. The
state of affairs may be seen more clearly if the two sets of
measures are plotted against one another. Fig. 21 is called a
scatter-diagram or *scattergram*. The marks have both been

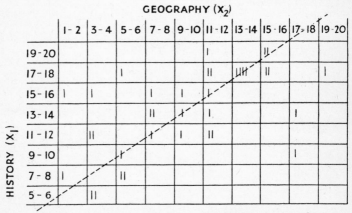

Fig. 21.—Scattergram, comparing two sets of school marks.

grouped into classes of 2. History marks (X_1) are shown on
the vertical axis, geography marks (X_2) on the horizontal axis.
Each pupil's position in the two exams is shown by a tick.
For example, Allan's 16 and 12 are represented by a tick
opposite the 15–16 mark in history, and below the 11–12 mark
in geography. Four pupils obtained either 17 or 18 in history
and either 13 or 14 in geography, hence there are four ticks in
this box or cell.

It will be seen that the majority of ticks tend to be grouped along the dotted diagonal line, although there are some rather extreme exceptions, for instance, the pupil with marks of 16 and 1, and the pupil with marks of 10 and 17. Obviously the closer the correspondence between the two sets, the more closely would the ticks fall along the diagonal, and the fewer would be the exceptions whose ticks are far removed from it. Fig. 26 (p. 154) and Ex. 45 (p. 131) show the scattergrams for a low correlation of + 0·146 and a high correlation of + 0·799 (the numbers in each cell represent the numbers of ticks). Only if each pupil got marks which exactly corresponded would the correlation be perfect and the coefficient be + 1·0. Note, however, that it is not necessary for the marks on the two variables to be *identical* for a perfect correlation to be obtained, since these marks may be arranged on different scales. In Fig. 21 the geography marks are on a different scale from the history marks ; 10 on the one corresponds, or is relatively equivalent, to 14 on the other. Consider another instance : the weights and heights of a class of children would certainly yield a very high correlation, although they would be measured on entirely different scales—pounds and inches. It is the closeness of agreement of *relative* scores or measures which governs the size of the correlation.

Very few correlations in educational or psychological investigations approximate to + 1·0. Usually there is only a general trend for high scores on one variable to go with high scores on the other, a trend which admits of many exceptions. Two tests of the same ability, e.g. two similar arithmetic papers, may perhaps give a coefficient of + 0·90 or over. Tests or exams in different subjects, e.g. arithmetic and English, or history and geography, are more likely to give moderate correlation coefficients of + 0·40 to + 0·70.

Occasionally one may find negative or inverse correspondence, when high scores on one variable go with low scores on another variable. For instance, in an ordinary school class intelligence or scholastic achievement and age are often negatively related, since the oldest pupils are rather dull, the youngest pupils very bright. Negative correlations are expressed, just as positive ones, by indices ranging from 0 to − 1·0.

Calculation of Correlations by the Product-moment Method (*sometimes called the Pearson-Bravais Method*).—The fundamental formula for the correlation coefficient, r, is :

$$r = \frac{\Sigma x_1 x_2}{N \sigma_1 \sigma_2}$$

Here σ_1 and σ_2 are the S.D.s of the two distributions. x_1 represents a score or measure expressed as a deviation from the mean of all the X_1 measures, x_2 is a measure expressed as a deviation from the mean of all the X_2 measures. $x_1 x_2$ is the product of a person's two measures, and $\Sigma x_1 x_2$ is the sum of all these products.

Since the means are seldom likely to be whole numbers, the computation of $\Sigma x_1 x_2$ would involve very troublesome arithmetic. Hence, just as in calculating S.D.s, it is usual to resort to the device of the arbitrary mean. Each of the quantities in the above formula then requires a correction. If x_1 is a deviation from an arbitrary mean, σ_1 is no longer

$$\sqrt{\frac{\Sigma x_1{}^2}{N}} \text{ but } \sqrt{\frac{\Sigma x_1{}^2}{N} - \left(\frac{\Sigma x_1}{N}\right)^2}$$

(cf. p. 56). A corresponding alteration is made in σ_2. $\dfrac{\Sigma x_1 x_2}{N}$ becomes $\dfrac{\Sigma x_1 x_2}{N} - \dfrac{\Sigma x_1}{N} \times \dfrac{\Sigma x_2}{N}$. Hence the full formula is :

$$r = \frac{\dfrac{\Sigma x_1 x_2}{N} - \dfrac{\Sigma x_1}{N} \times \dfrac{\Sigma x_2}{N}}{\sqrt{\dfrac{\Sigma x_1{}^2}{N} - \left(\dfrac{\Sigma x_1}{N}\right)^2} \sqrt{\dfrac{\Sigma x_2{}^2}{N} - \left(\dfrac{\Sigma x_2}{N}\right)^2}}$$

This same formula applies if the original scores are used, i.e. if X_1 and X_2 are substituted for x_1 and x_2. The only difference is that the arbitrary mean is now zero, instead of being some whole number chosen close to the true mean.

Statistical textbooks often provide modifications of this formula, or ' patent ' correlation techniques which are claimed to be simpler. The present writer prefers the direct method given here, both because it makes use of concepts such as the true and arbitrary mean, σ, and the correction required when σ is calculated from an arbitrary mean—concepts with which the student should already be familiar—and because errors in computation are fairly readily detected. Moreover, a coefficient accurate to three places of decimals can be obtained by this method if the multiplication and division, and the finding of squares and square roots, are done with a 10-inch slide-rule and/or four-figure logarithm tables.

Ex. 37.—The formula will be applied first to the original table of marks, given in Ex. 36, and later to the same marks grouped into classes (as in Fig. 21). This first method should generally be employed only when N is small, say less than 50, and when a high degree of accuracy is needed. In the following table, columns X_1 and X_2 list the original marks. As arbitrary means, 14 and 10 are selected. Columns x_1 and x_2 list the deviations of X_1 and X_2 from these A's. They are summed to give Σx_1 and Σx_2.

$$\frac{\Sigma x_1}{N} = \frac{+5}{36} = +0{\cdot}1389 \qquad \frac{\Sigma x_2}{N} = \frac{-2}{36} = -0{\cdot}0555$$

Therefore the true means are 14·139 and 9·945. Later we shall need

$$\left(\frac{\Sigma x_1}{N}\right)^2, \ \left(\frac{\Sigma x_2}{N}\right)^2 \text{ and } \frac{\Sigma x_1}{N} \times \frac{\Sigma x_2}{N}$$

These come to $+0{\cdot}019$, $+0{\cdot}003$, and $-0{\cdot}008$ respectively. Note that three places of decimals are sufficient for these corrections. Special attention should be paid to the sign ($+$ or $-$) of $\frac{\Sigma x_1}{N} \times \frac{\Sigma x_2}{N}$.

The next two columns, x_1^2 and x_2^2, give the deviations squared. These are summed and averaged.

$$\frac{\Sigma x_1^2}{N} = \frac{549}{36} = 15{\cdot}250 \qquad \frac{\Sigma x_2^2}{N} = \frac{836}{36} = 23{\cdot}222$$

X_1	X_2	x_1	x_2	$x_1{}^2$	$x_2{}^2$	$x_1 x_2$	
16	12	$+ 2$	$+ 2$	4	4	$+ 4$	
19	15	$+ 5$	$+ 5$	25	25	$+ 25$	
17	11	$+ 3$	$+ 1$	9	1	$+ 3$	
10	17	$- 4$	$+ 7$	16	49		$- 28$
18	14	$+ 4$	$+ 4$	16	16	$+ 16$	
18	16	$+ 4$	$+ 6$	16	36	$+ 24$	
15	4	$+ 1$	$- 6$	1	36		$- 6$
17	13	$+ 3$	$+ 3$	9	9	$+ 9$	
12	12	$- 2$	$+ 2$	4	4		$- 4$
16	8	$+ 2$	$- 2$	4	4		$- 4$
11	10	$- 3$	0	9	0	0	
14	9	0	$- 1$	0	1	0	
10	5	$- 4$	$- 5$	16	25	$+ 20$	
14	18	0	$+ 8$	0	64	0	
8	6	$- 6$	$- 4$	36	16	$+ 24$	
6	4	$- 8$	$- 6$	64	36	$+ 48$	
18	20	$+ 4$	$+ 10$	16	100	$+ 40$	
14	8	0	$- 2$	0	4	0	
12	4	$- 2$	$- 6$	4	36	$+ 12$	
18	14	$+ 4$	$+ 4$	16	16	$+ 16$	
16	10	$+ 2$	0	4	0	0	
6	4	$- 8$	$- 6$	64	36	$+ 48$	
18	14	$+ 4$	$+ 4$	16	16	$+ 16$	
12	11	$- 2$	$+ 1$	4	1		$- 2$
8	6	$- 6$	$- 4$	36	16	$+ 24$	
20	12	$+ 6$	$+ 2$	36	4	$+ 12$	
17	11	$+ 3$	$+ 1$	9	1	$+ 3$	
12	8	$- 2$	$- 2$	4	4	$+ 4$	
7	2	$- 7$	$- 8$	49	64	$+ 56$	
17	16	$+ 3$	$+ 6$	9	36	$+ 18$	
14	11	0	$+ 1$	0	1	0	
14	8	0	$- 2$	0	4	0	
12	3	$- 2$	$- 7$	4	49	$+ 14$	
16	1	$+ 2$	$- 9$	4	81		$- 18$
20	15	$+ 6$	$+ 5$	36	25	$+ 30$	
17	6	$+ 3$	$- 4$	9	16		$- 12$

$N = 36$ $+ 61$ $+ 72$ 549   836 $+ 466$

$- 56$ $- 74$ $- 74$

$= + 5$ $= - 2$ $= + 392$

Hence $\sigma_1 = \sqrt{\dfrac{\Sigma x_1{}^2}{N} - \left(\dfrac{\Sigma x_1}{N}\right)^2} = \sqrt{15 \cdot 250 - 0 \cdot 019} = 3 \cdot 903.$

$$\sigma_2 = \sqrt{23 \cdot 222 - 0 \cdot 003} = 4 \cdot 819.$$

The last pair of columns gives the products of the deviations ; the + and − products are separated merely for convenience in summing. Special attention to the signs is needed. When x_1 and x_2 are both + or both − the product is plus, when one is + the other − the product is minus. Notice how the exceptional cases, such as the pupil with 10 and 17, make large negative contributions to $\Sigma x_1 x_2$, and so ultimately reduce the size of r. The pupils who get very high marks on both variables, or very low marks on both, such as those with 6 and 4 or with 18 and 20, make large positive contributions to $\Sigma x_1 x_2$ and help to raise r.

$$\frac{\Sigma x_1 x_2}{N} = \frac{+ 392}{36} = 10 \cdot 889.$$

The correction, $\dfrac{\Sigma x_1}{N} \times \dfrac{\Sigma x_2}{N}$, is subtracted from this, but as its sign was −, it is in this case added.

$$\frac{\Sigma x_1 x_2}{N} - \frac{\Sigma x_1}{N} \times \frac{\Sigma x_2}{N} = 10 \cdot 889 - (- 0 \cdot 008) = 10 \cdot 897.$$

All the corrections indicated in the second formula have been made, hence we can finally apply the first, or fundamental, correlation formula :

$$r = \frac{\Sigma x_1 x_2}{N}\left(\frac{1}{\sigma_1 \sigma_2}\right) = \frac{10 \cdot 897}{4 \cdot 819 \times 3 \cdot 903} = + 0 \cdot 579.$$

Thus the coefficient shows moderate correspondence between the two sets of marks, as we guessed from looking at the scattergram.

Product-moment Correlation between Tabulated Measures. —When the measures are grouped into classes, the procedure is essentially identical, except that the computations are, of course, performed for all the measures in any one class at one time. We are no longer concerned with the deviations of single measures from their mean, and their products, but with deviations of classes from the mean class, and their products. At no time is it necessary to translate the results back into terms of the original measures, by multiplying by c (the size of the class).

The two sets of measures are first plotted in a scattergram, which should contain, if possible, between 11 and 19 rows and a similar number of columns. There is no need to have identical numbers of rows and columns. In Fig. 21 (p. 106) the data are, as a matter of fact, rather too coarsely grouped, since there are only 8 rows and 10 columns. Over-coarse grouping has the effect of reducing slightly the size of r (a formula for correcting this may be found in advanced statistical textbooks). By adding up the frequencies in each row, and in each column, we get the two frequency distributions of grouped measures. Fig. 21 is reproduced below with the frequency distribution of x_1 measures (F_1) written at the right-hand side of the rows, and the frequency distribution of x_2 measures (F_2) written at the foot of the columns. The frequencies in both these distributions should be checked by making sure that they add up to N.

$x_2 =$	-4	-3	-2	-1	0	$+1$	$+2$	$+3$	$+4$	$+5$	F_1
$x_1 = +3$					1		2				3
$+2$			1			2	4	2		1	10
$+1$	1	1		1	1	1					5
0				2	1	1		1			5
-1		2		1	1	2					6
-2			1					1			2
-3	1		2								3
-4		2									2
F_2	2	5	4	4	3	7	4	4	2	1	$36 = N$

An appropriate arbitrary mean is now chosen for the x_1 classes and for the x_2 classes, and the classes above and below these means are numbered $+ 1, + 2, \ldots - 1, - 2,$ . . . etc. These numberings are written at the left-hand side of the rows, and above the tops of the columns. Standards deviations are now calculated in the usual way.

x_1 and x_2	F_1	F_2	$F_1 x_1$	$F_2 x_2$	$F_1 x_1{}^2$	$F_2 x_2{}^2$
$+5$		1		$+5$		25
$+4$		2		8		32
$+3$	3	4	$+9$	12	27	36
$+2$	10	4	20	8	40	16
$+1$	5	7	5	7	5	7
0	5	3	$+34$	$+40$	0	0
-1	6	4	-6	-4	6	4
-2	2	4	4	8	8	16
-3	3	5	9	15	27	45
-4	2	2	8	8	32	32
	36	36	-27	-35	145	213

$$\Sigma F_1 x_1 = +7 \qquad \Sigma F_2 x_2 = +5$$

$$\frac{\Sigma F_1 x_1}{N} = \frac{+7}{36} = +0.1944 \qquad \left(\frac{\Sigma F_1 x_1}{N}\right)^2 = 0.0378$$

$$\frac{\Sigma F_2 x_2}{N} = \frac{+5}{36} = +0.1389 \qquad \left(\frac{\Sigma F_2 x_2}{N}\right)^2 = 0.0193.$$

The correction $\dfrac{\Sigma F_1 x_1}{N} \times \dfrac{\Sigma F_2 x_2}{N}$, which will be needed later in the numerator of the correlation formula, is :

$$+0.1944 \times +0.1389 = +0.027$$

$$\frac{\Sigma F_1 x_1{}^2}{N} = \frac{145}{36} = 4.028$$

$$\sigma_1 = \sqrt{4.028 - 0.038} = 1.997.$$

$$\frac{\Sigma F_2 x_2{}^2}{N} = \frac{213}{36} = 5.917$$

$$\sigma_2 = \sqrt{5.917 - 0.019} = 2.429.$$

Note that these S.D.s are approximately one-half those obtained in the previous computation of r (namely 3·903 and 4·819), the reason being that we have grouped the original measures into classes of 2. They are not exactly half because the grouping has produced some slight distortion of the distribution.

Now to obtain the products, the frequency in each cell must be multiplied by its x_1 value and by its x_2 value. For instance, the entry 2 in cell $x_1 = + 3$, $x_2 = + 3$ contributes $2 \times 3 \times 3 = + 18$ to $\Sigma F x_1 x_2$. The entry 1 in cell $x_1 = - 2$, $x_2 = + 4$ contributes $1 \times 4 \times - 2 = - 8$.

$x_1 x_2$	Cells corresponding to this value of $x_1 x_2$		Frequencies in these cells	Total F's	$F x_1 x_2$
0	$x_1 = + 1$	$x_2 =$ 0	1		
	0	0	1		
	$- 1$	0	1	7	0
	0	$- 1$	2		
	0	$+ 1$	1		
	0	$+ 4$	1		
$+ 1$	$x_1 = + 1$	$x_2 = + 1$	1	2	$+ 2$
	$- 1$	$- 1$	1		
$+ 2$	$x_1 = + 2$	$x_2 = + 1$	2	2	$+ 4$
$+ 3$	$x_1 = + 3$	$x_2 = + 1$	1	3	$+ 9$
	$- 1$	$- 3$	2		
$+ 4$	$x_1 = + 2$	$x_2 = + 2$	4	5	$+ 20$
	$- 2$	$- 2$	1		
$+ 6$	$x_1 = + 2$	$x_2 = + 3$	2	4	$+ 24$
	$- 3$	$- 2$	2		
$+ 9$	$x_1 = + 3$	$x_2 = + 3$	2	2	$+ 18$
$+ 10$	$x_1 = + 2$	$x_2 = + 5$	1	1	$+ 10$
$+ 12$	$x_1 = - 3$	$x_2 = - 4$	1	3	$+ 36$
	$- 4$	$- 3$	2		
					$+ 123$
$- 1$	$x_1 = + 1$	$x_2 = - 1$	1	3	$- 3$
	$- 1$	$+ 1$	2		
$- 3$	$x_1 = + 1$	$x_2 = - 3$	1	1	$- 3$
$- 4$	$x_1 = + 2$	$x_2 = - 2$	1	2	$- 8$
	$+ 1$	$- 4$	1		
$- 8$	$x_1 = - 2$	$x_2 = + 4$	1	1	$- 8$
					$- 22$
				$F x_1 x_2 =$	$+ 101$

It is unnecessary, however, to consider each cell in turn. Instead we take each possible value of $x_1 x_2$ in turn, as shown in the accompanying table. All the cells for which either $x_1 = 0$ or $x_2 = 0$ contribute zero to $\Sigma F x_1 x_2$. It will be seen that the total frequencies in such cells is 7. The total frequency in the cells where $x_1x_2 = +1$ is 2, hence $+2$ is entered in the last column.

As soon as the student becomes familiar with the method he will find it unnecessary to write out the second, third, and fourth columns of such a table. Only the first, and the last two are needed. The simplest plan is to draw a cross through each of the cells for which $x_1x_2 = 0$, and to count up the frequencies in these cells while doing so, and then enter the total in a table thus :

x_1x_2	F	Fx_1x_2
0	7	0
$+1$	2	$+2$
.	.	.
.	.	.
.	.	.

Next cross out the cells where $x_1x_2 = +1$, and enter in the table, and so on. At the end, sum the F column, in order to make sure that none of the entries in the cells have been omitted. The last column is summed to give ΣFx_1x_2, and the rest of the working is as before.

$\dfrac{\Sigma Fx_1x_2}{N} = \dfrac{+101}{36} = 2\cdot806$. The correction, to be subtracted, is $+0\cdot027$.

$$2\cdot806 - 0\cdot027 = 2\cdot779. \quad r = \frac{2\cdot779}{2\cdot429 \times 1\cdot997} = +0\cdot573.$$

It will be seen that in spite of the distortion due to grouping the scores into a rather coarse scattergram, the result is nearly identical with that obtained from the ungrouped measures, namely $+0\cdot579$.

There are, of course, numerous possibilities of error in working out product-moment correlations. All additions should be checked up and down ; multiplying, dividing, squaring, etc., may be done with logarithm tables and confirmed with a slide-rule. But a little practice will enable the student to predict r fairly closely from consideration of the scattergram, and so to judge whether or not the value he reaches is likely to be correct.

An Alternative Method of Calculating Correlation from the Scattergram.—We will describe one of the various alternative methods, which may be found simpler to use than the above, direct, method. It eliminates the collection of the contributions to $\Sigma F x_1 x_2$ from each cell, and substitutes the calculation of a third S.D., which we shall call σ_3. The formula for r is then :

$$r = \frac{\sigma_1{}^2 + \sigma_2{}^2 - \sigma_3{}^2}{2\sigma_1 \sigma_2}$$

Here σ_1 and σ_2 are the S.D.s of the F_1 and F_2 distributions, as before. The distribution whose S.D. is σ_3 is obtained by counting the total frequencies, not in the rows or columns, but along the diagonals. We start from the top left-hand corner and proceed to the bottom right-hand, counting all the entries along the diagonals at right angles to this line as we go. On the diagonal running from $x_1 = +1$, $x_2 = -4$ to $x_1 = +3$, $x_2 = -2$, there is one entry. The next diagonal runs from $x_2 = 0$, $x_2 = -4$ to $x_1 = +3$, $x_2 = -1$; this takes in two entries. The next diagonal includes no entries, the next 4, and so on. The complete distribution, which we shall call F_3, is given in the following table. We choose an arbitrary mean, and work out its S.D. in the usual manner.

F_3	d	$F_3 d$	$F_3 d^2$
1	+ 5	+ 5	25
2	4	8	32
0	3	0	0
4	2	8	16
6	1	6	6
10	0	+ 27	0
8	− 1	8	8
2	2	4	8
1	3	3	9
1	4	4	16
0	5	0	0
1	6	6	36
36		− 25	156

$$\frac{\Sigma F_3 d}{N} = \frac{27-25}{36} = 0\cdot 0555 \qquad \frac{\Sigma F_3 d^2}{N} = \frac{156}{36} = 4\cdot 3333.$$

$\sigma_3{}^2 = 4\cdot 3333 - (0\cdot 0555)^2 = 4\cdot 330.$

We already know $\sigma_1{}^2$ and $\sigma_2{}^2$ to be 3·990 and 5·898. Hence :

$$r = \frac{3\cdot 990 + 5\cdot 898 - 4\cdot 330}{2 \times 1\cdot 997 \times 2\cdot 429} = + \cdot 573.$$

This result is identical with that obtained above.

Rank-order Correlation.—A different method for determining correlations is available for data arranged in order, for example the orders of merit of a school class on two examinations. When the number of cases is greater than about 30, the figures involved become troublesomely big, but with a small number the method is much easier to use than the product-moment method. Often, therefore, sets of scores are turned into rank orders and the correlation between these orders is computed. The formula is as follows :

$$r = 1 - \frac{6\Sigma d^2}{N(N^2 - 1)}$$

where d is the difference between each person's two ranks. Such a correlation is often indicated by the Greek letter ρ (rho), instead of by r.

Ex. 38.—The second and third columns of the following table give the marks of eleven pupils on tests X_1 and X_2. The next

Pupil		X_1	X_2	Ranks		d	d^2
A .	.	65	75	6	4	2	4
B .	.	85	66	1	7	6	36
C .	.	64	58	7	9	2	4
D .	.	78	82	3	1	2	4
E .	.	60	58	8	9	1	1
F .	.	70	80	5	$2\frac{1}{2}$	$2\frac{1}{2}$	6·25
G .	.	83	80	2	$2\frac{1}{2}$	$\frac{1}{2}$	0·25
H .	.	55	71	10	5	5	25
I .	.	50	58	11	9	2	4
J .	.	72	55	4	11	7	49
K .	.	59	68	9	6	3	9
							142·5

9

two columns show the ranks, pupil A being 6th on X_1, 4th on X_2, and so on. The d column gives the differences in rank, regardless of sign. These are squared and summed. Substituting in the formula :

$$r = 1 - \frac{6 \times 142 \cdot 5}{11(121 - 1)} = 1 - 0 \cdot 648 = + 0 \cdot 352.$$

Clearly the bigger the differences in rank positions, the bigger will Σd^2 be, and the lower the value of r. If $6\Sigma d^2$ is greater than $N(N^2 - 1)$ the correlation will be negative.

Now there is no difficulty in turning scores into ranks when, as in X_1 in the above example, every person gets a different score. But when two (or more) persons tie with the same score, they then divide the two (or more) ranks between them, as in X_2. Thus pupils F and G must share 2nd and 3rd place, and are both called $2\frac{1}{2}$, whilst the next highest pupil, A, is called 4. Again, C, E, and I share the 8th, 9th, and 10th positions, and are all called 9, whilst J, the next highest, is 11. Such sharing is undesirable in that it distorts, and generally decreases, the size of the correlation. It follows, therefore, that the rank-order method should not be applied when there are a great many ties.

Other Methods of Measuring Correlation

The nature and the main uses of other methods will be indicated briefly, but they will not be described in detail. Full accounts of them may be found in more advanced textbooks.

Spearman's Foot-rule Method.—This, like the rank method, is applicable to data arranged in rank order. It is perhaps even simpler than the ordinary rank method, but the coefficients which it yields range only from $+ 1 \cdot 0$ to $- 0 \cdot 5$, not from $+ 1 \cdot 0$ to $- 1 \cdot 0$, and they often diverge rather widely from those obtained by the first two methods. A new and easy method, which possesses certain important statistical advantages over the rank method, has been described recently by Kendall, but has not yet been very widely used (cf. Kendall and Babington Smith, 1938).

Correlation Ratio.—This is denoted by the symbol η (eta), instead of by r.   We saw in Fig. 21 (p. 78), that the ticks in a scattergram tend to be grouped along a straight diagonal.   This is referred to as ' linear regression.'   When the regression is non-linear, that is, when the ticks tend to be grouped round a curve, a product-moment correlation fails to show the closeness of relationship, and the correlation ratio is used instead.   For example, when tests of motor perseveration are compared with assessments of

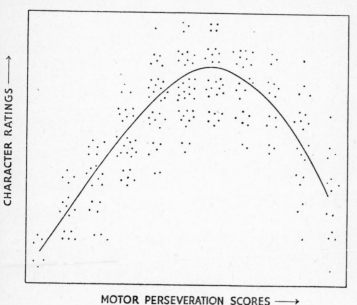

FIG. 22.—Scattergram of non-linear correlation.

desirable character traits, it is found that both the persons with high perseveration scores and those with low scores are often weak in character, whereas those with medium scores get the best character assessments.   This type of relationship is illustrated in the accompanying scattergram, Fig. 22.

Coefficients of Association and Colligation.—There are many variables which we may wish to compare, but to which we cannot apply any of the correlation techniques because they are not amenable to precise measurement. One instance is the colour of people's eyes. We can assign people to one of a number of more or less distinct groups or categories according to their eye-colour, even if we cannot measure the colour. The same can be done with hair-colour, and the two colours may then be compared. An appropriate technique will tell us the extent to which brown eyes and dark hair, blue or grey eyes and light hair, are associated or go together with one another. A further instance of a so-called ' categoric ' variable is sex. We might find that more men than women in a university take scientific courses of study, and that more women than men take literary courses. The coefficients of association or colligation would then provide a measure of the correspondence between sex and scientific versus literary interests.

Ex. 39.—Take the data from Ex. 36, and suppose that we do not know the actual marks, but only have the categories ' top half ' and ' bottom half ' on both examinations.[1] The following table may be drawn up :

GEOGRAPHY

		Top Half 11 or over	Bottom Half 10 or under	
HISTORY	Top Half 15 or over	$13 = a$	$5 = b$	18
	Bottom Half 10 or over	$5 = c$	$13 = d$	18
		18	18	36

Yule's coefficients of association (Q), and colligation (ω), are given by the formulæ :

$$Q = \frac{ad - bc}{ad + bc}$$

$$\omega = \frac{\sqrt{ad} - \sqrt{bc}}{\sqrt{ad} + \sqrt{bc}}$$

[1] There is no necessity for the proportions to be equal, as they are in the present instance.

where a, b, c, and d are the four frequencies in the table.

a	b
c	d

Substituting, we find $Q = + 0.742$, $\omega = + 0.444$. If all the pupils in the top half on one examination had been in the top half on the other, the table would have been

18	0
0	18

, and both coefficients would have been 1·0.

If there was no relationship, and the table had been

9	9
9	9

, both coefficients would have been zero. But with intermediate distributions the coefficients are clearly not comparable either with one another, or with the correlation coefficient.

What is known as *tetrachoric r* may sometimes be applied to these categoric classifications,[1] and this is supposed to be comparable to a product-moment coefficient. But it is far more difficult to compute than the above two coefficients. In the present instance it works out at $+ 0.642$. The discrepancy between this figure and our r of $+ 0.579$ is probably due to the small number of cases and the irregularity of their distribution.

Biserial r.—When one of the variables to be compared has been accurately measured and has yielded a normal distribution, but the other (though believed to be normally distributed) can only be expressed in the form of two categories, biserial r may be used. For instance, if we wish to compare intelligence-test scores with success or failure in a scholarship examination, we may not know the examination marks, but we do know the intelligence scores of scholars and non-scholars.

[1] Tetrachoric r can only be used when it can be assumed that the variables to be compared, although both expressed in the form of two classes, are really normally distributed. The assumption is true of examination marks, but not of sex or eye-colour and the like.

Ex. 40.—Suppose that we have all the history marks of Ex. 36, and that we know who fall into the top half, who into the bottom half, for geography. The average history marks of the top geographers is 16·4, that of the bottom ones is 11·9. From the difference in averages, 4·5, from the S.D. of the history marks, and from the proportions of pupils in the two groups,[1] we can find biserial r between history and geography marks to be $+$ 0·722.

Biserial r often fails to agree closely with product-moment r. In this instance the small size of N, and the irregularity of the distributions, accentuate the discrepancy.

Contingency.—When the data are grouped into two or more classes, but cannot be regarded as normally distributed, the measurement of correspondence is carried out by quite a different method, based on testing for goodness of fit, as described in Chap. V. For instance, we might wish to compare political and religious affiliations. We might classify a large group of persons into conservatives, liberals, socialists, communists, and re-classify into Roman Catholics, Anglicans, Free Church Protestants, Jews. We should then have a 4 $\times$ 4 table, to which the following method would apply.

We start by assuming that there is no relationship between the variables, and compute on the basis of this hypothesis how many persons would be expected to fall under each of our 16 categories. The actual frequencies are then compared with these F_e's. If they diverge from one another to an extent which cannot possibly be ascribed to chance errors of sampling, in other words, if the actual F's entirely fail to fit in with our initial hypothesis, then we have evidence suggesting that there is a relationship between the variables.

Ex. 41.—Take the data of Ex. 36, and suppose that the history marks consist only of A, B, C grades, the geography marks of A, B, C, D grades. The following 3 $\times$ 4 table is obtained.

Now if there was no relation between the two sets of marks, then we might expect the 13 pupils with A's in history to be

[1] There is no necessity for the proportions to be equal, as they are in the present instance.

GEOGRAPHY

		D	C	B	A	
HISTORY	A	0	1	7	5	13
	B	4	7	4	1	16
	C	3	3	0	1	7
		7	11	11	7	36

TABLE OF F's.

distributed, as regards their geography grades, in the proportions $7 : 11 : 11 : 7$. That is, the F_e in cell AD is $\dfrac{13 \times 7}{36}$, the F_e in cell AC is $\dfrac{13 \times 11}{36}$, and so on. Similarly the F_e's for the pupils with B in history are $\dfrac{16 \times 7}{36}$ in cell BD, $\dfrac{16 \times 11}{36}$ in cell BC, and so on. We arrive then at the following table of F_e's. The procedure now consists, as before, in computing $F - F_e$, $\dfrac{(F - F_e)^2}{F_e}$, and the sum of these quantities, chi squared.

	D	C	B	A	
A	2·53	3·97	3·97	2·53	13
B	3·11	4·89	4·89	3·11	16
C	1·36	2·14	2·14	1·36	7
	7	11	11	7	36

TABLE OF F_e's.

	D	C	B	A
A	2·53	2·97	3·03	2·47
B	0·89	2·11	0·89	2·11
C	1·64	0·86	2·14	0·36

TABLE OF $(F - F_e)$.

	D	C	B	A
A	2·53	2·23	2·31	2·41
B	0·26	0·91	0·16	1·43
C	1·98	0·35	2·14	0·10

TABLE OF $\dfrac{(F - F_e)^2}{F_e}$.

$\dfrac{\Sigma(F - F_e)^2}{F_e} = \chi^2 = 16\cdot81$. From tables of χ^2 it is found that
the probability of this value of χ^2 is $0\cdot01$, which means that
there is only one chance in a hundred that our obtained F's
could deviate as they do from the expected F_e's through chance
errors of sampling.

Chi squared may now be expressed as a coefficient, C, which
is called the coefficient of mean square contingency.

$C = \sqrt{\dfrac{\chi^2}{N + \chi^2}}$. Substituting, $C = \sqrt{\dfrac{16\cdot72}{36 + 16\cdot72}} = 0\cdot563$.

In this example C happens to be quite close to the r
which we obtained previously, but they are not usually
closely comparable to one another, for two reasons.   First,
the maximum possible value of C is always less than $1\cdot0$,
by an amount depending on the fewness of the number of
cells.   In this instance, with only 12 cells, C cannot exceed
$0\cdot775$.   Hence it is best, whenever possible, to adopt a
finer classification, e.g. 5×5 categories, which will yield
a maximum C of $0\cdot894$.

Secondly, we have seen that C is, strictly, a measure of
divergence, and such divergence does not necessarily prove
a relationship.   Suppose for example that our original
table of F's had been :

	D	C	B	A	
A	5	1	0	7	13
B	1	7	4	4	16
C	1	3	3	0	7
	7	11	7	11	36

TABLE OF F'S.

There is now no appreciable correspondence between
high scores in history and high scores in geography.   Yet
the contingency coefficient would be precisely the same as
before.   Contingency should then be used as a measure
of relationship only with great caution, if at all.

The Matching Method.—One context in which C is useful is in what are known as matching experiments. Suppose we wish to find whether style of English composition reflects the character of the writer. We would get, say, ten persons each to write a composition on a given theme, and then obtain from acquaintances as full and accurate descriptions as possible of the character of each writer. The character descriptions and compositions (which should be anonymous) would then be compared by a group of individuals who act as judges or matchers. Each judge would try to match or identify each composition with the appropriate character description. Some judges might ascribe A's composition to A, others to B or C, and so on. We would therefore arrive at a 10×10 table, similar to the contingency tables above, giving the frequency with which each composition was assigned to each character. By a modification of the mean square contingency technique, the accuracy of matchings, i.e. the extent to which the compositions appear to the judges to be related to the writers' characters, may be expressed as a coefficient, C. The present writer has described this technique and its applications elsewhere (Vernon, 1936).

Analysis of Variance.—There is an unfortunate tendency in contemporary educational and psychological investigations to make over-much use of correlation techniques, when other methods of statistical treatment of the results might be more appropriate. One very powerful tool which has so far been but little applied to educational statistics is known as the analysis of variance. This involves rather more advanced theory than we have space to discuss,[1] but the following is an instance of its application.

Ex. 42.—The writer's men students were divided, according to their various courses of training, into seven sections, each numbering about 22 students. The average level of ability in different sections seemed to differ considerably, and their average percentage marks on examinations in psychology are

---

[1] A good elementary description is given by Thouless (1937). See also Fisher (1930).

listed in the second column of the accompanying table. The third column shows, however, that the marks in any one section

Section	Mean Psychology Mark	S.D. of Marks
A . . .	72·89	8·25
B . . .	68·69	8·43
C . . .	65·59	7·88
D . . .	64·41	7·05
E . . .	63·95	8·58
F . . .	63·52	10·71
G . . .	63·48	10·71

were very variable, usually ranging from about 45% to 85%. Thus in order to answer the question whether there exists any relation between a student's ability and the section to which he is assigned, we must determine whether these differences between the means of the sections are significant or whether, in view of the variability of the marks within each section, such differences might arise merely through chance fluctuations of sampling. " Variance " is simply another term for spread, dispersion, or variability (actually the variance of a distribution of measures is the square of its S.D.). The technique of analysis of variance enables us to say how far these differences *between* sections can be ascribed to the effect of individual differences *within* sections. In this instance the probability of such differences between means arising by chance is quite small, approximately 0·01, so showing that there is a definite tendency for better students to be put into some sections, poorer students into others.[1]

The Probable Errors of Correlation Coefficients

A correlation coefficient is, like any other numerical psychological result, liable to vary on account of sampling errors, especially when the sample of persons, whose scores are inter-correlated, is of small size. The formula for the P.E. of a product-moment coefficient is :

$$\text{P.E.}_{\cdot_r} = \frac{0·6745(1 - r^2)}{\sqrt{N}}$$

Applying this to our r of $+ 0·579$, where $N = 36$, we get P.E. $= \pm 0·075$. It is usual to write the P.E. after the

[1] In Fisher's terminology z for the differences in variance is 0·610. Degrees of freedom are $n_1 = 6, n_2 = 145$. A value of z of 0·54 would under these conditions have a probability of 0·01.

coefficient, thus : $r = + 0.579 \pm 0.075$. The P.E. of a rank order coefficient is slightly greater than that of a product-moment one, and is usually calculated by the formula :

$$\text{P.E.}\rho = \frac{0.7063(1 - r^2)}{\sqrt{N}}$$

For the determination of the P.E.s or S.E.s of the other coefficients mentioned above, the reader should consult more advanced textbooks, such as Kelley (1924) or Guilford (1936).

The connotation of the P.E. of r or ρ is similar to that of an average or difference (cf. Chap. V). Thus $+ 0.579$ ± 0.075 signifies that if the same history and geography papers were set to much larger numbers of similar children, and the marks inter-correlated, the true value of r so obtained would be as likely as not to lie between $+ 0.654$ and $+ 0.504$ (i.e. $r + 1 \times$ P.E. and $r - 1 \times$ P.E.), but that there is a 1 in 370 probability that it might deviate as widely as $+ 0.916$ or $+ 0.242$ ($4\frac{1}{2} \times$ P.E.).

Just as a difference between averages should be three or more times its S.E. to be accepted as statistically significant, so a correlation should be $4\frac{1}{2}$ times its P.E. before it is regarded as showing a real relationship between the inter-correlated variables. A coefficient of, say, $+ 0.30$ ± 0.10 is on the borderline of significance. For if the true value of r was zero, the scores of a limited sample of persons might yield $+ 0.30$ once in 44 times.

In our previous illustration $+ 0.579$ is much greater than $4\frac{1}{2} \times$ P.E. Yet, as we have seen, this value is far from trustworthy, the reason being the small size of N. Most investigators consider a correlation calculated from less than 25 cases to be almost worthless because of its low reliability, and they prefer to have at least a hundred cases before they base any important conclusions on the results of an experiment involving correlations.

Fisher's z Method.—The P.E. method of indicating the reliability of r has been shown to be somewhat inaccurate, especially when N is small or r is large. Fisher (1930) presents a better method which is being widely adopted. It consists in transforming r into a new quantity called z, whose true P.E. is easily calculated.[1]   Applying this method to our $r = + 0.579$, we find that the limits within which true r is as likely as not to lie are almost identical with the limits derived, above, from P.E.$_r$, but that the extreme limits ($4\frac{1}{2} \times$ P.E.) should be $+ 0.831$ and $+ 0.132$ instead of $+ 0.916$ and $+ 0.242$.

Combined and Comparing Correlations.—The z method also provides a useful way of combining two or more correlations.

Ex. 43.—Suppose that another class of 43 pupils had taken the history and geography papers and yielded a coefficient of $+ 0.450 \pm 0.082$, what is the best estimate of the true correlation ?   The procedure is to determine z_1 and z_2 for the two r's, and then to compute the weighted average,
$$\frac{z_1(N_1 - 3) + z_2(N_2 - 3)}{N_1 + N_2 - 6}$$
Translating back from the average z gives us our answer, $r = + 0.512 \pm 0.057$.

It is often required to find whether a correlation in one group is appreciably different from that in another group, or whether the difference can be ascribed to errors of sampling.   When the numbers of cases are large the stock method may be used, $\sigma_d = \sqrt{\text{S.E.}r_1{}^2 + \text{S.E.}r_2{}^2}$.

Ex. 44.—What is the significance of the difference between $+ 0.579 \pm 0.075$ and $+ 0.450 \pm 0.082$?   The S.E.s of these coefficients are the $\dfrac{\text{P.E.s}}{0.6745}$, i.e. 0.1108 and 0.1216. $\sigma_d = 0.1645$. The difference is $0.579 - 0.450 = 0.129$, which is not as large as its own σ_d.   A difference as large as or larger than this would occur 43% of times as a mere matter of chance.

As the numbers are small, Fisher's z method should preferably be used.   This consists in computing z_1, z_2, and their

[1] $z = \frac{1}{2}\Big\{\log_e (1 + r) - \log_e (1 - r)\Big\}.$ The S.E. of $z = \dfrac{1}{\sqrt{N - 3}}.$
Fisher provides tables of z for various values of r.

S.E.s, and applying the stock formula to these S.E.s. The difference in z's is $+$ 0·1763 in the above example. S.E.$z_1 =$ 0·1741, S.E.$z_2 = $ 0·1581. $\sigma_d = \sqrt{0\cdot1741^2 + 0\cdot1581^2} = $ 0·2352. Here the difference is 0·75 times its σ_d, and it might occur 45% of times as a mere matter of chance.

CHAPTER VII

INTERPRETATION AND APPLICATIONS OF CORRELATIONS

A CORRELATION coefficient is never an end in itself, but always a means towards the proper interpretation of numerical data. By studying the correlations between tests of various abilities it is possible to analyse scientifically the nature of such abilities. This is one important application, which we shall consider in Chap. VIII. But the primary value of a correlation is that it enables us to make predictions. If abilities X_1 and X_2 are known to be inter-correlated, then we can use measures of X_1 to predict scores on X_2, and vice versa. For instance a pupil's probable scholastic success may be forecast from his performance on an intelligence test. This cannot, of course, be done with complete accuracy, but the correlation coefficient will also tell us how accurate is the forecast, or what are its limits of error.

Ex. 45.—The following scattergram shows the Intelligence Quotients of 440 children and adults on the Stanford-Binet scale, and their I.Q.s on the Vocabulary test from this scale. (The group or category 140 includes all testees with I.Q.s around 140, i.e. ranging from $135\frac{1}{2}$ to $145\frac{1}{2}$; similarly with the other groups.) Here the correlation is quite a high one, namely $+ 0.799 \pm 0.012$. Hence we would be justified in testing people only with the Vocabulary test, and predicting from their results what would be their Binet I.Q.s. Let us see how to make such predictions, and how good they would be.

Suppose a child to obtain a Vocabulary I.Q. of 120, his Binet I.Q. may, according to the scattergram, lie as high as the 140 class, i.e. up to 145, or as low as the 100 class,

X_2 = Vocabulary I.Q.

X_1 = Binet I.Q.	60	70	80	90	100	110	120	130	140	150		Average X_2
140						2	3	1	2	4	12	130·1
130				1		6	12	5	2	1	27	121·5
120			1	1	5	15	16	9	1		48	115·6
110			2	9	13	33	9	4	1		71	107·6
100			8	31	36	17	8				100	99·3
90		3	19	45	22	7					96	91·2
80	2	11	17	21	2	1					54	82·4
70	7	8	4	5	1						25	74·0
60	3	4									7	65·7
	12	26	51	112	80	81	48	19	6	5	440	
Average X_1	69·2	75·0	88·0	91·9	99·9	109·9	118·5	121·6	128·3	138·0		

i.e. down to 96. But presumably its most probable value
will be the average of the column :

X_1	F_1
140	3
130	12
120	16
110	9
100	8

This works out at 118·5. Similarly for a child whose
Vocabulary I.Q. is 70, the most likely value of his Binet
I.Q. is 75·0, though it may lie anywhere between 56 and 95.

Along the bottom of the scattergram are given the
averages of the columns, i.e. of the X_1 measures which most
probably correspond to the X_2 measures at the heads of the
columns. Fig. 23 is a graph of these figures. It will be
seen that the points on the graph lie approximately on a
straight line which runs through $X_1 = 100$, $X_2 = 100$.
That they do not all lie exactly on the line is due merely
to irregularities in the data. For though the numbers involved in our example are large, they are still not large
enough to yield really smooth normal distributions, or
regularly spaced averages.

Now as we approach the extreme values of X_2, the corresponding values of X_1 tend to lag behind ; 118·5 is smaller than 120, 138 is much smaller than 150. Similarly with values below 100, 75 is not so low as 70, 69 is much less low than 60. This is an important and characteristic feature of all correlations. It is known as the *regression* of X_1 towards the mean. The line drawn through the points on

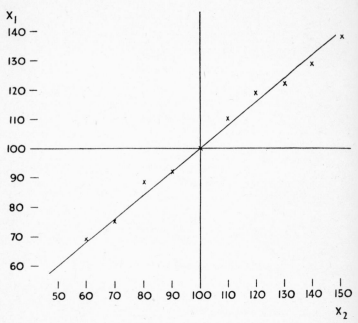

Fig. 23.—Graph showing the most probable values of X_1 for testees who obtain each value of X_2.

the graph is called a *regression line*, or a graph showing the regression of X_1 on X_2.

Suppose now that the correlation is a perfect one. The scores on X_2 and X_1 would be identical, and the slope of the regression line would be 45°. Next suppose that there is no correlation at all between X_1 and X_2. It would then obviously be impossible to predict scores on one variable from those on the other. If we took successive columns of the scattergram and averaged them, we should find that all these means lay close to the mean of X_1. Whatever the value of the Vocabulary I.Q., the average Binet I.Q. would be round about 100. In other words, the regression line would be horizontal. From these two hypothetical cases we can now see that the nearer the slope of the regression line is to 45°, the higher the correlation; the nearer it is to horizontal, the lower the correlation. Furthermore, when the correlation is perfect, there is *no* regression towards the mean, since each X_1 value is as big as each X_2 value. But when the correlation is zero, the regression is *complete*, since whatever the value of X_2, the value of X_1 is always the mean. Thus the greater the regression, the nearer the correlation approaches zero.

It has been assumed in the previous paragraph that the X_1 and X_2 measures are expressed in equivalent units. If the dispersions of the two distributions are very different, then the slope of the regression line corresponding to perfect correlation would not, of course, be 45°. However, as shown in Chap. IV, measures can be turned into equivalent units if they are expressed as deviations from their means, and divided by their standard deviations, i.e. as $\dfrac{x_1}{\sigma_1}$ and $\dfrac{x_2}{\sigma_2}$. If this is done the slope of the regression line is identical with r. When the slope is 45°, $\dfrac{x_1/\sigma_1}{x_2/\sigma_2} = 1 \cdot 0$, that is perfect correlation. When the slope is horizontal, $\dfrac{x_1/\sigma_1}{x_2/\sigma_2} = 0 \cdot 0$, that is zero correlation.

The slope of the regression line plotted in Fig. 23 is $0 \cdot 80$. σ_1 and σ_2 are $17 \cdot 49$ and $17 \cdot 84$ (i.e. the Vocabulary I.Q.s are slightly more spread out than the Binet I.Q.s). Hence $r = \dfrac{0 \cdot 80 \times 17 \cdot 84}{17 \cdot 49} = 0 \cdot 815$. This is very close to the figure already quoted for the correlation, as determined by the product-moment method. As a matter of historical fact, r was originally determined by plotting the regression line

10

and measuring its slope, before statisticians invented the product-moment method. The latter method is always employed now because, as we have seen, the regression line obtained by averaging the columns is somewhat inexact, even when N is large. It is more useful to reverse the historical procedure, to calculate σ_1, σ_2, and r, and from them to determine the regression line. If $\dfrac{x_1\sigma_2}{x_2\sigma_1} = r$, then $x_1 = rx_2\dfrac{\sigma_1}{\sigma_2}$. This is the algebraic equation of the regression line, and it can be used for predicting any individual's most probable x_1 score from his x_2 score. Alternatively, if we wish to predict in terms of original measures, instead of measures expressed as deviations from their means, the formula becomes :

$$(X_1 - M_1) = r(X_2 - M_2)\frac{\sigma_1}{\sigma_2}.$$

Ex. 46.—What is the most probable Binet I.Q. corresponding to a Vocabulary I.Q. of 140 ? According to the averages listed at the foot of the scattergram, the answer is 128·3. But this is based on only 6 cases and is therefore very unreliable. Applying the formula :

$$X_1 - 100 = 0\cdot799\,(140 - 100) \times \frac{17\cdot49}{17\cdot84}.$$

$$X_1 = 131\cdot3 \text{ is the correct answer.}$$

Regression of X_2 on X_1.—So far we have dealt only with

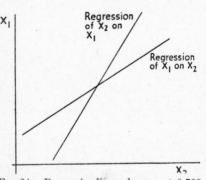

FIG. 24.—Regression lines when $r = +0\cdot799$.

the prediction of X_1, knowing X_2. The opposite is equally possible. On the right-hand side of the scattergram in Ex. 45 are listed the average values of X_2 which constitute the best estimates of the Vocabulary I.Q.s of persons with various Binet

I.Q.s. Here, too, there is regression towards the mean. The probable Vocabulary I.Q. corresponding to a Binet I.Q. of 120 is 115·6, and for a Binet I.Q. of 70 it is 74·0. A second graph may therefore be drawn, showing the regression of X_2 on X_1. Fig. 24 shows the two lines diagrammatically. If the correlation was perfect the two lines would coincide, both having a slope of 45° (provided, always, that X_1 and X_2 are measured in equivalent units). If the correlation was zero, the second line would be vertical, as in Fig. 25, since the only possible estimate of Vocabulary I.Q. from Binet I.Q. would be 100. With an intermediate correlation,

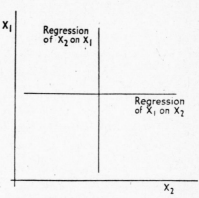

FIG. 25.—Regression lines when $r = 0·0$.

such as our $+ 0·799$, the second line makes the same slope with the vertical as does the first regression line with the horizontal; and the two cross at the means of X_1 and X_2. Thus the algebraic equation of the second line, which is also the formula for predicting X_2 from X_1, will be : $x_2 = rx_1\frac{\sigma_2}{\sigma_1}$, or, in terms of scores, $(X_2 - M_2) = r(X_1 - M_1)\frac{\sigma_2}{\sigma_1}$.

Ex. 47.—What is the probable Vocabulary I.Q. of a testee with Binet I.Q. 80 ? $X_2 = 100 + 0·799 (80 - 100) \times \frac{17·84}{17·49} = 83·7$. The estimate based on the scattergram was 82·4, which agrees quite closely with our answer.

P.E. of Estimated Scores.—The regression equations will tell us the *most probable* estimate of X_1 from X_2, or of X_2

from X_1. But it is obvious from the scattergram that the actual X_1 may fall within quite a wide range on either side of the estimated X_1, and that similarly an estimated X_2 is only the average of a wide range of possible X_2's. The ranges may be determined from the formulæ :

$$P.E._{estim.X_1} = 0 \cdot 6745 \sigma_1 \sqrt{1 - r^2}$$
$$P.E._{estim.X_2} = 0 \cdot 6745 \sigma_2 \sqrt{1 - r^2}$$

Applied to Exs. 46 and 47 : $P.E._{estim.X_1} = 0 \cdot 6745 \times 17 \cdot 49 \sqrt{1 - 0 \cdot 799^2} = 7 \cdot 1$, $P.E._{estim.X_2} = 7 \cdot 3$.

The P.E. of an estimated score has a slightly different meaning from previous P.E.s. It is best shown by the following example. Consider a very large group of persons whose Binet I.Q.s are 110, and whose estimated Vocabulary I.Q.s $108 \cdot 1 \pm 7 \cdot 3$. Then one half of them should have Vocabulary I.Q.s lying between $115 \cdot 4$ and $100 \cdot 8$, and practically all of them should lie within a range $\pm 4\frac{1}{2} \times$ P.E., i.e. between $140 \cdot 9$ and $75 \cdot 3$.

Actually we already know the Vocabulary I.Q.s of 71 persons with Binet I.Q.s round 110. This is not a very large group, but it should serve to test out our prediction. The scattergram is too coarse, but looking back to the original scores it appears that 37 of them, or 52%, had Vocabulary I.Q.s between 115 and 101 (inclusive), and that the two extreme Vocabulary I.Q.s were 138 and 80. This agreement is quite close.

It is important to note that the P.E. of an estimated score decreases as r increases. If the correlation were perfect there would be no error at all in estimating X_1 from X_2, or X_2 from X_1. The lower the correlation, the less accurate will be the predictions.

Ex. 48.—As an additional illustration, take the results from the 36 history and geography papers. Here N is far too small for accurate regression lines to be obtained by averaging rows or columns. But by the use of the formulæ given above, probable geography marks can be estimated from history marks, or vice versa. For instance : what geography mark (X_2) corresponds to a history mark (X_1) of 7, and what is its P.E. ?

$$M_1 = 14 \cdot 139 \quad M_2 = 9 \cdot 945$$
$$\sigma_1 = 3 \cdot 903 \quad \sigma_2 = 4 \cdot 819$$
$$r = + 0 \cdot 579$$

$$(X_2 - 9 \cdot 945) = 0 \cdot 579(7 - 14 \cdot 139) \times \frac{4 \cdot 819}{3 \cdot 903}$$

$$X_2 = 9 \cdot 945 - 5 \cdot 103 = 4 \cdot 84$$

$$\text{P.E.}_{\text{estim.}X_2} = 0 \cdot 6745 \times 4 \cdot 819\sqrt{1 - 0 \cdot 579^2}$$
$$= 2 \cdot 65$$

Therefore $X_2 = 4 \cdot 84 \pm 2 \cdot 65$.

Here the correlation is only moderate, hence the estimate is poor in reliability. All we can claim is that a pupil with a history mark of 7 would be very unlikely to get a geography mark as high as 17 ($X_2 + 4\frac{1}{2} \times$ P.E.), and would most probably get round about 2 to 7.

INTERPRETATION OF CORRELATIONS

In the light of the above discussion it is possible to give a much more precise meaning to the conception of correlation than heretofore. A correlation does not mean, as is sometimes supposed, the percentage agreement between the correlated variables. In the scattergram on p. 131, for example, only $37\frac{1}{2}\%$ of the testees get the same I.Q., or rather the same class of I.Q., on Binet and Vocabulary, although the correlation is $+ 0 \cdot 799$. It is possible to interpret a coefficient in terms of the number of factors or elements which are common to the two variables, which therefore cause them to correlate with one another,[1] but there is little practical point in so doing. What a correlation does indicate is *the amount of reduction of error in predicting scores on one variable from scores on the other variable.* When r is zero, the error is at its maximum, namely $0 \cdot 6745\sigma$. Predictions based on X_1 might fall anywhere within the whole range of X_2 scores, and would be no more accurate than drawing X_2 scores out of a hat. With a correlation of $1 \cdot 0$ the error is reduced to zero. The extent of reduction of error for intermediate r's is shown in the following table. The second column lists values of $100 (1 - \sqrt{1 - r^2})$, and so represents the reduction in percentage terms. These

[1] Cf. Garrett (1937), pp. 348 ff.

figures are sometimes referred to as the *forecasting efficiencies* of the *r*'s. It will be seen that the forecasting efficiency only becomes high enough to be of great practical value when *r* is in the neighbourhood of 0·8 to 0·9 or more. Great caution should be exercised therefore before predicting, say, scholastic success in a secondary school from elementary school examinations or from intelligence tests, since these usually give correlations of only + 0·4 to + 0·6 with what we wish to predict. Such deductions are only 8% to 20% more accurate than pure chance guesses.

r	Reduction of error, or forecasting efficiency %
0·00	0·0
0·10	0·5
0·20	2·0
0·30	4·6
0·40	8·4
0·50	13·4
0·60	20·0
0·70	28·6
0·80	40·0
0·90	56·4
0·95	68·8
1·00	100·0

The Influence upon Correlations of Irrelevant Common Factors.—A positive correlation which is statistically significant (i.e. 3 or preferably 4½ times its P.E.) always indicates some kind of causal connection, or some common factor or factors running through the two variables—even when the connection is not strong enough for us to be able to forecast one variable from the other. Considerable care is needed, however, in interpreting such a connection, for its real nature may be quite unsuspected, or the common factors may be of an entirely irrelevant kind. Suppose, for example, that we correlated the size of boots worn by all the children in a school with the speed of their handwriting, we should undoubtedly obtain a moderately high coefficient. Yet it would be absurd to say that big boots cause quick handwriting, or vice versa. The real reason for the correlation is an irrelevant common factor, in this case age.

The older children on the whole write more quickly and have larger feet than the younger ones. If we took children all of the same age and compared boots with handwriting, we should be likely to find that the correlation had fallen to zero.

Consider another, rather more complex, illustration. A positive correlation exists between backwardness in school work and unemployment among the children's parents. Idealists may at once jump to the conclusion that unemployment brings about malnutrition and anxiety among the children, and that these make their work fall off. But here also there is an important common element which goes some way to explain the connection. Unemployed parents are known to be on the whole less intelligent than employed ones, and unintelligent parents tend to have unintelligent children, and low intelligence is a far more important cause of backwardness than is malnutrition. We need to take two groups of children, one with parents employed, one unemployed, groups whose average intelligence level is identical, and then study their school work to see whether the former do better than the latter. Only when we have ' held the intelligence factor constant ' in this example, or ' held the age factor constant ' in the previous example, can we legitimately deduce some causal connection.

Partial Correlation.—The above type of problem or difficulty in interpretation is constantly occurring in psychology and education. Sometimes it can be met by applying what is known as the partial correlation technique. For this it is necessary to obtain measures of the suspected irrelevant factor, which we shall call X_3, and to work out the correlations between X_1 and X_3 (r_{13}), and between X_2 and X_3 (r_{23}), as well as between X_1 and X_2 (r_{12}).[1]   We

[1] Thouless (1939a) has recently pointed out that the partial correlation formula can only legitimately be used if X_3 can be measured without error. It is thus most appropriate for holding age constant, but not for, say, intelligence ; since measurements of the latter always involve some error. However, Thouless provides an alternative formula which may be used when the reliability of X_3 is known.

may then ' hold X_3 constant ' or ' partial it out ' by the following formula : $r_{12.3}$ (meaning the correlation of X_1 with X_2 when X_3 is eliminated) $=$

$$\frac{r_{12} - r_{13}r_{23}}{\sqrt{1 - r_{13}{}^2}\sqrt{1 - r_{23}{}^2}}.$$

Ex. 49.—Suppose the correlation between boots and handwriting speed to be $+ 0.45$, that between boots and age $+ 0.70$, and between handwriting and age $+ 0.60$. Then the correlation between boots and handwriting when the influence of age is removed is : $r = \dfrac{0.45 - 0.70 \times 0.60}{\sqrt{1 - 0.70^2}\sqrt{1 - 0.60^2}} = + 0.052.$

The Effect of Homogeneity and Heterogeneity upon Correlations.—We have just seen that when pupils are heterogeneous as regards age, the correlation between a pair of their characteristics may be spuriously raised. The same is true of other types of heterogeneity. Suppose we calculate the correlation between two tests in an ordinary school class, and then eliminate from consideration most of the pupils of medium ability on both tests, and re-calculate the correlation, the second figure will certainly be larger than the first. The distributions will not, of course, be normal, the diversity or heterogeneity of the pupils will be unduly large and this will increase the size of r. In ordinary practice the reverse, namely undue homogeneity, is more likely to occur without the investigator realizing it. Thus the correlations between intelligence tests and school work in an ordinary school class are usually lower than they would be in an unselected group of children of the same age. For such a school class is more homogeneous as regards intelligence and school work than is the population as a whole. The dullest children of that age are likely to be at a special school, and many of the brightest ones may be at private schools. Take an extreme case : if we selected a group of children all of precisely the same intelligence, any correlation between intelligence and work would disappear. One important reason why intelligence tests appear to be of much less value for predicting scholastic aptitude among secondary than among primary school pupils, and to be poorer still among university students, is that secondary pupils are more homogeneous or more highly selected than primary. Most of the children of I.Q. less than 100 are weeded out before the secondary stage is reached, and university entrance examinations remove many more from the lower end of the scale. Thus correlations necessarily sink as we pass from unselected children to the primary school, from the primary to the secondary, and from the secondary to the university level.

It is not easy to decide just what degree of heterogeneity should be regarded as normal and reasonable, nor to specify the extent to which any given group of persons exceed or fall short of this degree of heterogeneity. Hence the correction of correlations either for undue homogeneity or excessive heterogeneity is complicated. The reader may be referred to discussions by Kelley (1924), Sections 62–64, and Thomson (1939), p. 172 f.

The main conclusion to be drawn from the above sections is that the investigator should always scrutinize his correlational data very carefully, first in order to see whether any irrelevant common factors may be increasing spuriously the size of his coefficients, secondly to judge whether or not the diversity of scores in the group tested is unusually wide or restricted. He should realize that the absolute size of a correlation means very little, since this size may be so much altered by uncontrolled common factors or heterogeneity. His interpretation of the amount of relationship between the corrrelated variables should be made relative to the particular data with which he is working.

In contrast to the absolute size, the predictive value or forecasting efficiency of a correlation is but little affected by heterogeneity. For the latter, as we have seen, depends on $\sigma\sqrt{1 - r^2}$. Hence an increase in r on account of excessive heterogeneity may be offset by the increase in σ, and the P.E. remain much the same. It should be noted further that forecasting efficiency is not in the least upset by irrelevant common factors. True, it might be foolish to predict speed of handwriting from the size of boots, yet the correlation obtained between these variables would provide a valid means of making such predictions.

COMBINING TWO OR MORE TESTS

The educational statistician is frequently faced with the problem of combining the results of several examinations and tests, and using the total scores for the selection of the best pupils. We have already dealt rather fully with the point that the distributions to be combined should be expressed in equivalent units, i.e. that they should possess the same means and S.D.s, except when it is desired to give more weight to one set of marks than to another, in which case the former should have the larger S.D., not necessarily the larger mean. Here we must draw attention to an important fact which markers seldom realize, namely that the S.D. or dispersion of combined variables is always less than that of the separate variables by an amount depending on the lowness of correlation between these variables. This fact is a natural corollary of the facts of regression, outlined above.

Suppose, for example, that total marks are based on the average of six examinations, each with a mean mark of 60, a range of 30 to 90, and a S.D. of 10. If the average correlation between the six variables is $+ 0.70$, the final distribution will probably have a S.D. of 8.66 and the average totals will range from 34 to 86. But if the average inter-correlation is only $+ 0.30$, the final distribution will have a S.D. of 6.43, and the range will drop from 30–90 to 41–79. It is easy to see why this must be so. When the average inter-correlation is moderate or low, no pupil or student will get very high marks, or very low ones, on all the examinations. Hence the highest and lowest average marks will be distinctly nearer to the mean than the highest and lowest marks on each separate examination. The same phenomenon occurs when marks on different questions in a single examination are totalled. For instance, if five questions are marked, each with a range of 5–20 out of 20, the examination totals will probably range from about 40–85, and not from 25–100.

A chief examiner, head teacher, or other marking authority, should make allowance for these facts. If he wishes the distribution of final totals to show a certain proportion of very high (over 80%) marks, and a certain proportion of low (under 40%) marks, then he must either direct the markers of the component examinations to employ extra-wide distributions (i.e. to award much larger proportions of marks over 80% and under 40%), or else he must re-scale the final marks so as to spread them out again into a distribution with the required dispersion. The formula connecting σ, the S.D. of the component distributions, and $\sigma_{av.}$, the S.D. of these distributions averaged, is :

$$\sigma_{av.} = \sigma \sqrt{\frac{1 + R(n-1)}{n}}$$ where R is the average correlation

between all the sets of marks, and n the number of sets.[1]

Multiple Correlation.—If two tests or examinations each correlate moderately with a third, then the two combined will usually correlate higher with the third than either separately. For example, English and arithmetic examinations at 11 + usually yield correlations of about + 0·40 with subsequent secondary school achievement. The combined mark is likely to correlate about + 0·50 with such achievement. Every educationist has realized and applied this principle. With the aid of statistical methods we can formulate it more precisely.

Let there be n tests which give correlations r_{1A}, r_{2A}, r_{3A} . . . etc., with some measure of achievement, A, the sum of all these coefficients being Σr_{1A} ; and let the correlations of the tests with one another be r_{12}, r_{13}, r_{23} . . .,

---

[1] Alternatively, $\frac{\sigma_{sum}}{n}$ may be substituted for $\sigma_{av.}$, where σ_{sum} is the S.D. of the *total* scores. The same formula, turned around, is often useful for finding the average inter-correlation of n variables when their separate and combined S.D.s are known. Cf. Kelley (1924), Formula No. 171.

etc., their sum being Σr_{12}. Then the correlation of A with the combined tests is :

$$r_A(_1 + _2 + _3 + \cdots + _n) = \frac{\Sigma r_{1A}}{\sqrt{n + 2\Sigma r_{12}}}$$

Ex. 50.—Three different types of intelligence tests gave correlations of $+ 0.483$, $+ 0.456$, and $+ 0.337$ with students' marks in psychology. $\Sigma r_{1A} = 1.276$. Their inter-correlations were $+ 0.507$, $+ 0.468$, and $+ 0.508$. $\Sigma r_{12} = 1.483$. What will be the correlation of the combined tests with psychology marks ?

$$r_A(_1 + _2 + _3) = \frac{1.276}{\sqrt{3 + 2 \times 1.483}} = + 0.522.$$

The above method is a simple but crude way of combining tests so as to give better predictions of achievement. Naturally some of the tests are superior to others, and so should receive more weight in the total score. Further, the most useful tests will be the ones which, as well as correlating highly with A, do not correlate highly with the other tests that are being employed. For obviously, if tests 1 and 2 are measuring almost precisely the same thing, they will predict, as it were, the same aspect of A. Whereas what we want are tests which predict different aspects, and so between them cover the whole of A more thoroughly. Thus it may be better to leave out test 2, and substitute another which, while perhaps correlating less well with A, has the advantage of being almost independent of test 1. The method known as multiple correlation enables the educationist or psychologist to choose from a number of tests those which will in combination give the highest possible correlation with A, and to weight them suitably. Multiple regression equations can also be calculated which predict an individual's most probable score on A by combining his marks on the separate tests in appropriate proportions. The method is too elaborate to be given here, but the above discussion will, it is hoped, indicate its object and main principles.

The vocational psychologist applies an analogous procedure in selecting the best candidates for a certain occupation, that is, he gives a series of tests each of which has been found to correlate moderately with success at the occupation, and combines them by the multiple correlation method so as to obtain as accurate predictions as possible.

TEST RELIABILITY

If a test or examination is applied a second time under similar conditions, and the testees' scores differ widely from those previously obtained, the test is obviously a poor one. It is said to be reliable only if the two sets of scores correlate highly with one another. Further, if different testers apply and score a test or examination, they should arrive at the same, or nearly the same, scores. Repetition of a test may, however, give an unfair picture of its reliability, since the testees may remember their previous responses. Many tests are therefore supplied in two or more parallel forms, so that if a re-test is desired, different questions may be set which should, nevertheless, yield much the same results as did the questions of the first test. When no alternative form is available, a single test is often split into two equivalent halves. For instance, the scores on odd- and on even-numbered questions or items may be totalled separately, and then inter-correlated. But it is known that test reliability depends on the length of the test, hence the correlation between one half and the other half is unduly low, and is usually corrected by the formula :

$$R = \frac{2r}{1 + r}.$$ Here r is the obtained coefficient, and R the coefficient to be expected had it been possible to compare the whole of the test with another similar test.

In all these instances—namely repetition, application and scoring by a different tester, parallel form, and corrected split-half—we generally expect to get an inter-correlation of at least $+ 0.90$. For if this reliability coefficient is much lower it would indicate that the scores are too unstable to be trusted. Standardized educational and intelligence tests generally reach this level of reliability, but ordinary examinations often fail to do so, as we shall see in Chap. XI. Many performance tests, tests of occupational abilities, and character or temperament tests, are also often poor in reliability. However, by increasing the length of a test, or by combining several parallel tests, a more satisfactory coefficient may be attained.

Knowing the reliability coefficient it is possible to calculate the reliability, or the limits of variation, of individual scores, by the formula already given : $P.E._{estim.x_1} = 0.6745\sigma_1\sqrt{1 - r^2}$. For example, if parallel intelligence tests give a correlation of $+ 0.93$, and the S.D. of their I.Q.s is $16\frac{1}{2}$, then $P.E._{I.Q.} = 0.6745 \times 16.5\sqrt{1 - 0.93^2} = 4.08$. But if the reliability coefficient is only $+ 0.70$ $P.E._{I.Q.} = 7.94$, that is almost twice as large. Such a P.E. is, as we have already seen, an index of the extent to which scores on the second test may vary when predicted from scores on the first test. About half the testees will obtain I.Q.s on the second test within 4 points (if $r = 0.93$), or about 8 points (if $r = + 0.70$), of their I.Q.s on the first test. But some may alter by as much as $4\frac{1}{2} \times P.E.$, i.e. by 18 and 36 points respectively.

The application of two parallel forms of a test to the same individual yields, as we have seen, somewhat different results. If we possessed a large number of additional parallel forms and applied them, still other results would be obtained (quite apart from effects of practice). Such results for one individual would tend to conform to a normal distribution, and their grand average would, of course, be the best possible measure of the individual's standing on the test—what may be called his true score. The situation is exactly analogous to that which we discussed in connection with group differences (Chap. V), except that there we were concerned with variations among the means of sample groups, here with variations among an individual's scores on sample tests. An individual's score therefore possesses another P.E., which indicates its liability to deviate from his true score. The formula for this also involves the reliability of the test, and the S.D.

of the test scores of an unselected group of persons. P.E. $= 0.6745\sigma\sqrt{1-r}$. Thus the P.E.s of I.Q.s for tests with reliability coefficients of $+ 0.93$ and $+ 0.70$ are 2.96 and 6.11 respectively. Note that these P.E.s are smaller than those quoted above, since $\sqrt{1-r}$ is necessarily smaller than $\sqrt{1-r^2}$. This is to be expected, since the former P.E. represents the deviation of one sample score from another sample, whereas the latter represents the deviation from the mean of all the possible samples.

Factors Influencing Test Reliability.—Since the reliability of a test is almost synonymous with its thoroughness, it can be increased or lowered almost indefinitely by lengthening or shortening the test. The formula for predicting the reliability of a test whose length is doubled has already been cited. When it is lengthened n times, the formula becomes : $R = \dfrac{nr}{1 + (n-1)r}$. This is known as the Spearman-Brown prophecy formula.

Ex. 51.—A short educational test has a reliability coefficient of $+ 0.60$. How much must it be lengthened to attain a coefficient of $+ 0.90$? Turning the above formula round, we get :

$$n = \frac{R(1-r)}{r(1-R)} = \frac{0.90 \times 0.40}{0.60 \times 0.10} = 6.$$

It should be six times as long.

The same calculations would apply to the following example. If two examiners mark a set of examination scripts, and their marks inter-correlate $+ 0.60$, how many examiners should mark the scripts for their combined marking to attain a reasonable reliability of $+ 0.90$? The answer is six.

The formula assumes that the correlations between the additional tests (or examiners) would be the same as between the first pair of tests (or examiners). This condition seems generally to be satisfied by educational measurements.

A second important factor is the heterogeneity of the group whose scores provide the reliability coefficient.

Parallel forms of an intelligence test will inter-correlate much more highly if applied to school-children of several years' age range than when applied to a single class or to a single year-group (i.e. children whose ages range over only one year). Coefficients obtained from the latter groups are conventionally accepted as fairer indices of reliability than coefficients from the former. If we know σ, the S.D. of test scores in a group which is unduly homogeneous or heterogeneous, then it is possible to predict R, the reliability to be expected in a group with S.D. Σ, by

Kelly's formula : $R = 1 - \dfrac{\sigma^2}{\Sigma^2}(1 - r)$.

Ex. 52.—The reliability coefficient of an intelligence test when applied to a class of primary school-children was $+ 0.88$. The S.D. of their I.Q.s was 14. What would be its reliability in a secondary school class whose I.Q.s have a S.D. of only 9 ?

$$R = 1 - \frac{14^2}{9^2} \times 0.12 = + 0.71.$$

It can easily be shown algebraically that the P.E. of a score is not upset by this factor as is the reliability co-efficient. In the above example the two P.E.s would be $0.6745 \times 14 \sqrt{0.12}$, and $0.6745 \times 9 \sqrt{0.29}$, both of which $= 3.27$. Nor is the P.E. of the score on one test as estimated from the score on another much affected (this point was mentioned on p. 141). In our example, 0.6745σ $\sqrt{1 - r^2} = 4.48$ and 4.28 respectively.

Function Fluctuation.—Most reliability coefficients fall below 1·0 for two distinct reasons, first through the test being insufficiently thorough (i.e. liable to errors of sampling), and secondly because the persons tested or examined may alter in their level of achievement between one test and another. The latter factor has been termed ' individual variance,' or, ' function fluctuation ' (Thouless, 1936). Naturally it has a greater effect on coefficients obtained from parallel tests given on different occasions, or from repeated tests, than it does on coefficients obtained by the split-half method. Hence the difference between these two types of coefficient affords a means of distinguishing between the reliability of the test itself, and the tendency of testees to fluctuate in respect of the ability tested. Thouless provides a formula for estimating function fluctuation from this difference.

Effects of Test Reliability on Test Inter-correlations.—A test which is not perfectly reliable may be regarded as measuring so much of the function which a perfect test would measure, and so much error. The error part of it is quite useless, and will have the effect of reducing the correlation between this test and any other test. If both tests possess considerable errors through lack of reliability, their inter-correlation will be considerably reduced. In fact, the maximum possible value of such an inter-correlation will be, not 1·0, but the square root of the product of their reliability coefficients. Suppose we find a correlation of + 0·50 between special place examinations and subsequent secondary school achievement, and that the reliabilities of the examinations and the measure of achievement are only + 0·70 and + 0·80 (a common state of affairs). Then the true correlation, if it were possible to obtain perfectly reliable exams and measures of achievement, would be $\dfrac{+\ 0\cdot50}{\sqrt{0\cdot70 \times 0\cdot80}} = +\ 0\cdot67.$

Spearman has called this reduction effect of imperfect reliability—'attenuation,' and has provided formulæ by which it may be corrected or compensated. Such correction is, of course, of theoretical interest, since it tells us what correlations to expect between various psychological abilities if they could be accurately measured. But it is of little practical value, since completely accurate tests are unattainable, and for all purposes of prediction we have to employ the obtained, uncorrected, correlation coefficients (cf. Thouless, 1939a).

11

CHAPTER VIII

ANALYSIS OF ABILITIES

Fallacious Views of Mental Organization.—Correlational investigations have assumed especial importance in recent years, since they enable us to clarify our conceptions of human abilities, and of the organization or structure of the mind. The layman's notions as to what abilities exist, and what each ability includes or excludes, are extremely loose, and the same was true of psychological theory throughout most of last century. Teachers and parents are heard to remark : " Johnny is poor at book-learning, but he makes up for it by his cleverness with his hands. He will be a good mechanic when he grows up." " Mary has an excellent memory and good power of attention." " Willie is slow but sure," and so on. Such statements are now known, as a result of experimental investigation, to be largely fallacious. Only exact study can tell us how far the slow person is likely to be sure, whether manual ability in a boy has any predictive value for mechanical ability in a man, whether there is any such entity in the mind as memory. Again, the so-called faculty school of psychologists of a hundred years ago considered the mind to be made up of a number of distinct powers or faculties such as reasoning, judgment, imagination, etc. Indeed, it was at one time regarded as the main object of education to train each of these faculties by providing children with appropriate ' mental gymnastics.' As soon, however, as scientific psychologists tried to define the faculties precisely and measure them, and to determine the effects upon them of various types of training, they fell into discredit. *A priori* analysis has not even been able to decide what is the true nature of intelligence. The accounts of it given by different writers have been extremely varied and discrepant. Nowadays, therefore, such problems, both of theory and practice, are approached by means of experimental studies of correlations between tests. For they all eventually resolve into the question—what correlates with what ?

The Scientific Definition of An Ability.—First we must define what we mean by an ability, capacity, or faculty. It implies the existence of a group or category of performances which correlate highly with one another, and which are relatively distinct from (i.e. give low correlations with) other performances. Take, for example, mechanical ability. Some people are better than others at tasks involving manipulation of mechanisms, and this ability is fairly *consistent* or *general* in the sense that those who are good at one such task are also usually good at others. The consistency is not perfect. A may be especially good with meccano, less clever with locks, B the opposite, C the best with electrical fittings, and so on. But if there was no appreciable correlation between these and other similar performances, if they were all found to be *specific*, we should not be entitled to regard mechanical ability as a real entity. Another important condition is that the performances should be fairly reliable. We do not expect perfect stability, but if people fluctuated wildly in their success at mechanical tasks from day to day, we should hardly recognize the existence of mechanical ability. There is a further possibility, namely, that the various performances may inter-correlate well, but that the correlations may be accounted for by some other common factor such as general intelligence (the age factor, we will assume, has already been eliminated). Mechanical ability would not then be anything distinctive. However, intelligence tests can be applied to the same persons who take the mechanical tests, and intelligence can be partialed out or held constant. It is then found that the mechanical tests still overlap, or show positive correlations with one another over and above their correlations due to the intelligence factor (cf. Cox, 1934). We are, therefore, able to accept mechanical ability as something consistent and distinctive. Tests of it do correlate sufficiently well and reliably for us to postulate some common element running through them.

A common element such as this is often referred to as a *group factor*, since it occurs in a group of performances of a certain restricted type. It differs from a *general factor* like intelligence, which is found to run through an extremely wide range of tests, which indeed enters to some extent into all abilities.

Since the consistency or overlapping of different mechanical tests is not perfect, no one test can give a really adequate measurement of mechanical ability. But by combining several tests, we are likely to get a result much more representative of the group factor as a whole. The same applies, of course, in the measurement of educational abilities. We do not expect long-division sums alone to tell us how good pupils are at arithmetic, although they provide some indication of the ability. Instead we set several types of sums, and try to cover the whole field of arithmetic which the pupils are supposed to know.

Arithmetic is likely to yield a group factor similar to the mechanical ability factor.[1] But many of the faculties assumed by psychologists in the past, or by laymen at the present time, fail to stand up to the criteria enumerated above. Memory, for example, refers to so many different things, that it is meaningless to talk of so-and-so as having a good or bad memory in general, or of ' training children's memories.' The speeds with which people learn various sorts of material, and their retentiveness (i.e. the amounts of such material which they can recall after an interval) give only moderate or low inter-correlations, especially when the influence of intelligence is removed. Probably there exist several small group factors, each representing

---

[1] Experiments suggest, however, that, at least among younger children, the correlations between different arithmetic tests may be due to intelligence. It is possible, as will be seen below, that this and other educational group factors become more clearly differentiated during adolescence.

memory for a certain narrow range of material.[1] In other words, there may be several different types, but no single entity, of memory.

The notion that mental speed differs from, and is usually opposed to, mental accuracy or power, also appears to be fallacious. If there were two such distinct abilities, then tests of speed should give high correlations with one another, and low or negative correlations with tests of accuracy or power. In actual fact speed and power tests all inter-correlate to nearly the same extent, showing that they are both components of one and the same mental factor. It follows, then, that those who are 'slow' are more likely to be ' unsure ' than ' sure,' at least so far as mental work is concerned.

All Mental Abilities are Positively Inter-correlated.—Let us now turn to the wider problem—what abilities does the mind contain, and how are they organized or inter-related ? A first, extremely important, fact is that all tests of mental abilities tend to give positive inter-correlations. Even tests of manual, physical, and other non-intellectual functions also usually correlate positively with one another and with mental tests, though the coefficients are often very small, whereas the coefficients among tests of intellectual functions are generally moderate to high. Occasional negative correlations may arise, but they are not likely to be statistically significant, and so may be ascribed to errors of sampling. In other words, talent and versatility, more often than not, go together ; a person outstandingly good or bad in one field is usually above or below average, respectively, in all other fields. This fact at once serves to cast a great deal of doubt on the ' compensation theory,' i.e. the view that those who are poor at one thing make up for it by being good at something else. It does not entirely disprove it, for the following reasons.

First the reader should study the scattergram for a very low positive correlation, such as that shown in Fig. 26. This compares the marks of students in an examination in

[1] Cf., for example, Walters (1935).

hygiene with their intelligence-test scores, and yields an r of $+ 0.146$. It will be seen that, though there is still a slight tendency for high scores on X_1 to be associated with high scores on X_2, yet the correlation admits of many big exceptions. Students who are among the highest 3% for

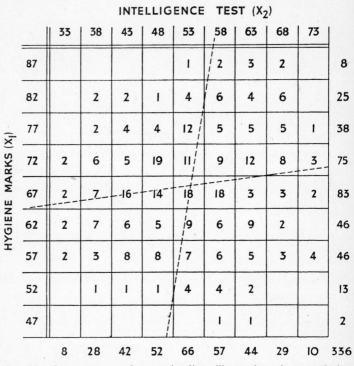

INTELLIGENCE   TEST (X_2)

	33	38	43	48	53	58	63	68	73	
87					1	2	3	2		8
82		2	2	1	4	6	4	6		25
77		2	4	4	12	5	5	5	1	38
72	2	6	5	19	11	9	12	8	3	75
67	2	7	16	14	18	18	3	3	2	83
62	2	7	6	5	9	6	9	2		46
57	2	3	8	8	7	6	5	3	4	46
52		1	1	1	4	4	2			13
47						1	1			2
	8	28	42	52	66	57	44	29	10	336

HYGIENE MARKS (X_1)

FIG. 26.—Scattergram and regression lines illustrating a low correlation, $r = + 0.146$.

intelligence may range right down to the lowest 18% for hygiene. The large amount of regression means that a fair proportion of persons can be high on one variable, low on the other. Such a state of affairs is certainly much more likely to occur here than it is when the correlation is high (as in Fig. 23).

Now ' book-learning ' and ' being clever with the hands '

are not highly correlated, hence it is quite possible for some children to be much better at one than at the other. But it is definitely false to suppose that they are inversely related, that those who are bad at one are therefore good at the other. On the contrary, those who are superior in intellectual abilities are on the average superior in practical ones also, though to a lesser extent.

A second reason is that age differences often obscure the issue. Some teachers are incredulous when told that children of superior intelligence tend to be superior also in growth and physical capacities to dull children, since they know well that the dullards in an ordinary school class are usually larger and stronger than the bright youngsters. But, then, they are forgetting that the dullards are far older than the bright ones, and so may be physically superior. If the dull children were compared with bright ones of the same age, the physical superiority of the latter would at once be obvious. Nevertheless, in this instance also the correlations are so low that a great many exceptions are possible.

Thirdly, ability is obviously to some extent a matter of interest and practice. Pupils who are backward at intellectual studies and who are on the average backward, but much less so, in physical and manual pursuits, naturally devote more time and energy to such pursuits. Bright pupils, though initially stronger and better at practical matters, may be more interested in intellectual matters, and so fall behind in other things. It is possible, therefore, for the differences that exist between abilities which give low inter-correlations to become accentuated, though there is still no evidence known to the writer that the correlations ever become negative.

We may conclude, then, that all the abilities with which teachers are concerned are, to a greater or lesser extent, positively correlated. As an example, we will quote some of Burt's (1917) results. He gave thirteen objective tests of achievement in various school subjects to 120 children aged 11 +, and calculated the inter-correlations. The following table shows the average correlation between each test and the other twelve tests.[1]

Composition	+ 0·505
History	+ 0·448
Geography	+ 0·456
Nature Study	+ 0·458
Mechanical Arithmetic . .	+ 0·283
Arithmetic Problems . . .	+ 0·457
Reading Fluency . . .	+ 0·323
Reading Comprehension . .	+ 0·369
Writing Speed	+ 0·323
Writing Quality . . .	+ 0·274
Dictation	+ 0·325
Drawing	+ 0·275
Handwork	+ 0·320

Composition, history, geography, nature study, and arithmetic problems overlap with the other tests to the largest extent. Mechanical arithmetic, drawing, and writing quality correlate to the smallest extent. This shows that there is a tendency for a pupil's achievements in all subjects to run on a fairly even level, though the correlations are low enough for some pupils to exhibit considerable divergences—special strengths in some subjects, special weaknesses in others. During the secondary school stage, correlations between subjects decrease, partly, of course, because the pupils form a more homogeneous group (cf. pp. 140–1), but also because abilities seem to differentiate during adolescence, and specialized talents develop. Nevertheless, the positive overlap of all intellectual abilities continues even beyond the university level. For example, the present writer inter-correlated the marks of 300 graduate students at a training college, and obtained small positive coefficients between subjects as widely different as teaching skill, arithmetic, hygiene, education, psycho-

---

[1] The average reliability of the tests was + 0·738. All these coefficients would, therefore, be larger by roughly 35% if the tests had been perfectly reliable (cf. p. 149). A recent repetition of the investigation with a much larger number of children has yielded closely similar results (Burt, 1939a).

logy, speech training, singing, physical training, etc. (cf. Vernon, 1939).

These facts are of considerable importance to examiners. They indicate that a School Certificate or Leaving Certificate, achieved at the age of 15 to 18, is some criterion of aptitude for any intellectual occupation, or for a university career, albeit not a very good one. Similarly, when the Civil Service requires persons to fill a wide variety of posts, it selects them, not by trying to test the aptitudes needed for each post, but by a general examination based largely on subjects studied at school or university. It believes that the possession of ' brains ' for one subject implies aptitude for all other subjects. And although, as we shall see later, the efficiency of these methods of selection leaves much to be desired, yet they are to this extent sound.

The General Factor Responsible for Positive Overlap.— Now when we find positive association, as in Burt's investigation, we are justified in assuming the existence of a general factor—general educational ability—which runs through all the separate subjects. Some subjects may be said to be more ' saturated ' with it than others, since they are more highly correlated with it. In the primary school we should get an excellent indication of this general factor from pupils' marks in composition and in arithmetic problems, a much poorer indication of it from drawing or handwriting quality. Statistical methods are available for assessing a pupil's standing on this general factor from his marks on all the component subjects (cf. p. 143). Further, it is quite easy to partial out the factor, and so to see whether or not it accounts for all the correlations between the separate subjects, whether, in other words, it is the only common element involved. When this is done, it is found that there are still a number of correlations over and above those due to the general factor. In Burt's study, the *residual* correlations indicated considerable overlapping within the following four groups of tests : (1) arithmetic problems and mechanical arithmetic ; (2) handwork, drawing, writing speed and quality ; (3) dictation, reading comprehension and speed ; (4) composition, history, geography, and nature study.   But there was little or no overlap, or even negative correlations, between the tests in one of these groups and those in another group.   Such results show clearly the existence of group factors, i.e. of distinctive types of educational abilities, over and above general ability.   In this instance there is an arithmetical factor, a manual one, a linguistic one, and one including all the higher, more integrative, school subjects.   As Burt points out, we have here a basis for cross-classification of pupils.   He suggests that they should be assigned to school classes in accordance with their achievements in the linguistic and ' integrative ' subjects, and that they might advantageously be reclassified for arithmetic lessons, and again for manual subjects.

Analogous findings were obtained in the writer's study of training college marks.   Three separate ' families ' of subjects could be distinguished, a practical one (teaching skill, speech training, and physical training), a scientific one (psychology, hygiene, arithmetic), and a literary one (English, speech training, education, history).   Few researches along these lines have been carried out in the industrial sphere, owing to the difficulties of measuring and correlating different vocational abilities.   But we might expect to get from them similar results, for example, group factors for the engineering type of occupation, for the salesmanship type, the clerical type, and so on.

FACTORIAL ANALYSIS

The statistical investigations of Spearman (1927) and others have shown that it is possible to account for practically the whole of a set of test inter-correlations by postulating appropriate common factors.[1]   It is legitimate,

[1] Note that we do not claim to be able to account for the *whole* of the correlations, for such correlations are, of course, always liable to errors of sampling.   Often the residual coefficients, which are left after a general factor and some group factors have been extracted, are so small relative to their P.E.s, that it is not worth while analysing them further.   Even with the most accurate techniques, such as

then, to regard each test as made up of two components, or as measuring two things. In so far as it correlates with other tests, it is measuring some factor or factors. This is often referred to as the test's *communality*. But in so far as it fails to correlate (and most test inter-correlations, be it remembered, are only moderately high), it is measuring a purely specific component, or something which is peculiar to that test alone and has no relationship to any other test. This is called the test's *specificity*. It includes, of course, the error which is present in the test on account of imperfect reliability [1] (cf. p. 149). Thus any test of an educational or vocational ability can be analysed into certain proportions of certain factors. For example, in Burt's research, the arithmetic problems test can be analysed into so much general educational ability, so much arithmetical group factor (these together make up its communality), and thirdly, a component specific to that particular test. The mechanical arithmetic test can be analysed into a rather smaller proportion of general factor, a large proportion of the arithmetic group factor, and a separate specific component. The presence of these specific components reduces the correlation between the two tests, but it is still quite high, namely $+ 0 \cdot 76$, because they have both a general and a group factor in common. A test of another subject, such as handwork, still correlates positively with arithmetic problems, because they are both partially saturated with the general factor, but the coefficient is a small one, namely $+ 0 \cdot 38$, since handwork embodies a different (manual) group factor, as well as a different specific component.

By means of factor analysis, then, it is possible to reduce a large number of test results to a few underlying common factors. Any psychological test, or measure of a scholastic

Hotelling's and Burt's, the later factors are generally so small that little significance can be attached to them.

[1] Thomson (1939) points out, however, that some of the influences producing unreliability, e.g. those of the function fluctuation type, may actually be common to several tests, and so contribute to their communality.

or occupational ability, can be regarded as made up of some of these factors, or as possessing a certain 'factor pattern.' Further, an individual person's standing on each factor can be derived from his test scores, and he, too, possesses a certain factor pattern. Thus, a pupil who is high in general educational factor will be above average in most of his school work, but his relative goodness at different subjects will depend on the strength or weakness of his group and specific factors.

Dangers of Factor Analysis.—At this point a strong warning should be given against carrying the factorial conception of abilities too far. Factors are not entities in the mind whose nature or constitution, and whose strength or weakness, are immutably fixed. Some writers do seem to assume that factorial analysis is revealing the fundamental elements of which human minds are compounded, much as chemical analysis reveals the elements from which chemical substances are compounded. We should realize that factors consist primarily of categories for classifying mental tests and examinations. Their value lies in the fact that they tell us objectively what correlates or overlaps with what, and so they take the place of unverified faculties and other subjective conceptions of human traits and abilities.

It is obviously illegitimate to compare factors in the educational field with chemical elements. For these factors, which are deduced from the correlations between various school subjects, must depend largely on how the subjects are taught and on the stage which the pupils have reached. Different factor patterns will, therefore, be found in different school classes, according as the teachers connect up, or bring about overlap in their pupils' minds between, the subjects. For example, Oldham (1937–38) found very diverse relationships between arithmetic, algebra, and geometry among different 12- to 13-year-old school classes, which could be ascribed to differences in teaching methods and in the pupils' attitudes towards the subjects. Others have proved that the factors extracted from a set of mental tests alter progressively with practice at the tests (e.g. Anastasi, 1936).

Like all other statistical constructs, factors will be liable to a good deal of variation if they are derived from measures of small numbers of persons. But apart from such sampling errors, they must be regarded as depending to a considerable extent on the particular group of persons measured. Thomson (1939) shows that they are markedly affected by the heterogeneity or homogeneity of this group of persons. In addition, they are dependent upon the particular set of tests used, since the factor pattern of a test is in essence an expression of the relations between this test and all the other tests in the set. Statistical analysis of a single test in isolation is incapable of telling us what factors it contains (though subjective analysis, or inspection of its content, may often give useful hints as to its probable factor pattern, which can later be verified by studying objectively its correlations with other tests). However, this limitation may not be very serious, since, as we shall see below, at least some of the most important factors emerge in almost identical form from a wide variety of sets of tests.

Then there is the more subtle difficulty that the same set of tests can always be factorized in a great many different ways. Most of these ways will lead to quite illogical results, so that the investigator has to choose from among the various possible factorizations the most meaningful and convenient pattern. Take, for example, the educational tests applied by Burt. We have so far regarded these as analysable into general educational ability, four group factors for related subjects, and separate specific factors for each test. Now Burt showed, incidentally, that the general factor was not identical with general intelligence as estimated by teachers, or as measured by intelligence tests, though the two overlapped closely. But it would have been quite legitimate to analyse measures of intelligence along with the educational measures, and to partial out intelligence first, so making it the principal factor underlying achievement. If this had been done, it is likely that a subsidiary general factor would have emerged representing, perhaps, the pupils' application to, and interest in, their work in general. Intelligence plus this subsidiary factor would then make up what we have previously denoted as the general educational ability factor. The group factors would also need to be somewhat modified, since most of the fourth one (composition, history, etc.) might have been absorbed into, or accounted for by, the intelligence factor.[1]

In investigating students' college marks, the writer obtained analogous results. The inter-correlations could be accounted for either by a very prominent general factor and group factors restricted to a few subjects, or else by three factors, all of about equal prominence, each entering into several subjects.

Certain other precautions which should be observed in interpreting the results of factorial analyses will be mentioned later.

Types of Factor Pattern.—Three main types of factor

I. BI-FACTOR PATTERN

Test	General Factor	Group Factors				Specific Factors
		A	B	C	D	
1	×	×				×
2	×	×				×
3	×	×				×
4	×		×			×
5	×		×			×
6	×			×		×
7	×			×		×
8	×			×		×
9	×			×		×
10	×				×	×
11	×				×	×
12	×				×	×

[1] In his later study (1939a), Burt describes several methods of factorizing which do yield numerically different, though logically consistent, results.

pattern recur very frequently in educational and psychological investigations. They may be represented by the following diagrams, each of which refers to twelve hypothetical tests, Nos. 1, 2, . . .

II. MULTIPLE-FACTOR PATTERN

Test	Common Factors				Specific Factors
	A	B	C	D	
1	X		X		X
2	X	X	X		X
3		X	X	X	X
4	X	X	X		X
5	X			X	X
6		X	X		X
7	X	X		X	X
8	X		X	X	X
9	X			X	X
10				X	X
11		X		X	X
12	X		X		X

III. UNI-FACTOR PATTERN

Test	General Factor	Specific Factors
1	X	X
2	X	X
3	X	X
4	X	X
5	X	X
6	X	X
7	X	X
8	X	X
9	X	X
10	X	X
11	X	X
12	X	X

In the first, which Holzinger (1937) calls the bi-factor pattern, there is a general factor running through all the tests, four different group factors, and specifics. This type of pattern is usually adequate for representing the results of tests of abilities, at least among children. For instance, it applies excellently to Burt's investigation.

The second, multiple-factor, pattern requires three, four, or more factors, none of them general, but all running through several tests, to account for the test inter-correlations. It will be seen that Test 1 involves factors A and C and a specific ; that some of the tests involve three, some only one factor. This type is usually required where tests of personality, character, or temperament, are concerned, since in these fields a general trait, running through all the tests, would seldom be appropriate. For example, Thurstone (1931) obtained measures of the interests of a group of students in a large number of different occupations—advertising, art, chemistry, etc.—and found that the interest scores could be classified under four main factors. These he roughly identified as interest in language, in science, in business, and in people. Each separate interest could be made up of appropriate proportions of these four factors. Other instances have been outlined by the present writer elsewhere (Vernon, 1938b).

Spearman's Two-factor Theory.—The third, unitary-factor, pattern, has aroused and still continues to arouse a great deal of controversy. Historically it was the first type to be discovered. Early in the present century, Spearman found that diverse tests of mental abilities usually gave inter-correlations which could be wholly accounted for (within the limits of their errors of sampling) by a single general factor plus specific factors. He enunciated certain criteria to which the correlations must conform if this is to be possible, the most important of which is called the tetrad difference criterion.[1] The general

---

[1] For an explanation, see Knight (1933), or Spearman's own book (1927). The apparent discrepancy between the names—Two-factor Theory and Unitary-factor Pattern—is merely due to the fact that Spearman includes the specific components as factors, whereas the terms we have used refer only to the communality of the factorized tests.

factor obviously corresponds to what we commonly mean by general intelligence, but Spearman preferred to symbolize it by the letter g, the specific factors by letters s_1, s_2, . . ., etc., so as to get over the difficulty, mentioned above, that the term ' intelligence ' has been so diversely defined by different psychologists. His g factor, it was claimed, would be the same whatever the tests used. It could be measured, for example, by a battery of tests consisting of Analogies, Completion, Vocabulary, and Directions, or equally well by a battery consisting of Abstraction, Mixed Sentences, Opposites, and Reasoning Problems. Each test would have its own independent s, but in so far as it overlapped with other tests, it would be measuring g. This view is widely known as the Two-factor Theory.

For a while it was thought that the Two-factor Theory would apply to all tests of abilities, not only to intellectual ones, and that very few additional group factors would be needed. Only occasionally would a few tests which were very similar in content (e.g. tests of musical aptitudes) be found to inter-correlate over and above their correlation due to g.

Different tests may differ considerably in their g-saturations. Those with the highest saturation seem to involve the capacity for seeing relationships, whilst tests which involve mainly mechanical or rote memory contain very little g. Among school subjects, classics is most dependent on g ; French, English, history and the like are also highly saturated. Manual subjects and music have much more prominent s's and relatively little g. Thus we find high correlations between classics and English, low correlations between handwork and music, and moderate correlations between classics and handwork, or English and music. The Two-factor Theory not only explains these and similar facts as to the relations between abilities, but also provides the mental tester with a scientific basis for choosing tests which will give the best measures of g. Although every sub-test in a battery of intelligence tests will involve a certain s-factor, tests can be selected in which these s's

12

are small, and when the tests are combined the s's will tend to cancel out, so leaving an almost pure measure of g.

Criticisms of the Two-factor Theory.—The theory has been subjected to much criticism, both on psychological and on statistical grounds. Spearman suggested that g might correspond to the conception of ' general mental energy.' Whether or not this is a psychologically sound explanation need not concern us here. On the statistical side, Thomson (1935, 1939) and others pointed out that, although the analysis into general and specific factors is legitimate when the tetrad difference criterion is satisfied, yet this is not the only possible mode of analysis ; that if mental abilities consisted of large numbers of overlapping group factors, the same criterion would still be satisfied. Thomson's view would seem to the present writer to be preferable from the psychological standpoint, but Spearman's view is perhaps more practically convenient, since we do already in everyday life assume the existence of something like g—whether we call it ' brains,' ' brightness,' ' intelligence,' or what not—and the Two-factor Theory provides a scientific basis for this common-sense assumption.

The theory, and the experiments which it has stimulated, at one time seemed to discredit all the mental faculties which had so often been abused in traditional psychology and in common parlance. But more recent research with modern factorial methods indicates that the theory requires considerable modifications in the matter of group factors. The evidence is still very far from complete, but it suggests that some at least of the faculties may re-emerge as scientifically established group—or multiple factors. For example, Thurstone (1938) applied a wide variety of psychological tests to university students, and obtained results which could be resolved into a set of multiple factors. These he identified as number facility, word fluency, visualization, memory, reasoning, perceptual speed, and induction. Spearman (1939), however, showed that a pattern of general + group factors would fit the same results as well, or better. Again, Guilford (1936) found that the sub-tests of a group test designed to measure adult general intelligence could be analysed into three multiple factors : verbal ability, numerical ability, and ability to use simple relationships.

It seems fairly safe to conclude now that *no* test measures nothing but *g* and a specific factor, since the type of test material employed always introduces some additional common element. All verbal intelligence tests, together with other tests depending on manipulations of words, involve a verbal factor, which has been named *v*. Certainly some, and possibly all, the common non-verbal performance tests bring in a practical factor, which Alexander (1935) calls *F*. In order to escape the influence of *v*, many mental testers are constructing tests out of abstract diagrams, pictures, and other non-verbal material. Experiments suggest, however, the existence of a factor, called *k*, which enters into such tests involving spatial relationships (cf. El Koussy, 1935). This overlaps, or may be identical with, *F*. School examinations and educational achievement tests depend (as Burt's research showed) on a factor which possibly represents the pupils' interest in and attitudes to work, or their character and temperament qualities. In addition there are probably group factors for families of school subjects, largely governed, as we have seen, by teaching methods. The main types—literary or humanistic, scientific and mathematical, practical and manual—are to be found not only among the abilities of school-children, but also among those of adults such as student teachers (cf. Vernon, 1939). In the vocational field we may expect to discover a similar differentiation, though the only group factors which have been at all fully investigated so far are those for mechanical ability (*m*-factor), and for routine manual operations (cf. Cox, 1934). In later adolescence and adulthood, however, the situation becomes very obscure. A *g*-factor can still be extracted from mental tests, but it seems to play a decreasingly important part both in educational and in vocational achievement. Abilities become so diversified, and interests, work attitudes, and temperament traits are so influential, that we can hardly hope to establish any simple scheme of mental organization.

Educational and Vocational Applications.—Such educational and vocational findings are of great practical importance, for if the Two-factor Theory were exclusively accepted, educational and vocational guidance by means of tests would scarcely be possible. If we wished to advise a child as to the type of education or the occupation for which he would be most suited, we could apply tests of g and so deduce the general intellectual level of the work he should take up. But we could not decide whether he would be likely to do better at classics or science, at a clerical job or an engineering trade, and so on, except by giving a vast number of tests of different s factors, or by letting him try each type of work in turn so as to find by practical experience which specific one suited him. There could be no recommending of general lines of occupation. To a certain extent this does seem to be true. Educational and vocational guidance among adolescents are extremely difficult and uncertain. They have to be based more upon a subjective analysis of interests and character traits than upon objective predictions by tests. Yet common experience strongly suggests that there do exist general categories or types of work, and that therefore a number of group factors, additional to m, could be established by further research. If this were done, guidance would become much more scientific. Full consideration of a candidate's interests and character would, of course, still be required, but his scores on a series of tests for each of these factors would give objective indications of his probable ability along each of the main lines of work.[1] Some

[1] Thomson (1939) has recently pointed out that when tests are given with the object of predicting educational or vocational achievement, the extraction of factors from the tests may constitute quite an unnecessary intermediate step. A much more efficient method would be to correlate the tests directly with measures of achievement and then to use multiple correlation for obtaining the most accurate predictions. While this view is, of course, perfectly true from the

overlap might also be found between the group factors in school work and those in different types of occupation, so that outstandingly good mathematicians, linguists, etc., might be directed to occupations which involve these abilities.

Conclusions about Factor Analysis.—Clearly an enormous amount of unavoidably complicated and expensive research will be needed before the whole realm of human abilities can, as it were, be mapped out. The difficulties are enhanced because, as we have seen, the factor patterns which an investigator extracts are often dependent on the particular tests and particular testees he employs, and because there is much room for subjective judgment in the type of factor pattern he chooses. Research at present is rather badly co-ordinated, since each investigator sets out to explore fresh territory, instead of trying to build on the factors already fairly well established by previous workers. Further, there is always the danger of mathematical rather than psychological considerations getting the upper hand. As already mentioned, factorial investigations are *not* revealing the elements out of which the mind is compounded, but are classifying test performances with a view to predicting more effectively other performances, e.g. in the educational or vocational sphere. But by no means all of the important facets of human nature are susceptible yet of accurate measurement. There may be abilities such as executive capacity, intuitive power, goodness of teaching, and social intelligence, which are generally recognized in

statistical standpoint, it would seem to the present writer to be practically applicable only in educational and vocational selection, not in guidance. It should certainly be used by the tester who wishes to select the best candidates for some single and definite educational course or job. But the problems of the vocational adviser are much too complex to be tackled as yet by this exact method. He is forced to predict a candidate's probable achievement in generalized terms, or factors. At the present time he is doing so largely in terms of unverified factors, derived from subjective considerations of tests and lines of work. The view put forward above is that his procedure could be made more systematic and scientific if more factors were experimentally established.

daily life, but which are not yet properly substantiated or analysed owing to the inadequacies of our tests. Still more is this true in the realm of emotional traits and interests, for reasons which the writer has described elsewhere (Vernon, 1938*b*). Yet we cannot hope to make successful predictions about an individual child or adult unless we know every side of his make-up. It may well be that all these attempts at analysing the measurable abilities and traits of human beings will never give us a picture of an individual personality considered as a whole, that we shall always need to supplement test results with subjective judgment and intuition in order to resynthesize them into a living entity. But this, too, is a matter of psychological controversy which the reader may follow up elsewhere (e.g. Vernon, 1937*a b* ; Cattell, 1937).

We have no space to describe the actual statistical techniques of factor analysis. Spearman has fully described his method in *The Abilities of Man* (1927). It is not difficult to apply, though rather laborious. It is the most accurate method of extracting unitary-factor patterns, but it is hardly suitable for bi- and multiple-factor patterns. Holzinger's (1937) method is an extension which deals readily with bi-factor patterns, though it does not seem to possess much advantage over the simple technique employed by Burt in 1917, and systematized by him in a recent article (1938). For multiple factor analysis, Thurstone's technique (which is well described by Guilford, 1936) is the easiest to acquire, but is less accurate than the techniques developed by Hotelling, Kelley, and Burt. The aims and the guiding principles of these latter methods are somewhat different from those dealt with in the present chapter. Since they are hardly comprehensible to any but advanced statisticians they have been omitted here. But a clear account of them is available in Thomson's book (1939).

CHAPTER IX

MENTAL TESTS

MENTAL testing is simply a more refined and scientific method of doing something which we all of us do every day of our lives, that is assessing one another's abilities and character traits. Our ordinary method is to observe a person's behaviour, including his facial expressions and gestures, in various situations and circumstances, and his speech or written productions. For example, we might watch a small boy playing with bricks, and from his skilfulness, or the elaborateness of the resulting construction, jump to the conclusion that he is quite a bright child. Obviously the basis for this, and other such judgments, is very haphazard and unreliable. There is no sure evidence that the boy is acting more, or less, intelligently than the majority of children. Nevertheless this performance may quite well be refined and turned into a scientific mental test. So-called performance tests of intelligence are based on just such activities with bricks, blocks, and other concrete material.

Let us then first consider the essential features of a mental test which distinguish it from such everyday judgments and from the, slightly more scientific, school examination.

(1) *Standardization of Test Situation.*—The first step which the tester takes is to standardize the test situation. He will, for example, adopt some standard set of bricks and give definite instructions, so that all children who are subjected to the test shall do it under as nearly as possible identical circumstances. Until this is done it is not legitimate to compare the performances of different children. With every good test there is published a detailed set of

instructions, to which the tester must closely adhere. School and university examiners, on the other hand, usually give no instructions beyond stating the number of questions to be answered, and they neglect to inform the examinees what type of answers they require. Because of this, and because of frequent ambiguities in the wording of questions, different examinees may conceive the tasks that are set them in a variety of different ways, and it becomes exceedingly difficult to compare and mark their answers.

The material of a test, its conditions of application, and its instructions, are further planned to be readily comprehensible to, and suitable to the mental level of, the children or adults for whom it is intended. This is another feature which some school examiners might be advised to copy instead of setting subjects for compositions, or other questions, which are far above the heads of the pupils.

We must, however, admit that several widely used tests do not entirely live up to these criteria. Some of them were originally constructed and standardized in America ; hence they require considerable modification or translation before they are suitable for British children. We are forced to employ these ' second-hand ' tests because the production of fresh tests is an extremely lengthy and expensive business. Unfortunately different British testers do the necessary ' re-modelling ' in different ways, so that the test situation is no longer identical for all.

(2) *Standardization of Scoring.*—The mental tester does not observe the child's behaviour, or his finished product, in the casual manner implied by our illustration, but obtains an accurate record of them. He insists on knowing definitely what was the *test response*, i.e. the child's reaction to the previously laid down test situation. Either the response is something which can be delimited in quantitative terms (e.g. so many bricks put into their correct positions in so many seconds), or else it is something which can be designated unequivocally as right or wrong.[1] It is

---

[1] So-called Quality Scales are tests whose scoring constitutes an exception to this rule, cf. p. 179.

most important that the personal opinion of the tester should play no part in this record. Any two testers observing and scoring the response should arrive at identical records. If this condition holds the test is called an *objective* one. All good mental tests, then, are provided with scoring keys or manuals of instructions which enable the recording and scoring to be done objectively.

Our everyday judgments of traits or abilities are, by contrast, decidedly subjective, for numerous investigations have demonstrated their liability to vary with the person who makes them. Some teachers are still convinced that they can assess the intelligence of their pupils better than can any test. But the fact is that different teachers, assessing the same pupils, give such different opinions that the scientific psychologist can put little trust in any of them. The same is true of many school and other examination marks, as will appear in Chap. XI.

(3) *Norms.*—The layman commonly seems to regard the observed behaviour as having some absolute value or significance. There is no doubt in his mind that it indicates high intelligence, or poor sociability, or whatever the trait may be. The more cautious psychologist realizes that such judgments must be based largely on more or less vague recollections of the behaviour of other similar children under similar circumstances, and so insists that all grading of abilities is essentially a comparative or relative matter (cf. Chaps. II and IV). Thus one of the most vital accompaniments of a mental test is the norms, by reference to which any child's goodness or poorness of performance may be assessed. Unfortunately it is also the feature in which many published tests are defective, on account of the difficulties already described (pp. 79–87).

In the nature of examining it is hardly possible to establish norms for examinations, since they cannot be applied to large numbers of pupils or students beforehand for this purpose, as is the standardized test. We have seen, however, that the process of rationalizing marks, which is essentially equivalent to the setting up of provisional norms, is necessary if the present ambiguities in the significance of school or examinations marks are to be avoided.

(4) *Reliability and Validity.*—A single piece of behaviour, casually observed, as in our illustration, would probably be very low in reliability. A discussion of the statistical methods of determining reliability was given above (p. 145), and the reliability of several of the more important tests is mentioned later in this chapter.

The most serious defect in the layman's everyday judgments is that he seldom has any good proof that the observed behaviour validly indicates the ability which he deduces from it. It may have arisen from some quite different trait or ability, or else from an ability which is almost wholly specific (in Spearman's sense), i.e. not correlated with anything else. To be *reliable* a test need only measure accurately the ability to perform that test, but to be *valid* it must also correlate effectively with other measures of whatever it is supposed to test. The mere inspection of the content of a test is seldom sufficient for the determination of its validity, although it is a necessary preliminary.

Such inspection of educational tests and examinations may reveal their failure to cover the ground which the pupils should have accomplished. Thus school and university examinations are often defective, because their questions are too few in number, or are badly set. It will be obvious also to a tester that the content of some of the published educational tests is unsatisfactory, either because they are designed for pupils whose tuition differs widely from that current among his testees, or because they are out-of-date. But apart from such flaws, many tests involve group or specific factors which detract from their effectiveness as measures of some general ability. For example, a test of reading may be based on the capacity for pronouncing difficult words. This may or may not indicate children's capacities in other aspects of reading, such as their fluency, or their comprehension of what they have read. Investigation by means of correlations is essential for establishing these points. Again, the technique of the test, i.e. the way in which the testee is required to express his ability, always seems to introduce an irrelevant factor. In Chap. XI we shall show that in an ordinary essay-type of examination, the translation of the examinees' knowledge into essay-form is one such factor, and in Chap. XII the examiner's translation of his questions into new-type or objective form will be recognized as another. Temperamental factors, health, fatigue, and the like also influence a testee's performances at many tests, and so reduce their validity as measures of ability.

Most educational and vocational tests are assumed not only to be valid indicators of some present general ability, but also to be prognostic of future achievement. Their predictions should then, of course, be followed up and compared with subsequently obtained measures of achievement. In the educational field there have been many such investigations whose results usually show our tests and examinations to possess disappointingly poor validity (cf. Chap. XI). Vocational psychologists have also tried to correlate their predictive tests with some measure of output, or with estimates of efficiency obtained from supervisors or foremen. As Farmer (1933) has shown, however, it is not always easy to secure a satisfactory criterion of success or failure in an occupation against which the test results can be checked.

The validation of intelligence tests, or of tests of capacities such as practical ability, verbal ability, and the like, is particularly difficult, since we possess no objective criterion of intelligence, etc., with which to compare them. Ratings have sometimes been used, that is, teachers' estimates of the intelligence of children in their charge, but these are highly fallible. If psychologists are unable to agree as to what they mean by intelligence, it is unlikely that laymen's views will be any more concordant. Indeed, if teachers could judge it accurately, there would be no need for tests. The main defect of such ratings is that they are strongly biased (often quite unwittingly) by considerations such as the children's industriousness and good school behaviour. Parents' judgments are still less trustworthy. Several group intelligence tests have been validated by comparing their results with the results of one of the Binet scales. But the validity of these scales is open to doubt. The items which they contain have always been chosen so as to differentiate older (hence presumably more intelligent) children from younger (less intelligent) ones. This criterion is, however, dubious in value, since it would admit tests of, say, height and weight, which have very little validity as indicators of intelligence. Yet we do not rely merely on subjective judgment when we state that these must be excluded from a test of intelligence, for in the absence of any external criterion of validity, we make use of what has been called the method of internal consistency.

This method consists either of factorial analysis, or of a modification thereof. All the test items or sub-tests are selected in the first place on the basis of subjective opinion ; they must appear to the tester to involve the exercise of intellect. Thereafter they are studied empirically. Either each item is compared with every other, or with the sum of all the rest of the items, or sets of items such as the sub-tests in a group intelligence test are compared with other sets. The inter-correlations will serve to show whether or not all the items are consistent with one another—whether they are measuring one and the same thing. And items that fail to conform to this criterion are excluded from the final, published, version of the test. The statistical conditions imposed by Spearman in his factorial analysis of group intelligence tests are much more rigorous than those used by Terman in revising the Binet scale. Both, however, prove that there is a general factor running through all their test items or sub-tests. Spearman and his followers wish to measure nothing but g, that is, they aim at a uni-factor pattern, and so exclude a number of sub-tests which fail to conform to such a pattern. The Binet test, on the other hand, although it certainly emodies a g-factor, contains a hotch-potch of heterogeneous tasks which would, if fully analysed, yield several group factors (a bi-factor pattern), or even a set of multiple factors (cf. Burt, 1939b). The effects of these different techniques of test construction will be discussed more fully below. What matters for our present purpose is that when a test, or a set of tests, is internally consistent, this signifies that it will validly predict any other behaviour which involves the same general factor. Intelligence tests work fairly effectively because scholastic success, and many of the other intellectual activities of everyday life, are known to be dependent largely on the g which they measure.

Test Construction.—Before proceeding, we would strongly urge amateur testers and teachers *not* to attempt to make up their own tests, apart from new-type ones for school examination purposes. To devise test items similar to those which appear in published tests is not difficult, but a great many technical features enter into the selection of suitable items and into their standardization, in addition to those described here. The points which we have outlined are meant, not to show how to construct a test, but to enable amateurs to choose more wisely the tests which will be most suitable for their purposes, and to give them some assistance in understanding what they are doing when they apply published tests.

TYPES OF TESTS

At the end of this chapter is given a classified list of most of the mental tests available in this country. The main headings are :

I. Attainment, Achievement, or Educational Tests.
    A. Examinations.
    B. Standardized educational tests.
        1. Quality scales.
        2–4. Individual tests.
        5–6. Group tests.

II. Individual Intelligence Tests.
      A. Versions of the Binet-Simon scale.
      B–E. Miscellaneous scales.
      F. Performance tests.
III. Group Intelligence Tests.
      A. Verbal.
      B. Non-verbal.
      C. Oral.
IV. Special Aptitude Tests.
V. Sensory-motor Tests.
VI. Temperament, Personality, and Character Tests.

The last three sections consist of little more than references, but the first three aim to be comprehensive
Although we shall not attempt to describe particular tests,
the following general explanations of, and comments on,
the main types may be useful to those who are not already
thoroughly familiar with the field.

Examinations and Educational Tests.—Examinations are
still the most important method of educational measurement, and so come at the head of our list. Their defects,
and the possibilities of improving them, or of employing
substitutes, are discussed in Chaps. XI–XIV. Standardized educational tests must be contrasted with them, for
although they are made up of the same kinds of items or
questions as occur in objective or new-type examinations,
their functions are quite different. They are not designed
to cover the work done by particular classes of pupils or
students, nor for the selection of those who are most likely
to ' make good ' in some future work. They serve to show
what is the standing of a class, or of an individual pupil,
relative to other similar pupils, either on some general
subject such as English or arithmetic, or on special branches
of, or stages within, a subject (these latter being known as
diagnostic,[1] or analytic, tests). The fact that they are
published, and their expense, obviously make them unsuit-

[1] Cf. the excellent discussion of diagnostic tests by Schonell (1935,
1937).

able for use as school examinations. By means of them,
however, a teacher can usefully grade his pupils at the
beginning of the school year, so as to find which ones will
need most coaching, or in which parts of a subject they are
most advanced or backward. If the norms are adequate
(cf. Chap. IV), they will tell him how his pupils compare
with pupils in general of the same age. The psychologist
at a Child Guidance Clinic, or the vocational adviser, finds
them especially valuable for assessing a child's strong and
weak points.

Quality Scales.—Although most educational tests consist
of large numbers of short items, both so as to cover the
subject as thoroughly as possible, and so as to admit of
objective scoring (cf. Chap. XII), some educational products
which are too complex to be assessed in this piecemeal
fashion can nevertheless be measured by ' quality ' or
' product scales.' Such standardized scales are available
for grading handwriting, composition, drawing, etc. Each
of these consists of a series of specimen products which have
been carefully chosen as representative of certain levels of
achievement. The testee is told to write or draw the same
matter in his normal manner, and his product is, as it were,
slid along the scale, or compared with the specimens, until
one is found to which it corresponds in achievement. It
is then given the score of this specimen. Such grading
cannot be made wholly objective, but there is evidence that
it improves with practice. Different testers will, when experienced, award the same or nearly the same score to a
child's product. Certainly the process is fairer than grading without any external standards. Hence the adoption
of a similar plan in the marking of school work was advocated in Chap. II.

Burt's scales all consist of specimens selected from a large
number as being typical of the work of average $5 +$, $6 +$,
. . . $14 +$ children. Cattell's handwriting scale for school-
leavers (13 to $15 +$), and his drawing scale for adults, include specimens typical of the best 6%, the next best 25%,
the middle 38%, the next 25%, and the poorest 6% of such

persons.   The scores assigned to these—I, II, III, IV, and V, respectively—represent equivalently spaced units (cf. p. 77).

Quantitative Tests and Scales.—The scoring of quantitative tests, either by the ' rate ' or ' power ' systems, or by a mixture of these, has already been described in Chap. II. It will be noted that scarcely any tests are available much above the 14-year level, and that very few deal with subjects outside the 3 R's.   One obvious reason for this is that the subjects taught in post-primary schools are of comparatively little importance to the majority of the population.   Another is that the matter included under history, languages, mathematics, science, etc., varies so much from one school to another, that it is scarcely possible to establish general standards of attainment.   Nevertheless it would not be difficult to devise and standardize tests suitable for some fairly homogeneous groups of pupils or students, such as those in English public schools, in provincial universities, in Scottish secondary schools, and so on.   Certainly our tests lag far behind those available for similar purposes in America.

INTELLIGENCE TESTS

Intelligence tests closely resemble quantitative educational tests (to which they are, of course, historically prior) in their construction and scoring.   Thus they may consist of :

(*a*) A series of tasks graded in difficulty (power plan).

(*b*) Tasks such as performance tests where the speed or number of moves are recorded (rate plan).

(*c*) Sets of questions which are roughly graded, but where the score depends on the number answered within a certain time limit.

Group tests generally include a ' battery ' of some half-dozen (between about four and twelve) ' sub-tests,' each containing some twenty (between ten and fifty) questions or items.   Alternatively they are arranged in ' omnibus ' form, where items of all kinds are mixed up. In the battery type, each sub-test has its own instructions and sample items, and is timed separately. In the omnibus form, the instructions and samples may be printed along with the questions, or included in a preliminary practice sheet, and one time limit suffices for the whole test. An omnibus test is therefore somewhat easier to give, but a test battery has the advantage of providing rest pauses every few minutes.

Almost all intelligence tests thus consist of rather large numbers of items. Performance tests are exceptional, but it is desirable to apply several, say, six or more, of these. The tests are always applied and scored in a standard manner, and the scores either take the form of Mental Age years (as in the Binet and some other tests), or can be translated into M.A.s and I.Q.s by means of tables of norms.

The Innateness of Intelligence.—The main difference between intelligence and educational tests is that the former aim to include tasks whose solution depends upon native ability rather than upon acquired experience. Although the precise definition of intelligence is still a matter of controversy—useful discussions are given by Ballard (1922) and Knight (1933)—most writers agree that some general innate capacity may be regarded as under-lying all our abilities. Some regard this capacity as con-stant and unalterable throughout life, but recent evidence suggests that, at least in early years, it may be greatly stimulated by a favourable environment, or depressed by an unfavourable upbringing (cf. Wellman, 1938). All, however, would admit that it remains fairly constant under normal circumstances which provide neither unusual stimulation nor inhibition. But quite apart from this problem of the stability of intelligence itself, we have to recognize that we can never get at it directly, that it ex-presses itself only through the medium of acquired know-ledge or skills. Therefore the tasks included in an intelli-gence test should as far as possible involve only those acquirements which are likely to be equally available to

13

all persons. For then if A scores well and B badly, we can claim that the difference is not due to A's having had more opportunity or better training than B, but to the underlying power which has enabled A to make better use of his opportunities and training. This conclusion fits in well with that reached in the previous chapter, namely that all measures of intelligence involve a group factor dependent upon the medium used in testing, as well as upon g.

Language is a fairly suitable medium from this point of view, and has been the most widely used of any. But verbal tests are clearly unfair to those who have not had normal opportunities for acquiring language, such as foreign-born or bilingual children, the deaf, and the children of gipsies or canal bargees who receive little or no schooling. Further, it is probable that there are innate differences in verbal capacities which therefore further distort the scores obtained in intelligence tests dependent on manipulations of words. Many testers therefore prefer non-verbal tests, where the media consist of pictures, abstract diagrams, or concrete (performance) material. These, of course, are open to analogous defects. A British or American child has much more opportunity than an African child for acquiring skills with pictures, blocks, etc., and so has a decided advantage when he is made to express his intelligence through tests which involve such material. Nadel (1939) shows convincingly the absurdity of assuming that racial differences in intelligence can be measured by such tests.

Tests of the concrete or pictorial type are valuable for application to young children, who are not so accustomed as older persons are to verbal thinking, and are not interested in verbal tasks. Non-verbal material may be essential also in testing the deaf or illiterate, and are useful as supplements to predominantly verbal tests. But since one of the most important, if not the most important, use of intelligence tests is that of predicting scholastic aptitude, and school work is itself predominantly verbal, verbal tests

re certainly the most useful. Though we know of no
onclusive evidence, yet it seems very likely that verbal
ests will correlate much better than pictorial or abstract
nes with school work. The latter, however, may have
nore value in scientific and technical education.

Versions of the Stanford-Binet Scale.—At the time of
writing, the majority of testers are still using the Stanford
Revision of the Binet-Simon scale, published by Terman
n 1916, or Burt's unpublished restandardization of this
Revision. But they are gradually changing over to the
New Stanford Revision, published in 1937 by Terman and
Merrill; and it is to be hoped that all persons who are
aking up individual testing for the first time will use this
version. We will therefore omit any discussion of the older
cales. The new one is superior to any other both because
t contains very full instructions for application and scoring,
which should obviate the confusions and errors previously
o common among inexperienced testers, and because of its
reater extensiveness. Both the L and M forms cover
lmost the whole range of intelligence from that of $1\frac{1}{2}$ year
hildren to that of adults.

Now the original American form of the New Revision
annot possibly be applied as it stands in this country,
ecause it is replete with words and phrases which require
translation ' into English. Most of them have been
ltered in the edition published here, but some still remain.
ince it would be unwise for every tester to make his or her
wn additional modifications, further revisions are being
rawn up by psychologists. A representative committee
nder Professor Burt has prepared a complete revision of
orm L, which often differs very widely from the present
British edition. It is hoped to publish this shortly. A
ommittee of the Scottish Council for Research in Educa-
ion has prepared a list of minimum alterations for Forms
and M, which can be obtained on request, and copied by
esters into their handbooks. None of these three British
ersions is at present standardized. Probably some of the
ests are distinctly easier, others more difficult, for British

than for American children of the same age.[1] But the
final scores (M.A.s or I.Q.s) yielded by the test are likely
to be nearly correct, since previous research with the 1916
Revision has shown that the Stanford-Binet norms for
America, Scotland, and England are practically identical.
There is, however, still some doubt as to the adequacy of
the tests for higher Mental Ages (12 years upwards). In
the earlier versions these tests were too difficult, and
high I.Q.s among older children and adults were generally
not high enough (cf. Vernon, 1937a). In the New Revision
the opposite is found; that is, the high I.Q.s tend to be
too high. But there is not yet sufficient evidence to enable us to specify the extent of this error. Until a proper
restandardization is carried out, the tester should be very
cautious at these higher levels. He must, in addition,
expect to find :

(a) That many of the tests are misplaced. A child may
fail all the tests in one year, but yet pass one or two in a
higher year. Hence thorough testing will necessarily take
rather a long time.

(b) That the items within any one test are often in wrong
order of difficulty. The Vocabulary words, some of the
Absurdities, and other sets of items, require rearrangement.

(c) That the typical responses quoted in the scoring instructions are of little use as they stand, since, even after

---

[1] The Vocabulary test in particular seems to be much too easy,
though this was not true of the same test in the 1916 Revision.
Preliminary research by the present writer has indicated that Terman
and Merrill's norms need to be adjusted as follows :

Mental Age level .	.	6	8	10	12	14	15 : 4	17 : 4	19 : 10	22 : 10
							A.A.	S.A.I.	S.A.II	S.A.III
Vocab. ⎱ Terman and Merrill	.	5	8	11	14	16	20	23	26	30
Words ⎰ British norms .		5	9	13	17	21	24	29	36	42

Burt (1939b) mentions several other instances of serious misplace-
ment, and finds that nearly half the tests are a year or more too high
or too low.

[2] Cf. Scottish Council for Research in Education (1933), and Burt
(1935).

some translation, they represent the thoughts and expressions of American children. The tester must try to decide whether his testees' responses correspond in intellectual level to these acceptable and unacceptable responses.

One other noteworthy disadvantage of the New Stanford Revision is the expensiveness of the concrete material needed for testing young children with Mental Ages of 4 : 0 or less. However, the tester who is concerned only with children of chronological age 6 or more can dispense with it. The only concrete material needed in later tests is the beads, blocks, and printed cards, and these can be obtained separately.

Performance Tests.—As we have already seen, these concrete tests may be employed when verbal ones are inapplicable, or may usefully supplement the predominantly verbal Stanford-Binet test. Their chief merits are their greater attractiveness to children, and their capacity for bringing out a variety of temperamental reactions. A testee's manner of approach to such tests, and his behaviour when confronted with difficulties, throws much light on his impulsiveness, persistence, complacency, and other qualities, which cannot as yet readily be tested or measured objectively.

The majority of performance tests suffer from the practical drawbacks that they are very unwieldy and difficult to transport, and extremely costly. Some testers are suspicious of them because different tests often give very inconsistent results. A child with a Binet M.A. of 9 years may, for instance, pass performance tests at anywhere from the 7- to the 12-year levels. One reason for this is their poor standardization. The published norms may be inadequate (cf. Vernon, 1937a), or the American standards may be incorrect for this country. Often also the test material or method of application differ in certain small respects from those current when the test was standardized, so that the test is thereby rendered somewhat easier or more difficult. As performance tests have to be applied individually, the task of providing accurate British age norms has as yet hardly been attempted. Even if they were perfectly standardized, we should still expect considerable inconsistencies, since their inter-correlations show that each test involves a large specific factor, or unknown group factors. Most of them are also poor in reliability and the evaluation of this feature is difficult, because they can hardly be applied twice to the same testees, except after an interval which is long enough to wipe out memories of the earlier testing.

Undoubtedly then their validity, either as measures of g or of some practical group factor such as Alexander's F, is poor. The conception of ' practical ability ' in everyday life is even more obscure than the conception of general intelligence. Quite frankly, we cannot as yet say what type of ability in daily life they serve to measure. It is interesting to note that several of them are markedly affected by emotional maladjustment or neuroticism. Children or adults tested at a Psychological Clinic tend to make poorer scores on them than on the Binet test. This dependence on affective group factors constitutes another reason why they are not very efficient measures of ability. Thus the mental tester should never place much reliance on a single performance test, nor on two or three. A small number may be sufficient to indicate whether a Binet test result is likely to have been distorted by some verbal defect in the child, but the median or mean score from at least half a dozen of them, or the total result from a comprehensive battery such as Drever and Collins's, should be taken if a reliable performance test M.A. is desired.

Group Tests versus Individual Tests

The merits and the defects both of individual tests such as Stanford-Binet or performance tests, and of group verbal or non-verbal tests, may best be brought out by contrasting them under the following series of headings :

(1) *Age Range.*—Individual tests must be used with very young children because it is practically impossible to hold

the attention of a group, or to get them all to act alike at the same moment. Further, it is not natural for children to apply their intelligence to symbols on paper—either words, pictures, or diagrams—until they have settled down to formal schooling. Manipulation of concrete objects or individual conversation with the tester constitute much more appropriate testing media. Group tests are available which claim to measure Mental Ages down to 6 or even 5 years. The instructions for these must, of course, be given orally. But their value is very doubtful, for the above reasons. They may sometimes be useful for classifying pupils aged 7 +, i.e. children whose M.A.s are likely to run from 5 to 9.

By 9, or better 10, years, children can read instructions for themselves, are thoroughly accustomed to class work, and can readily deal with a variety of verbal problems. This is therefore a very suitable age at which to begin group testing. Above 14, group tests have definite advantages over individual, both because they can readily be made difficult enough even for the highest intelligence levels, and because their items are much less apt to appear silly and childish to suspicious adolescents or adults.

(2) *Ease of Application.*—Group tests are easier to procure, to apply and to score, and they demand much less training and experience on the part of the tester. Possibly however, these are disadvantages, since so many unskilled persons misapply and misinterpret them (cf. Chap. X).

(3) *Time.*—Needless to say, the time saved by applying group instead of individual tests is enormous. For instance, a class of forty can usually be tested in less than an hour, and their answers scored in four to eight hours, whereas an experienced Binet tester needs about half an hour for each young child, three-quarters for an older one, and an inexperienced tester much longer still. The point, however, is whether this three-quarters of an hour per child is worth while. The great majority of psychologists would certainly say that it is, and that an individual test can reveal much better than a group test things which the child's

teachers and parents may have failed to recognize even after years of acquaintanceship. Probably the best compromise would be for the school psychologist or infants' mistress to test each child individually at 6, for group tests to be applied in class at 10, and possibly at 12 and 14, and for individual tests to be given at these later ages only to exceptional pupils whose group test results are very puzzling, or about whom some important decision has to be made for purposes of educational or vocational guidance.

(4) *Time Limits.*—Most of the items in the Binet scale and many individual performance or educational tests are untimed, whereas the great majority of group tests have to be done at maximum speed. Are not, the critics ask, some children slower but surer than those who score well on these timed tests ? That the answer is probably in the negative has already been indicated in the previous chapter. A large body of research shows that ' speed ' and ' power ' factors cannot be effectively distinguished.[1] Certainly if time allowances were increased the slower testees would improve their scores, but experiment proves that they would still remain relatively poorer than the quick testees, and (according to the principles of Chaps. II and IV) it is relative, not absolute scores that matter. Untimed group tests have been constructed, but they are inconvenient both because the questions have to be made more difficult, and because different testees finish them at different times. Possibly also they may introduce the temperamental factor of persistence or willingness to go on trying, which is irrelevant in measuring intelligence.

At the same time, it should be remembered that factorial studies of ' speed versus power ' are based on correlations between scores of *groups* of persons, and that even quite high coefficients may admit big exceptions in individual cases (cf. Chap. VII). It is conceivable then that the tim-

---

[1] A group factor of mental speed has emerged from Holzinger's extensive investigations (1934), but it appears to be very small. For a useful summary of earlier work on the problem, see Spearman (1927).

ing may unfairly affect a few children or adults, especially those who are emotionally maladjusted. This is one reason, if rather a dubious one, why Clinic psychologists prefer to use individual tests.

(5) *Objectivity*.—With good group tests the conditions of application and the scoring are much better standardized than with most individual tests. Very little is left to the personal decision of the tester, and the marking is, or should be, completely foolproof. In actual practice many group testers still manage to commit gross errors, some of which will be pointed out in the next chapter. And modern individual tests like the New Stanford Revision afford much less scope for subjective whims than did the older ones. Nevertheless individual testers often have to judge the correctness of doubtful responses, and may, without departing from the instructions in the handbook, alter the testing conditions in a variety of ways. Clearly, then, if different testers are liable to arrive at different results when testing the same children, their results are not objective or reliable. Yet there seems to be no evidence of serious discrepancies between the results of trained testers, although untrained ones may make grave mistakes. The reliabilities of the 1916 Stanford and Burt-Stanford Revisions were very high so long as the testees were in the middle range of Mental Ages, and were not suffering from serious emotional disorders. The New Revision should be even better. Greater difficulties, and therefore less reliability, occur in testing children below the age of 5 years, or adolescents of 13 + and adults. Also occasional children at a Psychological Clinic are so unco-operative or unstable that their results cannot be trusted. But the experienced tester should be able to recognize when his judgments are uncertain and try to obtain a re-test by someone else who may be able to handle such cases better.

Actually the rigid objectivity of the group test is distrusted by Clinic psychologists, since they know that the same physical situation may mean very different things to different children. The flexibility of individual testing is to them a great advantage which, so far as is known, they do not abuse.[1]

(6) *Dependence on Health and Mood*.—Both group and individual tests seem to be much less affected by these factors than might be anticipated. Experiments show little and often no difference between the scores of children when they are fatigued or ill, and when in good health, nor between those who are strongly motivated (e.g. by the promise of monetary rewards) and those who are merely encouraged in the ordinary way. Studies of the latter type sometimes show that testees who are making more effort may attempt more test items, but they also make more mistakes so that their scores are scarcely altered. There seems then to be little evidence for such statements as that the examination conditions of group testing make some testees unduly nervous, or that others are stimulated to do better by the competitive nature of the testing situation. All such conclusions, however, are based on average tendencies, which admit occasional individual exceptions, and Binet testing certainly indicates that a few testees are so resistant or timid that they fail to do themselves justice. More extreme differences in attitude to the test can undoubtedly distort the scores,[2] and certain physical conditions such as bad eyesight must have a like effect. No intelligence test possesses perfect reliability; and conditions such as these may be at least partly responsible. Test reliability is known to be particularly low among unstable testees (cf. Tulchin, 1934).

The great advantage of individual over group testing is that in the former the tester can generally discern the influence of abnormal conditions, whereas in the latter he

[1] For a fuller discussion of this, and the two following, sections, see Cattell (1937) and Vernon (1937*b*).

[2] This was found by Barron in an experiment on strict and slack conditions of supervision in group testing, carried out under the present writer's direction. The correlations between two forms of a group test applied under similar conditions averaged + 0·930. But the same tests given under different conditions only correlated + 0·573, showing that the conditions have a marked effect on what the tests measure.

has scarcely any control over, or insight into, them. It may be that while high scores on group tests are relatively stable and significant, low scores can arise from a variety of sources other than poor intelligence. However, a lot more careful research is needed in order to determine definitely the part played by such factors.

(7) *Dependence upon Acquired Influences.*—The Stanford-Binet test has in the past been especially strongly criticized for including tests of information which might depend on schooling, social background, and the like. Many of these tests (e.g. Names of Coins, Days of the Week, etc.) have disappeared from the 1937 Revision, and there seems now little to choose between individual and group tests in this respect. Indeed the new Binet test may be superior in that it involves a wider variety of mental operations than the manipulations of words which go to make up most group tests, and which are very likely to be affected by schooling. It possesses the further advantage that the individual tester can often gauge the incidence of environmental factors such as poor social background, lack of verbal facility, etc., which the group tester cannot do. The former cannot, of course, make any scientific correction for abnormal upbringing and environment, but he can apply additional non-verbal tests, and can discount the verbal ones if their results seem unreliable for such reasons. As we have already seen, no test measures innate intelligence directly, and the results of tests only hold good for those who have had similar experience, or similar opportunities for acquiring facility with the various media— words, pictures, or concrete material—through which intelligence may be expressed.

(8) *Dependence on Practice or Coaching.*—Most intelligence tests are published, hence anyone can procure them, coach testees on them, and ensure considerably increased scores. It is a most foolish thing to do, since a child who is made to appear unduly intelligent may also legitimately be expected to be capable of unduly difficult school work. But whenever examinations for secondary school entrance,

or for other purposes, include intelligence tests, the teachers who wish their pupils to do well will naturally be tempted. In Binet testing it is fortunately not difficult to recognize when children have been coached, since their glib answers are very different from the answers of children who are puzzling out the tests for themselves. With group tests, on the other hand, this is seldom possible unless (as has actually occurred) a whole class answers 19 test items out of 20 correctly, the 20th being one where the teacher was mistaken. In order to prevent coaching, many Education Authorities obtain unpublished tests from Moray House, Edinburgh, where they are constructed and standardized privately.

Apart from coaching on a particular test, evidence is accumulating of a considerable practice effect among tests in general. The fact of having recently done Test A tends to improve scores on Test B, and when Tests A and B are similarly constructed, coaching on Test A seems to send up Test B scores still more.[1] Whether, when A and B are rather dissimilar tests, over-coaching on A may reduce scores on B, is not yet known. But this seems quite possible in the light of experiments on transfer. Terman and Merrill (1937) have found a practice effect of 2 to 3 points of I.Q. if Form M of the New Stanford Revision is taken shortly after Form L, or vice versa. The effect in group tests may be considerably larger, at least among testees of superior intelligence (cf. Vernon, 1938c), since group test questions are generally presented in a more roundabout form, a form which seems very strange to naïve testees. In the Binet test the questions are asked naturally and directly, and the testee usually supplies an answer in his own words. But in group tests the items are of the ' closed ' or ' recognition ' type. The testee has to select the best of a number of answers, in accordance with instructions printed at the top of the page. The sophisticated testee is likely to become familiar with the

---

[1] Cf. work by H. Macrae, carried out at Jordanhill College School, Glasgow, not yet published.

instructions commonly used, and to pick up various more efficient methods of selecting the right answers quickly. Much as the cross-word puzzle habitué becomes used to the ' language ' in which cross-word clues are set, the testee may become progressively accustomed to the ' language ' in which mental tests are set.

The magnitude of such practice effects is not yet precisely known, but it is probably large enough to make the use of the same norms for naïve and for sophisticated testees unfair. The school psychologist, therefore, had better not test children more frequently than, say, once in two years, and should keep careful check of any practice the children may get on educational, or other similarly constructed, tests.

(9) *Validity.*—The Binet test, as already mentioned, measures an unanalysed hotch-potch of abilities, and it has been severely criticized by Spearman, Cattell, and others on account of the weaknesses of its statistical construction and theoretical foundations. A properly constructed group test, on the other hand, is claimed to yield a measure of almost pure g. And yet most psychologists prefer the Binet test to any group test when they are called on to make any decision involving the intelligence of an individual child. They regard it as their most valid mental measuring instrument, i.e. as giving the best available index of a child's ' general intelligence.' Few experienced persons appear to put much trust in an individual's group test score, not merely because of prejudice or conservatism, but also because different group tests are known to yield remarkably discrepant results. Correlations between them are usually around $+ 0.7$ to $+ 0.8$, and a child who is given two or more may obtain I.Q.s differing by as much as 30 or even 40 points. In the present writer's view, group tests are very useful for testing groups, e.g. for comparing a whole class of children with the norms, or for large-scale experiments, but not for obtaining trustworthy information about individuals. What reasons may be advanced for this paradoxical state of affairs ?

It seems probable that the intelligence which we recognize in daily life, in school work and other activities, and which we wish to measure or predict by our tests, is never pure g, but is always admixed with various group factors. And that very similar impurities occur in the items of the Binet scale, so that the M.A.s and I.Q.s which it yields correspond excellently with our conceptions of intelligence. From the factorist's point of view this is a most unsystematic and haphazard state of affairs, but it happens to work well. In more colloquial terms, Binet and his followers chose items very largely from children's everyday life experiences, regardless of their factor content, and therefore the test as a whole gives a much better measure of everyday intelligence than would perfect tests of unadulterated g. Further it would seem that intelligence in daily life is not a purely cognitive process, but is closely bound up with the child's or adult's emotions and interests. Only under favourable affective conditions are its full powers displayed. Now the Binet tester, through his personal contact with the child, has considerable control over his state of mind ; he can produce favourable conditions and can judge, albeit subjectively, whether the child's responses are typical of the best that he can do. From general conversation and from the child's manner of approach to difficulties (particularly those offered by performance tests) he builds up a picture of the child's whole personality, and observes how that personality actually applies his available intelligence. He therefore obtains a much more complete and practically useful view than he could from a more scientific measure of cognitive intellectual ability.

In group tests, on the other hand, the items are mostly of a much more restricted and artificial type. The child is forced to express his intelligence through a less natural medium. All that the tester gets is the numerical score, with none of the additional indications which are so useful in interpreting Binet test scores. If such tests do measure pure g, then the general intelligence which psychologists

nd teachers want to measure must be very impure.
Actually the discrepancies between the results of different
ests either show that most of them are not good measures
of g, or suggest that (despite the small effects of mood and
health conditions) there must be many uncontrolled factors
which upset the scores in unknown fashion.

In the present writer's view, testing must be done individually. Yet he would agree with Spearman, Cattell, and
Kent (1937) that the New Stanford Revision is a distress-
ingly unscientific instrument owing to the heterogeneity of
its content.[1] Burt (1939b) has recently published a preliminary account of an analysis of its items by modern
factorial methods, which both demonstrates this heterogeneity and shows that it is responsible for great irregularities in the order of difficulty of the items among different
testees. Boys and girls, bright and dull pupils, and children from higher and lower social grades, all tend to give
somewhat different orders, because they possess different
patterns of the group factors upon which the items depend
in addition to g). A further consequence of this heterogeneity is that it tempts testers to make dubious subjective
analyses of types of items, as when they note that a child
does especially well on the practical items, or badly on the
memory items, and deduce, without any evidence, that he
is a ' practical ' child in daily life, or has poor ' memory '
for school work. Burt's investigation should help considerably in clearing up these ambiguities. Nevertheless
the writer believes that an alternative method of testing,
advocated by Kent, would be much preferable. A series
of individual scales should be collected gradually, each of
which should measure some homogeneous ability, but which

[1] A personal note of explanation seems to be needed here. In a
recent article (1937b) I put forward the strongest arguments I could
muster against factor theories, and in favour of the Binet test.
Actually I was attempting to express the views of clinic psychologists, more than my own, which have always been sympathetic to
factor theory. But I must admit that I have been influenced, partly
by Cattell's reply to my article and partly by Kent's able criticism
of the Binet test, and therefore appear less favourable towards it in
this book than previously.—P. E. V.

should also be sufficiently different from one another and
varied in character, to cover as wide a range of intellectua
operations as the present Binet and performance tests
Such homogeneous abilities need not be pure factors in th
statistical sense, nor independent of one another, but thei
diagnostic worth could be scientifically verified.   The teste
would choose the scales most appropriate to his particula
testing purpose, and to his testee's age and temperament
This method would require greater training and skill or
the part of the tester, but it would seem to be by far the
soundest way, both from the theoretical and practica
viewpoints, in which testing might develop.

List of Tests and Methods of Measurement in Educational Psychology

The following list includes most of the mental tests avail
able in this country, together with some particulars of age
limits, times, publishers, prices, and references to literature
A few may be omitted through pure ignorance on the part
of the writer.   But usually tests are excluded either
because no reasonable norms are available, or because they
are likely to be too unreliable or too inaccurate to be worth
using.   Apart from a few performance tests, no American
or other foreign tests are included, unless they are also published in this country.   It is not possible to provide full
and uniform information regarding every test, nor can
complete accuracy be guaranteed, although every item has
been checked.   Age limits usually refer to the ages for
which norms are provided, not to the ages for which the
tests are suitable.   We shall see later (Chap. X) that the
latter are much more restricted than the former.   When a
definite figure for the time is given, this usually means the
actual working time.   An approximate figure, e.g. c. 20–30
mins., usually means the total time, including the distribution of test blanks, reading of instructions, etc.   Prices are,
of course, subject to alteration.   The prices of tests issued
by American firms are doubtful on account of the exchange,

and are liable to an increase owing to customs duty.[1] The
list does not usually include the price of the test manual
and scoring key, but most publishers provide these, together with a sample copy of the test blank, for about
1/- per test. References to books or articles where
descriptions of, or norms for, the test may be found are
generally listed after the name of the author of the test.
Additional references and notes are often needed, and these
are put in footnotes.

Publishers' names are abbreviated as follows : B =
Baird, Edinburgh. E = Experimental Instruments Co.,
Sudbury, Suffolk. G = Gibson, Glasgow. H = Harrap.
K = Bar-Knight Model Engineering Co., Glasgow. L =
Lewis, London. N = National Institute of Industrial
Psychology, London. O = Oliver and Boyd, Edinburgh.
S = Stoelting, Chicago. U = University of London Press.

An asterisk (*) in the prices column indicates that the
answers to this test can be written on blank paper, and the
printed blanks used over again.

[1] Testers are advised to order American tests through their own
educational bookseller. Customs officials will often allow material
so ordered to be ' educational ' and therefore free of duty, but may
demand duty from a private purchaser.

14

I. ATTAINMENT, ACHIEVEMENT, OR EDUCATIONAL TESTS

A. Examinations, constructed as a basis for school or college marks (cf. Chaps. XI–XIV).
  1. 'Old-type', or essay-form examinations.
  2. 'New-type', or objective examinations.
B. Standardized tests for grading classes, or individual children or adults, in comparison with norms for average persons of the same age.
  1. Quality scales, individual or group tests.

			Age limits
(i)	*Handwriting (cursive).*		
	Burt [1] (1921, Test XVI). Time *c.* 2–5 mins. Ages $5\frac{1}{2}$–$14\frac{1}{2}$ years.		
	Cattell (1936). School-leaving age standards.		
(ii)	*Composition.*		
	Boyd (1924). Scottish qualifying standards.		
	Burt (1921, Text XX). Time 30 mins. Ages $7\frac{1}{2}$–$14\frac{1}{2}$.		
	Williams [2] English 11 + standards.		
(iii)	*Drawing.*		
	Burt (1921, Test XVII). Time *c.* 3–10 mins. Ages $3\frac{1}{2}$–$14\frac{1}{2}$.		
	Cattell (1936). Time 10 mins. Adult standards.		

  2. Individual tests, constructed on the power system.

			Age limits
(i)	*Reading Quality or Pronunciation.*		
	Burt (1923, Test I), Graded Vocabulary Test. Time *c.* 5–10 mins.	.	4–15
	Vernon (1938a). Revision of Burt's test for Scottish children	.	4–15
	Vernon (1938a). Graded Word Reading Test, for Scottish children and adults	.	5–21
(ii)	*Reading Comprehension.*		
	Burt (1923, Test IV), Graded Directions Test. Time *c.* 5–10 mins.	.	$5\frac{1}{2}$–$13\frac{1}{2}$
(iii)	*Oral Arithmetic.*		
	Burt (1923, Test VIII), Graded Oral Test. Time *c.* 5–15 mins. Shortened form given in Burt (1935)	.	4–15
	Cattell's Midland Reading and Arithmetic Tests can either be given as individual,		

Burt[3] (1921, 1923, Test III), Monosyllables Test	$6\frac{1}{2}$–$14\frac{1}{2}$	1
Ballard (1920, 1923), One-minute Reading Test[4]	$5\frac{1}{2}$–16	1
(ii) *Arithmetic*.		
Ballard (1920, 1923), One-minute Addition Test[4]	5–12	1
Ballard (1920, 1923), One-minute Subtraction Test[4]	$5\frac{1}{2}$–$13\frac{1}{2}$	1
4. Individual test for fluency, accuracy, and comprehension in reading.		
Burt (1921, 1923, Test V), Continuous Prose Test	$7\frac{1}{2}$–$14\frac{1}{2}$	c. 4–10
5. Group tests, suitable also for individual testing.		
(i) *Reading*.		
Cattell (1936), Midland Attainment Test,[5] Vocabulary	6–14	5
Cattell (1936), Midland Attainment Test,[5] Comprehension	6–14	10
(ii) *Spelling*.		
Burt (1923, Test VI), Graded Vocabulary Test.[6]	5–15	c. 5–10
Burt (1921, 1923, Test VII), Graded Dictation Test	$6\frac{1}{2}$–$14\frac{1}{2}$	c. 5
Cattell (1936), Midland Attainment Test.	5–14	10
Schonell (1932), Regular and Irregular Words Tests	$7\frac{1}{2}$–$13\frac{1}{2}$	c. 5–10
Schonell (1932), Graded Dictation Test	$7\frac{1}{2}$–$13\frac{1}{2}$	c. 5–10

[1] Reference is made to Burt (1923), i.e. the *Handbook of Tests*, when the test can be given and scored from this book. Reference is made to Burt (1921), i.e. *Mental and Scholastic Tests*, when the test material, instructions, and scoring can only be found in this larger volume. All the tests referred to Burt (1923) are also included in Burt (1921). The reference Burt (1921, 1923) signifies that the 1923 book contains the test material, but that the norms for scoring must be obtained from the 1921 book.

[2] Williams, G. P., *Northamptonshire Composition Scale*. Harrap. Price 5/-.

[3] Cf. footnote 1.

[4] Ballard's One-minute Tests are published separately from his books. Publisher U. Prices 1d. each, 1/9 for 25, 6/- for 100 copies.

[5] The Midland Attainment Tests are published separately from Cattell's book. Publisher U. Prices 2d. each, 1/6 doz., 2/9 for 25, 8/6 for 100 copies.

[6] Restandardized for Scottish children by Dr. W. B. Inglis. Norms on request.

I. ATTAINMENT, ACHIEVEMENT, OR EDUCATIONAL TESTS (continued)

	Age limits	Time (mins.)
(iii) *Writing Speed.*		
Burt (1921, Test XV)	6½–14½	2
(iv) *English.*		
Cattell (1936), Midland Attainment Test, Grammar and Style [1] . .	6½–14	20
Cattell (1936), Knowledge of Literature [2] . .	6½–14	15
Cattell (1936), General Knowledge Test . .	14 and Sup. adult	30–40
(v) *Mechanical Arithmetic.*		
Burt (1923, Test IX), Written Graded Test .	7–15	c. 15
Burt (1921, 1923, Tests XI–XIV), Four Rules Tests [3] .	6½–14½	5 each
Cattell (1936), Midland Attainment Test [1] .	6½–14	8

	Age limits	Time	Publisher	Price per 12	25	100
(vi) *Arithmetic Reasoning.*	7–15	c. 15				
Burt [4] (1923, Test X), Written Graded Problems						
Cattell (1936), Midland Attainment Test,[1] Knowledge of Method	6½–14	60				
(vii) *Diagnostic Arithmetic* (separate norms for each sub-test).						
Burt, Northumberland Standardized Test I [5] .	7½–14½	50	U	2/-	3/6	10/-
Schonell (1937) Diagnostic Arithmetic Tests .	7–13	1–4 hrs.	O	—	6/-	21/-
6. Group tests, usually in the form of printed booklets, containing batteries of sub-tests.						
(i) *English Tests of Vocabulary, Silent Reading, Comprehension, Grammar, etc.*						
Alexander, Thanet Test .	10½–12½	45	U	—	3/6	10/-
Ballard (1923), Silent Reading Test	9–14	15	II	1/3	2/6	8/-*

Ballard (1923), English Comprehension Test .	10–14	60	U	1/3	2/6	8/–*
Ballard (1923), English Construction Test .	10–14	60	U	1/3	2/6	8/–*
Brighton Reading Tests [6]	9–14	30–40	U	2/–	—	6/–*
Burt, Northumberland Standardized Test II	7½–14½	50	U	2/9	5/–	17/6
Dingwall Test in English Usage, Form for 9 + .	9 +	50	U	4/6	8/–	25/–
Dingwall Test in English Usage, Form for 10 + to 12 .	11	50	U	4/–	7/–	20/–
Fleming, Kelvin Measurement of Reading Ability	8–12	20	G	—	—	8/6 [7]
Fleming, Kelvin Measurement of Spelling Ability	8–12	30	G	—	—	8/6
Lothian English Test [8]	11–12 +	56	H	—	4/–	15/–
(ii) *Arithmetic Tests.*						
Alexander, Thanet Test	10½–12½	34	U	—	7/–	20/–
Ballard (1923), Mechanical Arithmetic Test	9–14	50	U	1/3	2/6	8/–*
Ballard (1923), Arithmetic Reasoning Test.	9–14	60	U	2/–	3/6	12/–*
Fleming, Kelvin Measurement of Arithmetic Ability	7–12	25	G	—	—	8/6 [7]

[1] The Midland Attainment Tests are published separately from Cattell's book. Publisher U. Prices 2d. each, 1/6 doz., 2/9 for 25, 8/6 for 100 copies.
[2] Prices for separate copies 3d. each, 2/6 doz., 4/6 for 25, 15/– for 100.
[3] Restandardized for Scottish children by Dr. W. B. Inglis. Norms on request.
[4] Cf. footnote 1, p. 199.
[5] For norms for Scottish children, see Murray (1933).
[6] There are six forms of these tests. Both Question and Answer blanks may be obtained separately at half the quoted prices, i.e. at 1d. each.
[7] Prices for smaller quantities of all tests published by Gibson, 20 copies for 2/6, 50 copies for 4/6.
[8] Norms on request from the East Lothian Branch of the Educational Institute of Scotland.

I. ATTAINMENT, ACHIEVEMENT, OR EDUCATIONAL TESTS (*continued*)

(iii) *Unpublished, but Standardized, Tests.*

	Age limits	Time
Earle (1936), Test of Ability in the Use of Words [1]	12 +	30
Earle (1936), Test of Ability in Algebra [1]	12 +	60
George Combe Standardized Tests in English and Arithmetic (MacDonald, 1938)	13–15	

Moray House English Test 7.[2] Time 30 mins.

Moray House Arithmetic Test 7.[2] Time 40 mins.

National Institute of Industrial Psychology Tests of English and Arithmetic Achievement. Ages 10–11 +.

II. INDIVIDUAL INTELLIGENCE TESTS

A. Binet-Simon scale (mainly verbal).

1. Early versions, now largely discarded.

Binet-Simon, 1905, 1908, 1911.

Burt-Binet (1923), 1921.

Herring Point Scale, 1922.

Terman's Stanford Revision, 1916.

Burt-Stanford Revision, 1929 (unpublished).

Age limits for two latter versions 3–19½. Time *c.* 15–50 mins.

2. Present versions.

Terman and Merrill's New Stanford Revision, Forms L and M. English edition [3] (1937), 1937.

Burt's version of Form L (unstandardized and unpublished), 1938.

Age limits 2–23. Time *c.* 20–80 mins.

Test				
Stutsman's (1931) Merrill-Palmer Scale. (Partly verbal, mainly play material) . . .	1½-6	c. 15-40	S	c. £10
Cattell's Dartington Intelligence Scale O (non-verbal material)	4-11	c. 45	H	17/6
D. Non-verbal scale.				
Penrose and Raven's R.E.C.I. Perceptual Tests (Progressive Matrices). Cf. Raven (1939) . .	6-14	c. 20-60	L	10/6
E. Performance test scales.				
Drever-Collins Scales (1936). Battery of eight tests .	5½-15½	c. 40-60	B	£11/6/0
Supplementary battery of six tests . .	4-7	c. 20-40	B	£6/17/0
Alexander's Scale (1935, 1938). Three tests .	7-19	c. 15-45	BU	45/-
F. Performance tests				
1. Formboard type.				
Seguin-Goddard Formboard, small model. Cf. Stutsman (1931) .	2¾-6	c. 2-8	E	42/-
Seguin-Goddard Formboard, standard model.[4] Cf. Cattell (1936) .	5-14	c. 1-3	E	42/-
Dearborn Formboard No. 3. Cf. Gaw (1925) .	6-15	c. 5-10	E	30/-
Oakley Formboard. Cf. Oakley (1935) .	Aver. adult	c. 2-10	K	42/-
Moorrees Formboard. Cf. Vernon (1937a).	12– Sup. ad.	c. 2-12	—	—

[1] Published privately by the Scottish Council for Research in Education. Norms are being collected for entrants to Scottish secondary schools.

[2] Obtainable from University of London Press on recommendation from a Director of Education.

[3] Manual and material published by Harrap. Prices: Manual, 10/6. Printed card material for Form L, 4/6. Performance test material (chiefly for young children), 45/-. Blue beads, 1/6. Record blanks, 25 for 3/6, 100 for 12/6. Ditto for Form M. Files for printed card material: Hunt and Broadhurst's 'Loxon Loose-leaf Notebook S739/D,' price 1/6, is recommended.

[4] A third, extra-large, model is included by Baird in the Drever-Collins scale. No norms for it are available. For description of other variants, cf. Vernon (1937a). The best norms for the standard model over 5-14 years seem to be Cattell's (1936).

II. INDIVIDUAL INTELLIGENCE TESTS (*continued*)

	Age limits	Time	Publisher	Price of material
2. Picture and jigsaw type.				
Manikin. Cf. Stutsman (1931), Gaw (1925)	4–8	c. 1–5	B	12/6
Mare and Foal. Cf. Vernon (1937a)	4–9	c. 1–4	B	31/–
Ship Test. Cf. Vernon (1937a)	5–10	c. 1–5	S	c. 30/–
Healy Picture Completion II.[1] Cf. Vernon (1937a)	7– Sup. ad.	c. 5–15	N	66/–
Feature Profile. Cf. Arthur (1930)	8–16	c. 1–5	B	16/3
3. Cube pattern type.				
Knox Cube Imitation. Cf. Arthur (1930)	4–8	c. 1–3	B	1/6
Cube Construction.[2] Cf. Alexander (1935)	12–16	c. 4–12	B	8/6
Kohs's Block Design.[3] Cf. Alexander (1935)	12–16	c. 10–20	B	15/6
Alexander's (1932) Passalong Test.	7½–18½	c. 10–20	U	21/–
4. Drawing type.				
Goodenough's (1926) Drawing a Man Test.	3–13	c. 2–8	H	7/6
Porteus's Maze Test.[4] Cf. Burt (1921, 1923), Vernon (1937a)	3–16	c. 3–15	E	1/–

III. GROUP INTELLIGENCE TESTS

A. Verbal tests, or tests with occasional non-verbal problems.

	Age limits	Time	Publisher	Price per 12	25	100
Alexander, Thanet School Aptitude Test	6½–16	30	U	—	5/–	15/–
Ballard (1922), Chelsea Test.	11–14	not timed	U	3/–	6/–	18/6*

		timed				
Burt, Northumberland Standardized Test III .	9½–16½	60	U	2/6	4/6	16/6
Cattell Intelligence Tests, Forms A, B. Scale II .	7½–ad.	70	H	—	5/-	17/6
Cattell Intelligence Tests, Forms A, B. Scale III .	12½–Sup. ad.	70	H	—	5/-	17/6
Dale, Bristol Group Reasoning Tests, Forms A, B, C	10½–14	c. 60	U	1/-	1/8	5/6
Dawson Mental Tests, Forms A, B. .	9–ad.	40	H	—	3/6	12/6
Fleming, Kelvin Measurement of Mental Ability .	8–12	25	G	—	—	8/6 [5]
Group Test 33 (National Institute of Industrial Psychology[6])	14 upwards	30	N	—	—	20/-
Group Test 34 (National Institute of Industrial Psychology[6])	10½–16½	40	N	—	—	40/-
Houghton, Orton Intelligence Test . .	10–14	70	G	—	—	8/6 [5]

[1] Healy Picture Completion Test I is omitted since the several sets of norms which have been published are utterly discordant.

[2] Drever and Collins (1936) describe a much simpler method of applying and scoring this test, but unfortunately provide no separate norms. Gaw (1925) gives yet a third, rather complicated method. Her 6–16 year norms are not reliable enough to be recommended here.

[3] Drever and Collins (1936) describe a simpler method of scoring, but provide no norms. Kohs's original version gives far more extensive (American) norms, namely 7-adult, than does Alexander, but it requires a longer series of cards, and very complex scoring.

[4] Various methods of applying and scoring are summarized by Vernon (1937a). Probably the most convenient, and cheapest, is that described by Burt (1923), who includes the test material. But if his method is followed, his revised norms (1921) should be used.

[5] Cf. footnote 7, p. 201.

[6] These tests do not have M.A. norms, but deciles are given for various types of schools. Prices for smaller quantities, 3d. and 6d. a copy. Other group tests used by the N.I.I.P., but not yet published, include No. 35 (a parallel test to No. 33), No. 36 (a verbal test for 11–15-year elementary school pupils), and No. 42 (an omnibus test for a similar age range).

III. GROUP INTELLIGENCE TESTS (*continued*)

	Age limits	Time	Publisher	Price per		
				12	25	100
National Intelligence Tests (National Research Council, U.S.A.). Forms A2, B2	8–15	c. 25	H	—	6/–	21/–
Otis Advanced Group Intelligence Scale, Forms A, B [1]	8–17	c. 50	H	—	5/–	17/6
Otis Quick-scoring Mental Ability Tests [2]:						
Beta Test, Forms A, B	8–17	30	H	—	5/–	—
Gamma Test, Forms A, B	11–ad.	30	H	—	5/–	—
Richardson, Simplex Group Intelligence Scale	9–ad.	90	H	—	6/–	21/–
Richardson, Simplex Junior Intelligence Scale	5½–18	45	H	—	5/–	17/6
Terman, Group Test of Mental Ability, Forms A, B	10–ad.	30	H	—	5/–	21/–
Thomson, Mental Survey Test, 1932 [3]	10½–11½	55	U	2/6	4/6	15/–
Thomson, Moray House Tests Nos. 10, 11A, 20 [3]	10½–12½	55	U	2/9	5/–	17/6
Thomson, Northumberland Mental Test, No. I	9–16½	60	H	—	5/–	17/6
Thomson, Northumberland Mental Test, No. II	10½–13½	60	H	—	5/–	17/6
Tomlinson, Northern Test of Educability	7½–15½	50	U	3/6	6/6	21/–*
Tomlinson, West Riding Tests of Mental Ability, Forms Y, Z	7–ad.	60	U	3/6	6/6	21/–*
Williams, Oxton Group Intelligence Test (mainly non-verbal)	10–13	30	H	—	6/–	21/–
B. Non-verbal material, instructions given orally.						
Alexander, Junior School Grading Test	4¾–12½	c. 25	U	3/6	6/6	20/–
Cattell, Intelligence Test Scale I, Forms A, B	7–ad.	c. 45	H	—	6/–	21/–
Fleming, Kelvin Measurement of Ability in Infant Classes	5–8	30	G	—	—	8/6 [4]
Otis Primary Group Intelligence Scale, Forms A, B	5½–15½	c. 40	H	—	5/–	17/6

Otis Quick-scoring Mental Ability Tests.

Alpha Test, Forms A, B . . . 5–13 20 H — 5/- —

Sleight, Non-verbal Intelligence Test. . . 6–12 c. 35 H — 10/6 35/-

C. Oral tests. Verbal items are read to the pupils, who write their answers on blank paper.

Ballard (1922), Group Test for Juniors.[5] Ages $8\frac{1}{2}$–$13\frac{1}{2}$. Time c. 120 mins.

Spearman, Measure of Intelligence.[6] Ages 9–15. Time c. 75 mins. Cf. Walters and Thomas (1929).

[1] For more accurate British norms between $9\frac{1}{2}$–$13\frac{1}{4}$, cf. Fraser Roberts (1935).
[2] The Otis Quick-scoring Tests are revisions and extensions of the old Otis Self-administering Tests. The latter are therefore omitted from this list.
[3] These tests have full I.Q. norms for the age ranges indicated.
[4] Cf. footnote 7, p. 201.
[5] For norms see Kent Education Gazette, 1934, XIV, No. 10, pp. 182–183. They differ considerably from those listed by Ballard.
[6] Publisher: Methuen. Price 1/-.

IV. SPECIAL APTITUDE TESTS

Almost the only special aptitude tests standardized for use in this country, and worth using, are those of the National Institute of Industrial Psychology, to whom application should be made. They include the following : Mechanical Aptitude and Manual Ability Tests (Cox), Group Tests of Clerical Aptitude and of Form Relations Ability ; Tests for Motor Drivers, etc. For descriptions of these and other tests see Oakley and Macrae (1937), and the files of *The Human Factor* (Journal of the N.I.I.P.). For a description of tests of artistic and musical abilities, see Vernon (1935*b*).

V. SENSORY-MOTOR TESTS

A. Bodily physique ; strength, quickness, and steadiness of movement ; fatigability. The best-known tests include dynamometers, tapping tests, aiming tests, reaction time, pursuit-meter, dotting machine, etc., few of which, however, are adequately standardized.   References : Whipple (1919), Oakley and Macrae (1937), Sutcliffe and Canham (1937).

B. Right- or left-handedness. Cf. Burt (1937).

C. Vision. 1. Colour blindness. Tests include Holmgren wools ;   Edridge-Green lantern ;   Collins-Drever, Ishihara, and other figure tests. Cf. Collins (1937).

2. Right or left eye dominance. Cf. Burt (1937).

D. Hearing. 1. Auditory acuity. Tests include whispered speech, audiometer, etc. Cf. Whipple (1919), Burt (1937).

2. Sense of pitch, intensity, rhythm. Cf. Vernon (1935*b*).

In addition, oculists, speech therapists, doctors, and other specialists use a number of tests which would fall within this group.

VI. TEMPERAMENT, PERSONALITY, AND CHARACTER TESTS

A. Ratings or assessments of personality traits by acquaintances. Cf. Vernon (1938b), Symonds (1931), Hunt and Smith (1935).

B. Performance tests, e.g. Downey Will-temperament, tests of perseveration and fluency of association, tests of character. Cf. Vernon (1935a), Symonds (1931), Cattell (1936).

C. Questionnaires, attitude scales, inventories, and interest blanks. Cf. Vernon (1938b).

D. Qualitative approaches : observations of manner during testing or interview ; free word association ; Rorschach inkblots ; Mosaics test ; drawings. Cf. Earl (1939), Burt (1935), Vernon (1935c, 1938b).

CHAPTER X

HINTS TO TESTERS

1. *Choice of a Test.*—In choosing a test for some particular purpose, the tester's first consideration should, of course, be its validity for that purpose. As we have seen in Chap. IX, he may be able to judge its validity to some extent by inspection of its content, but he would be better advised to seek out experimental proof of what it is that the test measures. Investigations by its author, or by others who have used the test, should be consulted. The mere fact that it is called a test of such-and-such an ability does not constitute evidence. The second consideration (which greatly affects the first) is the test's reliability. Generally speaking, a test must be fairly long, and its scoring must be objective, if it is to be satisfactory in this respect. Most authors of good tests publish evidence of their reliability in the accompanying manuals. Little trust should be placed in tests whose scores are not known to yield a reliability coefficient of $+0 \cdot 90$ or over.

2. *Age Range.*—Few, if any, tests presume to cover *all* ranges of ability, and most educational and intelligence tests are only intended to cover quite a limited range. Thus the tester should be careful to choose from among the available tests those which will, when applied to a large group of his testees, be likely to yield a normal distribution of scores, and which will not unduly curtail this distribution at either end. For instance, in testing an ordinary school class, he should first estimate roughly the range of M.A.s or E.A.s which it contains. A class of average C.A. 10 years may often include individuals with M.A.s (on a group test) of 6 to 14 years, though the great

majority should lie between 7½ and 12½ years. He should
then study the ages for which the various tests provide
norms, and pick one which covers as much of this predicted range as possible. If he has reason to believe that
the average M.A. or E.A. of the class will be, perhaps, a
year above or below its average C.A., he must correspond-
ingly adjust his choice of test.

The ' differentiating power ' of the test norms should
also be noted. They should show a fairly large and even
increase in score from one age level to the next. Suppose
a test containing, say, 200 items, to provide the following
norms from 6 to 13 years. The increases are large up to
9 or 10, but then tail off, till there is only a difference of 5
items between the 12 and 13 year scores. Such a test will
clearly not discriminate or differentiate well at the upper
end, and its effective range of norms is from 6 to 11 rather
than from 6 to 13.

Years :	.	6	7	8	9	10	11	12	13
Score :	.	40	71	101	128	151	168	179	184

Similar considerations apply to the choice of tests whose
norms are issued in percentile, or other, forms.

3. *Convenience of Arrangement and Scoring.*—If a test is
to be used extensively, attention should be paid to its
general arrangement from the point of view of ease in
applying and scoring. With some performance tests and
tests of special aptitudes, much time is wasted in setting
out the material, or the instructions are very elaborate, or
the scoring unnecessarily detailed. More modern American tests usually try to reduce these inconveniences.

Group tests of attainment or intelligence may also vary
greatly in ' mechanics ' or ' lay-out.' Some of the older
ones have insufficient instructions and sample items or
practice sheets, so that testees often fail to understand
what they have to do, and a lot of additional oral explanation is needed. Sometimes the testees have to answer in
their own words, and the scoring manual never allows for
all the possible answers which turn up, so that much time

is wasted in deciding whether or not an answer shall be
counted.   The positions of the answers are often scattered
all over the page, instead of being arranged in the right
hand margin. True, stencils are often provided which, when
laid over the test page, show up the correct answers.   But
according to the present writer's experience, it is far more
trouble to fit the stencils over each successive page than
it is to compare the testee's booklet with a booklet on
which all the correct answers are clearly marked.

Many American group tests are now issued with an inter-
leaved carbon-paper device, so arranged that all the correct
answers, and none of the incorrect ones, are automatically
shown as crosses on the back of the page.   The scorer then
merely has to count the number of crosses.   Alternatively,
testees may check their answers with a special carbon
pencil ; their blanks are then passed through an electrical
machine which counts instantaneously the number of
carbon marks in correct positions, through the amount of
current which passes.   In this country, however, testing is
seldom carried out on so large a scale as to warrant such
ingenuity, and its consequent expense.

4. *Procedure.*—Many of the following hints may seem
puerile to some readers, yet they are all based on the
writer's experience of mistakes actually committed by
amateur testers.   Such mistakes may often lead to quite
serious consequences.

The tester should first study the instructions and the
test material carefully with a view to seeing precisely how
the test works, and should then follow these instructions to
the letter.   Often it is worth the tester's while to take the
test himself.   In Binet testing, the results should not be
trusted until such time as the tester practically knows the
instructions, and the essentials of scoring, by heart, and
until he has given the test to, say, twenty cases.

5. *Modification of Instructions or Materials.*—The inexperienced tester is very apt to find flaws in the test or
instructions which, he thinks, could be eliminated by some
simple modifications.   Very likely the test could be im-

proved, but then it would no longer be the same test, and the published norms would no longer hold good. For the same reason a printed group test must not be duplicated or mimeographed in order to save expense. Quite apart from the probable infringement of copyright, the difficulty of the test is likely to be altered thereby.

6. *Timing.*—Accurate timing is essential. In some group tests a mistake of 5 seconds may quite possibly lead to an error of 1% or 2% in average I.Q. Testers who do not own stop-watches are advised to use omnibus tests when feasible, since these require only a single timing. If times are kept by a watch with a seconds hand, the exact minute and second at which a test is to stop should be *written down* as soon as the test has started. Mistakes very easily occur if the tester trusts to his memory.

7. *Underlining and Erasing.*—Before giving a group test to a class, all rulers and indiarubbers should be firmly removed, otherwise the pupils will waste several minutes in ruling their underlinings, or rubbing out responses when they change their minds. If the test instructions do not already say so, the tester should explain to the pupils that, in order to change a response, they should scribble out the first choice rapidly, and then mark or underline the new choice clearly.

8. *Distractions and Copying.*—In all testing, possible sources of distraction should be avoided. For instance, a group test should not be given when a singing lesson is due to occur in the next classroom. The testees should be spaced as far apart as possible, since it is very easy, in multiple-choice tests, for one to overlook and copy the answers of another. Often the younger children have no intention of cheating, but are yet extremely anxious to write down the same as their neighbours, simply because the whole situation is unfamiliar to them, and they are afraid of doing the ' wrong thing.' The motive behind such copying is a desire for social conformity.

9. *Practice Sheets and Samples.*—In most group tests for children there are preliminary practice sheets or sample

15

items, where help may be given. The tester should make sure that even the dullest testees understand what to do, and that they can manage at least one or two of the sample items by themselves.

10. *Coaching.*—No practice or coaching of any kind, beyond what is specified, should be given. Testees who gain an advantage by such means will no longer be comparable with those on whom the test was standardized, and the norms will be useless.

11. *The 'Subjective' Situation.*—At the same time as adhering to the standard objective conditions of testing, the tester should try to obtain, even in a group test, a favourable subjective atmosphere. If the tester himself is apprehensive, or bored, his mood is likely to communicate itself to a group of children. The testees should not be excited and anxious, nor, of course, lackadaisical, in their attitude to the test. Teachers should not peer over children's shoulders while they are working to see how they are getting on ; it inevitably upsets them.

12. *Testing and Teaching.*—Many teachers make bad testers because the teaching attitude is so ingrained in them that they cannot refrain from drawing morals, or pointing out mistakes. A test is not a kind of lesson, and children should not be expected to learn anything whatsoever from it. Rather it is a matter of stock-taking. The essential object is to obtain a record of the testees' performances under certain standard conditions, so that these performances may be compared with those of other similar testees who have been tested under the same conditions.

13. *Scoring.*—The scoring instructions must be followed as meticulously as the instructions for applying the test. The tester may sometimes disagree with the response provided in the scoring key, and think that some alternative is just as good or better. This may be so, but once personal opinion enters the scoring ceases to be objective, and the results again cannot be compared with the test norms. The scoring of most group tests is quite mechanical, but errors very readily creep in, both in checking the right

sponses and in adding up correct checks.   It is extremely
esirable for such tests to be scored twice, preferably by
ifferent persons.

14. *The Subjective Situation in Individual Testing.*—The
onditions of individual testing require still more tact and
ympathy than those of group testing.   By means of pre-
minary conversation the child should be put at ease, and
interspersed irrelevancies should keep him interested and
sponsive throughout.   If he shows signs of fatigue, dis-
action, or resistance the testing should be broken off.
he good tester develops a kind of ' bedside manner,' and
voids formalities.   He does not read the oral tests from
ie handbook, but, knowing them by heart, says them in
conversational tone.   In order to keep the child interested
e must himself sound interesting.   Encouragement should
ollow every response, but some caution is needed in prais-
ig incorrect responses, since many children may realize
hen they are wrong and become careless or discouraged
 there is no criticism nor stimulus to do better.   The
resence of a third person, particularly the mother or head
eacher, constitutes a distraction which should always be
voided.

In giving the older versions of the Binet scale, it was the
ommon practice among trained testers to jump about from
ne part of the scale to another.   This enabled the tester
o choose the test which seemed to him to be most appro-
riate to the child's mood at the moment, also to save time
y grouping together tests with identical instructions
.g. the digit memory tests) ; and it prevented all the most
ifficult tests from coming at the end of the session.   Un-
ortunately Terman and Merrill (1937) have now forbidden
iis procedure.   However, their book contains several other
seful hints on obtaining good *rapport,* while at the same
me adhering strictly to the standard instructions and
coring.

15. *Record Keeping.*—The following principle is com-
only adopted by experienced testers : never spend *any of
e child's time* in making records of his responses.   Notes

should certainly be made, not only of test responses, but also of manner, speech, etc. All the recording, however should be done while the child is engaged either in doing a test, in irrelevant conversation, or in listening to the instructions for another test ; and it should be so unobtrusive that it never constitutes a distraction. Poor testers not only waste time in recording responses and looking up the scoring, but also allow awkward gaps to occur which entirely spoil the favourable atmosphere of alertness and interest. The reason for this is usually mere lack of familiarity with instructions and scoring.

16. *Impartiality.*—While the good tester enters very fully into the thoughts and feelings of the child he is testing, yet he also needs to exert considerable self-control. There are various ways in which he may (quite unwittingly) give illegitimate hints, for instance, by over-emphasizing the crucial words in an oral test, or by making emphatic movements in the direction of the correct blocks, holes, etc., of a performance test. Further, he cannot help but feel more sympathetic with some children than with others. He should, therefore, frequently ask himself : " Am I in any way being prejudiced by my liking for this child ; am I giving hints or crediting him with doubtful passes because I believe that he is bright, which I would not do if I believed that he was dull ? "

17. *Studying the Whole Child.*—The tester should never regard his job merely as measurement of the I.Q. or other test scores (although many doctors, teachers, and others may seem to regard that as his sole function). Rather he should try to understand, and to build up a picture of, each child's whole personality. By doing so his test results are more likely to be accurate, since he will realize when they are being distorted by emotional or other factors ; and he will certainly be better able to interpret their significance when the guidance or treatment of the child is under consideration. Although, as we have seen, he is not justified in analysing a heterogeneous test like the Binet scale into tests of hypothetical discrete abilities (memory, verbal

ractical, etc.), yet he can pick up innumerable hints
egarding the child's intellectual and emotional character-
stics, which can later be explored more thoroughly.   Sug-
estions of specific educational difficulties may readily be
ollowed up.   Bühler (1938) shows that responses to the
Ball and Field (or Purse and Field) test may give valuable
liagnostic indications.   Other Binet items and, still more,
performance tests like the Porteus Mazes, may be equally
evealing (cf. Vernon, 1937a ; Earl, 1939).   These deduc-
ions should, of course, be checked later by comparing
hem with other sources of information, such as the
psychiatrist's case-record, when available.   In this way a
ester can always be extending his methods and improving
heir validity.

18. *Interpretation of Test Results : Unreliability.*—No
mental test score should ever be accepted at its face value,
nor trusted in the same way as physical measurements are
rusted.   Even the best tests, it should be remembered,
only measure to within a certain Probable Error.   In
other words, a test score should be regarded as the centre
of a range of possible scores.   It may be correct to within,
say, 5%, but also it may be in error by as much as 20%,
unless it has been confirmed by the results of other tests
which narrow the range of uncertainty.

19. *Units of Measurement.*—The imperfections of men-
al units should also be borne in mind, for example, the
ack of equivalence of M.A. and E.A. units (cf. p. 84).
The I.Q. is still more open to criticism.   It is misinterpreted by a very large proportion of testers, and by almost
all teachers and laymen.   It is not an index (even an
naccurate index) of the amount of intelligence that a child
actually possesses.   The M.A. is such an index.   The I.Q.,
being a ratio, is a measure of rate, namely, rate of mental
levelopment.   The point may be brought out by the
ollowing example of the test scores of two children,
A and B.

| A : | . | . | C.A. 9 : 0 | M.A. 11 : 0 | I.Q. 122 |
| B : | . | . | C.A. 8 : 0 | M.A. 10 : 6 | I.Q. 131 |

Here it is A, not B, who is the more intelligent, since h
can do more difficult intellectual tasks, and can be ex
pected to be superior in school work.   It is true, howevei
that B is growing more rapidly in mental powers than A i:
that in about another four years he will catch up with A
and that he will probably be, as an adult, the more intell
gent of the two.

In actual practical work of educational guidance o
emotional treatment, the tester need hardly bother t
calculate the I.Q. or E.Q.s, since what matters is the presen
level of the child's intelligence and educational capacities
The only proper use of the I.Q. is for predicting a testee'
future career, i.e. for assessing approximately his ultimat
educational or vocational level.

20. *Dependence of I.Q. on the Test Employed.*—The naïv
tester or layman usually assumes that a child would obtai
the same I.Q. whatever the test employed.   This is so fa
from true that the test employed should invariably b
quoted along with an M.A., E.A., I.Q., or E.Q.   Th
reasons for these discrepancies have already been given
and will merely be summarized here.

(*a*) Chance errors of measurement, due to the fact tha
no test is perfectly reliable (cf. pp. 145–9).

(*b*) Many tests are not well standardized.   For instance
American group tests may give results which are too
lenient (cf. pp. 80–1).

(*c*) Different intelligence tests have different dispersion
of M.A.s and I.Q.s, so that one test makes a bright chil
out to be much brighter, a dull child to be much duller
than to does another test (cf. pp. 85–6).

(*d*) All test scores seem to be liable to distortion by
various unknown group factors, or by emotional or othe
influences, about which we possess little exact knowledge
and which we are not able to control (cf. pp. 190–5).

In view of this uncertainty over the norms and the dis
persion of group intelligence tests, the inexperienced teste
would be well advised never to calculate individual I.Q.
from them, but to treat their results in purely relativ

fashion, i.e. in the way which was recommended for educational tests (cf. p. 82). The class teacher can obtain from a group test practically all the information which it is capable of yielding if he or she simply finds which child in the class has the highest score (corresponding to the highest M.A.), which the next highest, and so on. When test results are thus confined to rank orders, they are far less likely to be misinterpreted than is common at present.

21. *Conclusion.*—Mental tests have been widely, and often unfairly, criticized. But the progress of testing is probably hindered to a greater extent by its friends, who are ignorant of its limitations, than by its enemies. One of the main objects of this book is to analyse these limitations and to explain the underlying principles which must be understood if tests are to be applied and interpreted properly. No one ought to use tests who is not willing to familiarize himself with these matters, and with the literature which bears on the particular tests that he employs. In skilled hands, testing provides a far surer and more accurate tool for the assessment of abilities than do subjective impressions or the ordinary examination paper. But human nature is far too complex to be measured in the simple and direct ways in which physical quantities can be measured, and the over-enthusiastic but unskilled tester is only too likely to make serious mistakes.

CHAPTER XI

EXAMINATIONS

Functions of Examinations.—The chief functions of ordinary written examinations may be summarized as follows :

1. They are employed as tests of achievement, to prove that an individual pupil has, or has not, acquired a certain amount of knowledge of a subject.

2. They are given to a whole class, or school, for a similar purpose, or for assessing the efficiency of the teachers whose pupils are examined. Although ' payment by results ' has disappeared, schools are still commonly judged by the public on the basis of their examination successes. And both head teachers and inspectors try to ensure the maintenance of certain standards by means of periodic oral or written examinations.

3. Many of the most important examinations are assumed to possess a prognostic function, i.e. to be capable of predicting future achievements. Thus they are used to bar the gates between the primary and the secondary school, between the secondary school and the university, between the university and many professions ; and they are supposed to select the few who are best fitted for these higher stages.

4. Many qualities besides achievement, or promise of achievement, in particular scholastic subjects, are believed to manifest themselves in examination success. The business employers who insist that their clerks shall have passed Matriculation or the Leaving Certificate do not actually desire employees who are good at Latin, biology, and the like. When asked why they attach such importance to academic examinations, their answers show that

they hope, rather, to acquire clerks of good general all-round ability in non-academic as well as in academic subjects. They say also that success at an examination requires a certain amount of perseverance and industry, some docility to discipline, and calmness under pressure ; and that these qualities of character are desirable also in their employees (cf. Harding, 1933). The significance attached to a university degree is often almost as variegated. Employers are probably quite as much to blame for the stranglehold of the contemporary examination system as are the teaching profession and the education authorities.

5. Another function of examinations whose existence is seldom explicitly admitted is that they constitute an incentive for stimulating pupils and students to work, particularly in the secondary school and university ; also for keeping teachers up to the mark. Indeed, some would maintain that the prospect of having to do examinations must still be employed as one of the chief motives in education, even if their results are entirely worthless. Clearly, then, examinations are an essential feature of the whole educational system which relies largely upon extraneous motives, such as competition, fear of punishment, and blame. And they can hardly be discarded until the more progressive ideal of appealing to the pupils' or students' spontaneous interests becomes a practical reality.

6. Many American writers (e.g. Kandel, 1936) believe that the only legitimate function of examinations should be that of guidance. By checking up the results of his instruction the teacher can see where he has failed to make some topic clear, and can improve his methods. By examining a pupil's accomplishments he can both diagnose the pupil's weak points which require special attention, and can direct his endeavours along the lines for which he is most suited. Secondary schools and universities should apply examinations to entering candidates, not so as to keep out all but a select few, but to discover the fields of work in which each candidate is likely to do best, and should dissuade

from entering only those who could profit from no kind of advanced study. From so democratic a conception of education our own and other European countries are as yet far removed.

Unfortunately, the traditional written examination fails very badly in its attempts to fulfil these many different functions. We will consider first the criticisms which have been levelled against it, and later ask whether other measuring instruments would serve the purpose better, or whether its adequacy can in any way be improved.

Criticism of the Effects of Examinations upon Education. —The first and commonest complaint is that examinations dominate and distort the whole curriculum. Although scarcely 15% of the primary and preparatory school population enter secondary schools, and only 1·5% eventually reach the university, yet every pupil has to work as if his ultimate objectives were a School Certificate and a university degree. The proportions in Scotland which attain these higher stages of education are more than double those in England, yet the same harmful effects are found. No teacher or school can afford to give to the majority of pupils the knowledge which would be of most value to them in after-life because, as we have seen, both are judged by the results of the minority who must sit examinations concerned almost exclusively with formal, academic subjects. Even the infant schools tend to become preparatory departments for training in the three R's. Homework is set at far too early an age. Brighter children are prematurely promoted, in order that as many successes as possible may be secured in the special place examination. Similarly, for the sake of university scholarships, narrow specialization occurs in the secondary and public schools.

Furthermore, these examinations stimulate an unhealthy, competitive spirit in children, and at all ages they encourage the cramming of set books and rote memorization, rather than education in its best sense. Doubtless they act as an incentive (Function No. 5), but not an incentive to learning for its own sake.   Indeed, examinations are an inefficient type of incentive, since most pupils and students regard them as too remote to bother about until a few weeks or days beforehand.   A few candidates, however, take them much too seriously, or are forced by their parents and teachers to over-work ; with the result that many of the maladjusted children who come to Psychological Clinics for advice and treatment show signs of this examination strain.

Apparently the only reason, apart from mere conservatism, which is put forward to excuse this state of affairs, is the old fallacy of formal discipline.   It is said that although the passing of examinations in academic school subjects is of no direct value to 85% or more of the population, yet the pupils' minds are trained thereby so that they become better able to learn other subjects, to reason, to write good English, and so forth.   A large body of experimental evidence not only proves that this spread of training in one field of study to other fields is usually extremely limited in extent, but also suggests that the very opposite may occur.   The system may indeed train pupils and students in the best methods of passing examinations in other subjects, but it is more likely to stunt ' reasoning power ' owing to its emphasis on mechanical memorization. Often it produces a dislike of everything associated with school, and so discourages the desire for further education. It does not help to develop writing of good English, since the English style in which most examination answers are written is known to be, on the average, markedly inferior to the style in which the same pupils can write compositions at leisure.

INADEQUATE RELIABILITY OF EXAMINATIONS

We will not, however, dwell on these points since, for the purposes of this book, it is a more serious matter that most examinations are very defective methods of measuring the achievements or the future promise which they set out to measure.   Their chief, though not their only, flaw is inadequate reliability. The following facts are well established :

(*a*) When examinees sit two different examinations dealing with the same scholastic subject, both set and marked by the same examiner, they are likely to obtain distinctly different marks on the two occasions.

(*b*) When a single set of scripts is marked by two different examiners, the resulting marks are liable to show wide discrepancies.

The main causes of poor reliability are :

(1) Actual changes in the examinees' mental and physical states which affect their examination performances.

(2) Inadequate sampling of the examinees' knowledge and ability by the particular questions set.

(3) Inconsistencies in the standards of marking adopted by different examiners, or by the same examiner on different occasions.

(4) Differences of opinion between different examiners regarding the relative merit of the examinees' answers.

1. *Changes in the Examinees.*—This was described above (p. 148) as ' function fluctuation.' Two closely parallel examinations sat on consecutive days will always give somewhat divergent results, because some examinees will be feeling more fit, or in a better frame of mind, at the first of the two, others at the second. Many external and irrelevant happenings may temporarily depress or improve the work of a few individuals. Over longer intervals the examinees' abilities will naturally show considerable developments and alterations. On the whole, however, the uncertainties occasioned by such factors are probably smaller and less important than those due to the other three causes.

2. *Inadequate Sampling.*—This factor is responsible for the common complaint among examinees, namely, that the questions ' did not suit them,' that on another set of questions they might do better (or worse). A pupil's capacities in the various special branches or aspects of a subject are always somewhat uneven. And no examina-

tion is capable of bringing out everything that the pupil can do in that subject, or of measuring all his strong and weak points. Hence, the half-dozen or so questions which he answers are never more than a sample of the questions which would be needed to cover the whole field. Common sense, as well as statistical principles, tell us that the more lengthy the examination, and the greater the number of questions, the more representative will the sample be, and the better will the ground be covered. Thus in certain university honours examinations where the students' marks are based on twenty-four hours of examination work, their marks would be unlikely to alter to any great extent if they sat another similar series of papers. But when, as in the special place examination, the pupils only take one short paper in English and one in arithmetic, quite large alterations might easily occur in further parallel papers. The typical correlation coefficient between results on ordinary two-hour papers in the same subject is known, from many experiments, to be no higher than $+ 0.70$, and often less than this. We can therefore predict, by applying the Spearman-Brown formula (p. 147), that examinees would require to take at least four such papers before the ground was sufficiently covered for the reliability coefficient to rise to the fairly respectable figure of $+ 0.90$.

Suppose that one hundred pupils take such an examination, with a reliability coefficient of $+ 0.66$; and that their range of marks is from 30 to 90, their average 60, and their standard deviation 12 marks. The P.E.estim. of an individual mark will then be approximately $\pm 6\%$. Now if this is an examination in which the passing mark is fixed at 70%, we can predict that all those who scored 70 to 75 have an even chance of scoring *below* 70% on a second similar paper, and that those who scored 64 to 69 have an even chance of gaining 70% *or more* on a second paper. This means that only 10 of the pupils would pass according to both papers, 61 would fail on both, and as many as 29 would pass on the first and fail on the second, or vice versa. This hypothetical, but only too typical, illustration demonstrates the unfairness which inevitably results from the lack of thoroughness of many examinations, and in particular the difficulties which arise when the examination is supposed to divide the candidates into two distinct categories at an arbitrary pass mark.

An additional reason for the variability of a pupil's level in answering different questions or sets of questions is that the majority of examination answers consist of English compositions or essays. (This does not usually apply to papers in mathematics or in foreign languages ; but it does to English, history, geography, science, and other subjects.) And the English essay is known to be a particularly variable production. The compositions written by a pupil weekly throughout a school year fluctuate widely in their merits. As Ballard (1923) points out, teachers may refuse to accept this statement, and claim that *their* pupils *are* fairly consistent from week to week. But the fact that a teacher marks any one pupil's work on a dead level probably indicates that, unwittingly, he has formed a stereotyped conception regarding his ability, and is marking the successive compositions not on their own merits but in the light of his knowledge of the pupil's average achievement. The truth of this suggestion is borne out by the many stories of the two pupils who regularly received, one a good, the other a bad, mark, and who continued to do so even when they exchanged their essays.

An outside examiner does not possess this knowledge of the pupil's average work, and so will give poor marks to those who happen to write answers much below their normal level, good marks to those who rise above it. Moreover, under the stress of examination conditions, such deviations are likely to be exaggerated. Probably much more representative products would be forthcoming if the examination could be answered at leisure, under conditions similar to those which apply when pupils do written work at home, or at school.

3. *Divergent Scales of Marks.*—This factor has already been discussed fully in Chaps. II and IV, hence we will not

ause to re-argue the illogicality and injustice of a system which permits a far higher proportion of passes, or a higher verage mark, to be awarded in one university or School ertificate subject than in another subject. If a mark of 0%, or a first class or credit, signifies to one examiner the tandard achieved by a quarter of the examinees, and to nother the standard reached by only 1% of the examinees, hen it is obvious that this mark means different things o different people. And it follows that an examinee's nark will vary with the particular examiner who happens o read his papers, unless all the marks given by all the xaminers are uniformly standardized in accordance with he principles outlined above.

The standards of marking even of a single examiner are able to alter with fatigue and mood. When marking arge numbers of answers to the same question, he may egin very strictly and gradually become more lenient, or ice versa. The same script might receive a different nark if read after, instead of before, dinner.

4. *Differences in Opinion as to Relative Merit.*—The most mportant source of unreliability (which is usually found n combination with No. 3) is the personal element which nters into every examiner's evaluation of a script. We vill first summarize some of the evidence regarding this ubjectivity. The classical experiments were carried out n America as far back as 1912. Starch and Elliot (1913) ent copies of a single geometry paper to the chief geometry eachers of 116 high schools, with the request that they hould mark it in accordance with their usual practice. The marks awarded varied all the way from 28% to 92%. Two of the teachers gave it more than 90%, 18 gave it etween 80% and 90%, 18 gave it between 60% and 30%, nd 2 under 30%. Similar results were obtained with apers in English and in history. Equally striking is the necdote related by Wood (1921) of the papers which were narked in the usual way by six examiners. The first xaminer, for his own guidance, wrote out a set of (what he egarded as) model answers to the questions ; but he un-

fortunately left this among the candidates' papers. He was subsequently awarded marks varying from 40 % to 90 % by the other five examiners ! Many experiments, con ducted under far more strictly controlled conditions than these, have substantially confirmed their findings.   Euro pean educationists, however, were so little impressed by them, that it was necessary for further elaborate studies to be carried out recently in England and in France, under the auspices of the International Examinations Enquiry Committee.

Hartog and Rhodes (1935) arranged for typical groups of scripts to be marked by experienced examiners under normal examination conditions.   Special place, School Certificate, and university honours examinations were represented, and several different subjects were studied Generalizing from a number of their results, it appears that when half a dozen examiners independently mark a set of scripts, the lowest and highest marks given to any one script differ on the average by about 10 to 12 %. Among a few of the scripts the discrepancies may be quite small, but among others they may be far larger, often greater than 20 %. The authors show that part of the divergence may be ascribed to the different standards of leniency adopted by different examiners (No. 3, above), but that even when this factor is eliminated, large variations remain. In several of the experiments the examiners drew up an agreed scheme of instructions for marking, listing both the general characteristics and the detailed points which were to be looked for in the scripts.   In the marking of English compositions, where this was scarcely possible, the incon- sistencies were much greater.

Now Hartog and Rhodes doubtless desired to shock the public conscience with regard to examinations, and so did their best to emphasize the disagreements.[1]   The present

[1] As most reviewers of *An Examination of Examinations* pointed out, some of the experiments were rendered quite futile by the selection of unduly homogeneous sets of scripts for the examiners to mark.

writer is more impressed by the smallness than by the largeness of the discrepancies, and would conclude from his study of the results that important public examinations, like the School Certificate and university honours, are marked much more consistently than is usually the case. Instead of laying their chief emphasis on the extreme discrepancies, the authors might have pointed out that the median disagreement between any two examiners is not more than 3% in the best-conducted examinations. Since this figure represents the Probable Error of an examinee's mark, a few examinees will naturally show discrepancies four or five times as large. It represents an average correlation between different examiners of $+ 0.80$, when the standard deviation of their marks is 10%. And decidedly lower figures have been obtained by other investigators. The authors also omit to point out that the reliability of an examinee's final total mark is generally very much higher than their results indicate, since it may be based on half a dozen or more papers, each marked by two or more examiners. Their results mostly refer to single three-hour, or two two-hour, papers.

Nevertheless, this study deserves to be taken very seriously, since it indicates that the special place, and other less thorough, examinations are deplorably unreliable ; that in the absence of a scheme of instructions drawn up and applied by experienced examiners, much worse discrepancies may arise ; that when the average and the dispersion of marks are not standardized, gross differences may appear in the proportions of Credits, Passes, Fails, etc., which are awarded ; and that even a P.E. of 3% may frequently make all the difference between a Pass and a Fail, or a First and a Second Class.

Another example will be quoted which better illustrates the subjectivity of marking under ordinary school conditions. Boyd (1924) collected large numbers of essays on ' A Day at the Seaside ' from 11-year-old Scottish schoolchildren (i.e. children at the qualifying stage). From these he selected 26 as representing the whole range of merit, and

16

had them marked independently by 271 teachers. The marks were not numerical, but consisted of seven grades, ranging from Excellent to Unsatisfactory. On comparing the results of different markers, it was found that almost every essay received at least 6 of the 7 possible grades. The following instance is typical : 3 teachers marked it Excellent ; 31 VG +, 80 VG, 125 G +, 28 G, and 4 marked it Moderate (the lowest grade but one). Boyd shows that part of the discrepancy was due to differing standards. But even when the 20% most lenient markers and the 20% most severe were excluded, the average essay was still awarded at least 4 out of the 7 grades. He also points out that the *average* grade given to an essay by a large number of markers is highly consistent, and that the various divergent individual grades are distributed around this average more or less in accordance with the normal distribution curve.

Other experiments, including one of Hartog's, indicate that when the same examiner re-marks a set of scripts after an interval, the discrepancies between his first and second opinions are likely to be almost as great as those between two independent examiners. Some of the studies by the French members of the International Examinations Enquiry are also worth quoting. A set of papers in science were marked by three trained scientists (one of them doing it twice over), and also by a student who had no scientific training. When the markings were compared, the average correlation coefficient between the scientists was + 0·63, whilst the correlations between the student and the scientists averaged + 0·51. The latter figure is lower than the former, but so little lower that it casts some suspicion on the value of an examiner's knowledge of his subject.

Particularly striking was a study of the philosophy examination in the Baccalauréat. One hundred scripts were marked by six examiners. Only 10 of the candidates were passed by all the examiners, only 9 failed by all of them. The remaining 71 were passed by some, failed by others.[1] It is, of course, always the examinees of medium ability whose true standing is most uncertain. The few best or few worst are recognized as such by all examiners. But only too frequently an arbitrary dividing line—the pass mark—has to be erected in the middle of this region of maximum uncertainty. Undoubtedly, therefore, a large number of candidates who *just* succeed, or *just* fail, to gain a School Certificate or a special place might very easily obtain the opposite result if they were marked by a different examiner, or if they sat an alternative set of papers. In many instances their whole educational or vocational career may be blighted owing to the unreliability of their marks.

Reasons for the Subjectivity of Marks.—The prime reason for the discrepancies which we have described is that different markers conceive differently the desirable or undesirable characteristics of examination answers. In other words, they attempt to assess many diverse types of abilities. One examiner may give chief credit for evidence of work done, and for the comprehensiveness and accuracy of the facts contained in the answers. Another may look rather for signs of future promise, originality, and grasp of general principles. One may insist on clarity of expression of ideas, another may try to assess the profoundness of the ideas irrespective of their good or bad expression. Some may search for emotional rather than strictly intellectual qualities, such as the examinee's interest in the subject. Whenever a candidate states his attitudes or opinions, these are liable to coincide, or clash with, the attitudes or opinions of the examiner; and however desirous the examiner may be of maintaining impartiality, he is liable to bias if his pet theories are approved or attacked by the candidates. Often, if he would take the trouble to formulate explicitly his notion of the aim of the examination, he would find that he means by a good examinee the one who closely approximates to himself, and as a poor candidate

[1] This result suggests that the correlation between any pair of examiners averaged only + 0·60.

the one who shows none of the intellectual or emotiona
qualities which he himself idealizes. Is it to be wondered
then, that different examiners differ in their opinions of a
candidate ?

We must recognize that any one script may manifest an
extreme complexity of features, good and bad, and so can
be looked at from a multitude of different points of view
Its merit can never be assessed in the same way that a
physical object is measured. An examiner ordinaril
splits it up into its chief components, notes the facts whic
it contains or omits, its elements of originality, style o
expression, the mechanics of its grammar or computation
and so on. He attaches a certain weight to each of thes
possible components (a weight which is likely to be highl
individualistic, unless a detailed scheme of marking ha
been adopted), and finally re-synthesizes the candidate
performance on each component into a single mark for th
answer as a whole. Some examiners do not attempt
systematic analysis of this kind, and merely mark on th
basis of a general impression. But as Ballard (1923) an
Hamilton (1929) show, every general impression involves
more or less vague analysis.

Even in such subjects as arithmetic, or the translatio
of foreign languages, the weightings assigned to the variou
analysable features of an answer, and the penalties given t
various possible mistakes, are liable to differ among di
ferent markers. But the complexity is far greater in th
case of English composition, or in those subjects such a
history, science, etc., where the answers consist chiefly o
compositions. The essay-type of answer has been ver
widely, and justifiably, criticized. Examinees have t
waste a large proportion of the available time in translatin
their historical or scientific knowledge into readable essa
form, and in the mere process of writing. This latter
particularly unfair, because some can write much faste
than others without necessarily being better historians o
scientists. A considerable proportion of the written word
(for instance, the a's, the's, and's, etc.) add nothing to th

evidence of the examinee's good or poor ability. Investigation shows that the average examinee puts into writing less than one fact or idea per minute of examination time, since the process of expressing these facts or ideas takes so long. The examiner, then, has the still more difficult task of translating the product back again, of trying to penetrate through the verbiage to the signs of ability and knowledge beneath. Few examiners can remain entirely uninfluenced by the literary style or the handwriting of an answer (there is direct experimental proof of this), although they are presumably trying to mark the product for its historical or scientific merit, not *qua* essay.

INADEQUATE VALIDITY OF EXAMINATIONS

The poor reliability of examinations greatly reduces their value for any and every purpose. For if they cannot even measure examination success without serious errors, they naturally cannot validly predict anything else. Even, however, if perfect reliability were established, validity would still be diminished by the dependence of examination success on factors other than ability, knowledge, and industry.

One such factor is, obviously, the efficiency of the examinee's teachers as examination coaches, and their cleverness in guessing the kinds of questions which examiners will set. It is manifestly unfair that a pupil at one school, where the teachers are specially adept at instilling examination knowledge, should succeed when a pupil of equal ability fails because he attends another school, where the teachers are either less skilled, or more humane in the education which they provide.

There is also the old complaint that some pupils are 'good examinees,' while others become unduly 'nervous,' and 'fail to do themselves justice.' One wonders whether it is not usually the weaker candidates who make this complaint, and whether they would do better if subjected to any other kind of test, including the tests of real life. However, we may admit that certain temperamental

qualities, which we can as yet hardly specify, together
with good physical health, may confer some advantage on
certain candidates, which other candidates lack.

Examinations, then, certainly fail to fulfil the first two
functions with which we started, namely, the measurement
of achievement, both because of poor reliability and
because of the other considerations just mentioned. How
imperfect they are we cannot determine. We can, however, study their validity as measures of future ability by
directly correlating their marks with the results of the same
pupils at later stages in their careers. Comprehensive
investigations into this matter have been carried out by
Valentine and Emmett (1932), with almost uniformly dis-
heartening results. By comparing the subsequent secondary school achievement of groups of pupils who had been
awarded, or who had failed to obtain, scholarships at the
time of the special place examination, it was found that
many of the latter ultimately surpassed the former group.
Similarly, at the university level, Valentine found that
roughly two-fifths of all those awarded scholarships failed
to justify their promise, since they eventually obtained
only third-class honours or pass degrees. They were
beaten by as many as one-third of the non-scholars, who
achieved first- or second-class honours. Of those who won
scholarships given by the universities, only about one-
fifth failed to live up to expectations, of State scholars only
one-tenth. But this meant that practically one-half of
those who obtained other types of scholarships (from their
schools or from local authorities) did not justify themselves
(cf. Valentine, 1938).

In a further study by the Scottish Council for Research
in Education (1936), marks gained by secondary school
pupils at the Leaving Certificate examination, together
with teachers' marks and the head masters' estimates of
the pupils' general standing, were correlated with subsequent class marks and degree marks at the universities.
It was found that on the whole those who got first-class
honours had been rated higher by the school head masters

than those who got second class, and that honours students had been rated higher than ordinary degree students ; but that, as in Valentine's research, there were a great many exceptions. The actual correlation coefficients between school and university marks varied from about + 0·30 to + 0·70, and the average of several such results was + 0·48. In the light of our discussion of correlations (Chap. VII), this figure implies very poor predictive validity.

It should be remembered, however, that the above investigations (together with most of the studies of reliability) dealt with highly selected groups. A random sample of the population might be expected to show a range of ability at least twice as great as that of university students. This means that, if it were possible for a random sample to receive a secondary and university education, and to take both the Leaving Certificate, or entrance scholarship, examinations and the degree examinations, the coefficient of + 0·48 might rise to + 0·75 or more (cf. p. 140).

It would be unreasonable to expect perfect correlations between marks at successive stages in pupils' careers, since the subjects studied at a secondary school differ distinctly from those studied at a primary or preparatory school, even when called by the same names. And the conditions of work at a university differ from those at a school, being more congenial to some, less stimulating to others. Again, every individual changes to some extent as he grows older, some of his abilities becoming relatively weaker, new ones developing. All in all, then, the inability of entrance and scholarship examinations to choose those candidates who will profit most from higher education is not very surprising to the psychologist. Yet their validity for this purpose is certainly much poorer than is generally supposed by the educational authorities who set the examinations, and who base their awards and selections upon them. The universities would scarcely continue to dictate the present constitution of the School Certificate, Leaving Certificate, and Matriculation examinations, if they did not believe that these instruments picked out the most suitable entrants.

Still more unjustified is the belief embodied in the fourth of the functions outlined above (p. 165), namely that these examinations are adequate criteria of vocational fitness. It is indeed true, as employers assert, that successful candidates will on the average be better in general all-round ability than those who have failed to gain the Certificates, since all scholastic abilities are to some extent positively correlated with intelligence. It is probably true, also, that vocationally desirable temperamental and character qualities may aid in examination success. But so do a great many other factors. Some pupils with extremely undesirable characters may do well at examinations through intellectual brilliance ; others through efficient coaching on the part of their teachers, or through over-cramming ; still others through the pure chance factors introduced by the subjectivity of marking and other forms of unreliability. The conclusion follows, then, that success or failure may depend on so many diverse qualities, that it does not provide trustworthy evidence of any of them. The employer would be far better advised to make use of the services of a scientific vocational psychologist, who would measure or obtain the best available assessments, both of intelligence and other aptitudes, of educational achievements and of temperamental traits ; and would give each of these qualities its due weight in deciding on the suitability of prospective employees. Undoubtedly the adoption of a similar scientific study of each individual candidate for secondary or university education would lead to many more just selections, and more accurate predictions of future achievement, than do the present methods.

Although this chapter has consisted mainly of destructive criticism, certain hints have been given as to possible ways and means of improving examinations. These will be followed up, and expanded in the next, and in the final, chapters.

CHAPTER XII

RELATIVE ADVANTAGES OF NEW-TYPE AND ESSAY-TYPE EXAMINATIONS

It has been widely claimed that the worst defects of the traditional type of written examination may be overcome by adopting in its place the objective or new-type test for measuring achievement. Such tests came into common use in the United States many years ago, but are still little known in this country, in spite of Ballard's (1923) able advocacy. Americans, however, realize now that they also are liable to certain defects when used undiscriminatingly, and that there are still functions which can better be performed by the old- or essay-type of examination. Thus we are in a position to profit both from their researches and from their errors, to devise our tests in accordance with the principles they have already worked out, and to apply them to the fields of educational measurement where they will be most useful and most valid.

Now it is clear that some educational products can be marked much more objectively and reliably than others. In the early stages of school arithmetic, when children are given a series of short sums to do, there is no subjective element involved in deciding which ones, and how many, they do correctly. But before long arithmetic becomes more complex ; each sum involves a number of different operations, partial credits are essential, and different markers are now liable to differ. An English composition, or an examination answer written in essay form, brings in a still greater personal element, since it is still more complex and cannot ever be considered merely from the point of view of right or wrong. The new-type tester argues, therefore, let us refrain from setting sums or essay questions which involve many operations, and instead ask questions which evoke each operation separately, questions to which only one right answer is possible. And instead of leaving to the marker's personal taste the analysis which must be made of a complex product, and the weighting which must be attached to its component elements, let the person who sets the questions make the analysis beforehand, and decide systematically just now many marks (i.e. how many questions) shall be allotted to each element.

Advantages of New-type Examinations.—So we arrive at the new-type examination which contains a large number of brief questions, instead of a few long ones. Every question is so arranged that all markers will agree as to the rightness or wrongness of an answer. This elimination of the personal element is not the only advantage. For the hundred or more questions of the new-type test are capable of sampling the whole field of knowledge much more comprehensively than can the half-dozen or so questions of the orthodox examination. Candidates can no longer complain that the particular questions failed to suit them, since all their strong and weak points are probed. This fact should help to reduce the ' spotting ' and cramming of likely questions. Again, the subjectivity of standards of marking need no longer cause trouble, since the examinees' marks are pure ' count scores ' (cf. p. 24). So long as the questions are designed to cover all levels of difficulty evenly, the distribution of marks is sure to approximate to normality, and can readily be converted into any desired percentage or other scale. The examiner may, of course, draw an arbitrary pass line at any point in the distribution that he wishes, so as to cut off the examinees who fail to come up to his minimum standards.

A full description of the various sorts of questions which may be employed in new-type tests is given in the next chapter. Here it will be sufficient to distinguish between the so-called ' open ' or ' recall ' type of question and the ' closed ' or ' recognition ' type. In the former the desired answer consists of a single word, or a few words, or numbers, which the examinee must write either in a space provided on the examination paper itself, or on a separate sheet.   Questions 1–16 on pp. 240–1 are of this type.   Since, however, there is always some danger of partially right or alternative answers being given, whose marking would involve subjective judgment, the other type of question is more commonly adopted, where the examinee has to identify the right answer from among two or more answers printed on the examination paper.   Either he may underline or put a check beside the answer he believes to be correct, or else merely write down its letter or number.   Questions 17–54 on pp. 241–6 are of this type.

This latter system has the additional advantage that practically all writing is eliminated.   So that when geography or history is being examined, irrelevant factors such as speed of writing or literary style do not distort the examiner's marking.   It has been claimed that the average examinee, instead of expressing less than one idea or fact per minute (as in an essay-paper), can deal with three to six new-type questions a minute.   But this naturally depends on the level of difficulty of the questions.   A further advantage is that the examinee who knows scarcely anything about the subject, but who bluffs by 'free-associating' around an essay-type question, and who often gains several marks by doing so, is entirely foiled.   Older students realize how much fairer is the new-type test, and on the whole prefer it to the orthodox examination. Younger pupils, also, according to several American investigations, enjoy it more.

A short test is appended below, dealing with the subject-matter of the previous chapters in this book, which the reader is advised to try to answer.   It is not meant to be a complete examination on mental testing and statistics (hence it violates several of the rules of construction given in the next chapter).   But it introduces several of the main varieties of new-type questions, some easy, some fairly difficult, and should give the reader who is not already familiar with such questions a better insight into them.

Nos. 1–8 are simple-recall type, Nos. 9–16 completion type, Nos. 17–25 true-false type, Nos. 26–36 multiple-choice type, Nos. 37–47 matching type, and Nos. 48–54 rearrangement type. The correct answers are listed on pp. 290–1.

EXAMINATION ON MENTAL MEASUREMENT AND STATISTICS. Time : One Hour

Please read the following directions carefully before starting :
Answer as many questions as possible, in any order. The answers should be written in the right-hand margin on the blank spaces provided. Any rough figuring may be done on blank paper.

The answer to every question (except Nos. 37–42) consists of *one* letter, word, or number.

You may guess if you are not certain of an answer; but as marks will be deducted for wrong answers, random guessing is not advisable.

1. Eight pupils obtained the following school marks :

A	B	C	D	E	F	G	H
15	10	12	10	9	12	10	18

  What is their median ? . . . .
2. If the above marks were put into rank order form, what would B's rank position be ?. . . . .
3–5. The following is an extract from the norms for a group intelligence test :

Score .	.	48	58	68	77	84	89	93
Mental Age .		9	10	11	12	13	14	15 and adult

  What are the respective intelligence quotients of :
  3. A child aged 8·0 who scores 77 ? . . ..
  4. A child aged 10·0 who scores 63 ? . . ..
  5. An adult aged 20·0 who scores 77 ? . ...
6–8. In a certain secondary school all the marks are transposed into the following standard scale. A pupil obtains marks of 60%, 47%, and 63% respectively in English, French, and Mathematics. In his English class there are 41 pupils, in his French class 35, and in his Mathematics class 44.

Percentile			Mark
90	.	.	. 73%
75	.	.	. 67%
50	.	.	. 60%
25	.	.	. 53%
10	.	.	. 47%

What is his approximate place (i.e. his rank position in the class) in :

6. English ? . . . .
7. French ? . . . .
8. Mathematics ? . . . .

9–16. In each of the numbered spaces in the following paragraph, one word or letter is needed to complete the statements. Do not write anything in the actual spaces, but opposite No. 9 in the right-hand margin write the word or letter which is needed to fill up space (9). Fill in the other words or letters similarly.

The compensation theory of mental organization is disproved by the fact that all correlations between mental abilities are (9). The results of correlational investigations also disprove the view that the mind is made up of distinct (10). The Two-factor theory, proposed by (11), regards each ability as made up of a factor common to all abilities, called (12), and a factor (13) to that ability alone, called *s*. However, when verbal tests, performance tests, and other tests of intelligence are compared, it is doubtful whether (14) will account for all the inter-correlations. Residual correlations indicate the presence of (15) factors, such as verbal ability, *v*, and practical ability (16).

9. . . . .
10. . . . .
11. . . . .
12. . . . .
13. . . . .
14. . . . .
15. . . . .
16. . . . .

17–25. Write a + sign in the margin after any of the following statements which are true, and a — sign after those which are false.

17. An omnibus test is a group intelligence test in which items of many kinds are mixed up . . . .

18. A majority of very dull children are below average in health and physical development . . . .

19. Performance tests are applied by psychologists chiefly in order to measure a child's practical ability in everyday life . . . .

20. In order to measure the average intelligence of a class of 7-year-old children, a teacher would be best advised to use a group test with pictorial material . . . .

21. In a normal frequency distribution curve the semi-interquartile range and the standard deviation are identical . ...

22. University students who obtain scholarships on the basis of competitive examinations as often as not obtain no better degree marks than those who fail to win such scholarships . . ..

23. The advantage of scoring abilities in terms of Mental Age or Educational Age is that the units of measurement are all equal to one another . . ..

24. A group of a hundred children picked out as being especially superior in one school subject will practically never show as great an amount of average superiority in any other subject . ...

25. The Probable Error of a pupil's English composition mark is generally likely to be smaller than that of his arithmetic mark . . . .

26–36. Write the letter (A, B, or C, etc.) of the correct answer in the margin.

26. Group intelligence tests, as contrasted with the Stanford-Binet test, are : ....

(A) More varied in content
(B) Better measures of children's intelligence
(C) More objectively scored
(D) More difficult to apply
(E) Less suitable for application to superior adults

27–32. A set of 51 pupils took three examinations, A, B, and C. The following distributions of marks were obtained :

Mark	A	B	C
87 + .	. 1	1	3
80 + .	. 3	2	5
73 + .	. 4	4	7
66 + .	. 18	7	11
59 + .	. 17	11	11
52 + .	. 5	14	8
45 + .	. 2	9	4
38 + .	. 1	3	2
	51	51	51

27. Which of the distributions approximates fairly closely to normal, A, B, C, or None ? . . . .

28. Which of the distributions is negatively skewed, A, B, C, or None ? ....

29. Which of the distributions is likely to have the smallest standard deviation ? . . . .

30. A certain pupil happened to get 70% on all three examinations. In which of them did he do relatively best ? . . . .

31. If you were calculating the average of Distribution C, what figure would you take as your arbitrary mean ? . . . .

32. In calculating this same average, what figure would be multiplied by 2 (i.e. by the number of pupils who scored 38 +) ? . . . .

33. A group intelligence test was applied in a secondary school, and the occupational preferences of all the pupils were ascertained and classified under ten headings. In order to find whether there is any correspondence between occupational preference and intelligence, which of the following statistical techniques could best be applied ? ....

(A) Biserial r.

(B) Product moment correlation.

(C) Analysis of variance.

(D) Contingency coefficient.

(E) Correlation ratio.

(F) Multiple correlation.

34. Which is the *least* serious of the following defects in intelligence quotients obtained from group intelligence tests ? ....

(A) Group test scores are considerably affected by previous practice on similar tests.

(B) The standard deviation of group test I.Q.s differs considerably in different tests.

(C) Few of the published tests are adequately standardized, or have reliable norms.

(D) Group tests are generally given with a time limit, and the child who is quickest is not necessarily the most intelligent.

35. Which *one* of the following statements is untrue ? The distribution of marks given by an examiner to a class of fifty pupils may be very irregular or skewed because : ....

(A) The number of cases is too small for a smooth, normal distribution to be expected.

(B) The examiner's opinion of the relative merits of the compositions is a personal one.

(C) The pupils' abilities may be asymmetrically distributed, as when, for example, the class contains a long tail.

(D) The scale of marks which the examiner adopts may be lacking in any rational basis.

36. In an experiment on the scores of graduate and non-graduate teachers on verbal and non-verbal group intelligence tests, these results were obtained :

	Verbal Tests	Non-verbal Tests
Graduates . . .	153·9	78·6
Non-graduates . .	143·5	77·0
P.E. of the difference between means . .	2·1	1·2

Which of the following conclusions may legitimately be drawn ? ....

(A) Graduates do better than non-graduates at intelligence tests.

(B) All teachers do better at verbal than at non-verbal tests.

(C) Scores on verbal tests are improved by taking a university degree.

(D) Teachers with university training have no appreciable advantage over others on non-verbal tests.

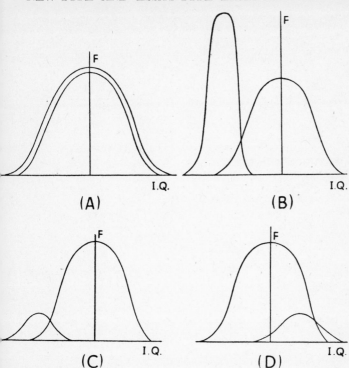

37–41. The above pairs of curves (A–D) represent the approximate frequency distributions of the intelligence quotients of various groups of children. Below are listed several such groups. Opposite four of them write the letter of the pair of curves which corresponds. Write ' None ' opposite the groups to which no pair of curves corresponds.

37. One thousand elementary school pupils, and one thousand special school pupils . . . .

38. All elementary school pupils and all special school pupils in the country . . . .

39. All elementary school pupils and all children in the country . . . .

40. All special school and all secondary school pupils in the country . . . .

41. All elementary school and all secondary school pupils in the country . . . .

17

42–47. Below is given a list of psychologists (A–F), togethe
with a list of important pieces of work in educationa
psychology. After each of the latter write the letter o
the psychologist who was mainly responsible for, or whom
you chiefly associate with, this piece of work. Tw
letters may be written if two psychologists were pro
minently associated. Some letters may be used twice o
more, some not at all.

(A) Ballard
(B) Binet
(C) Burt
(D) Drever-Collins
(E) Terman
(F) Thurstone

42. Development of the conception of the Intelligence Quotient . . . .

43. Development of a scale of performance tests . . . .

44. Investigations by correlations into the factors underlying abilities . . . .

45. Advocacy of new-type examinations . . . .

46. Construction of educational attainments tests . . . .

47. Re-standardization of the Binet-Simon scale . . . .

48–54. An arithmetic test, a handwriting test, and two grou
intelligence tests were given to an ordinary school class
and the following inter-correlations were worked out :

(A) Combined intelligence tests with handwriting test
(B) Combined intelligence tests with arithmetic test.
(C) Combined intelligence tests with chronological age
(D) One intelligence test with the other.
(E) Arithmetic test with handwriting test.
(F) Handwriting test with chronological age.
(G) One intelligence test with arithmetic test.

Which pair would you expect to yield :

48. The highest correlation ? . . . .
49. The second highest ? . . . .
50. The third ? . . . .
51. The fourth ? . . . .
52. The fifth ? . . . .
53. The sixth ? . . . .
54. The lowest correlation ? . . . .

DEFECTS OF NEW-TYPE EXAMINATIONS

So far only the advantages of new-type examination
have been mentioned, and we must now consider criticism

of them in detail. Two minor objections will be admitted at once. First, the cost of printing or duplicating a new-type test is considerably greater than that of an essay-type examination. For classroom purposes, however, oral presentation of the questions can often be adopted. If several groups of pupils or students are to be examined, they can write their answers on blank sheets, and their test papers can be used several times over.

Secondly, much greater time and skill are needed for constructing a *good* new-type test. The major criticisms which are to be discussed below apply only too often to inferior tests which have been rapidly constructed by inexperienced amateurs. It is highly desirable that teachers should be trained in the principles of testing during their training college courses. The time needed in setting a paper is, however, more than offset by the time saved in marking, when the number of examinees is large. Indeed, since the marking should be fool-proof, there is no reason why it should not be done by clerks or secretaries. In large public examinations, the authorities could save much expense by paying professional examiners only to set, not to correct, the papers. The present writer finds that the construction of a one-hour's new-type test in educational psychology (such as that appended above) takes him about twenty hours. Setting an essay-examination scarcely needs one hour. But in marking these one-hour examinations he can easily do thirty of the former as against ten or less of the latter scripts per hour. He, therefore, finds no saving in total hours of work unless the number of examinees approximates to 300 or more. But the setting of a new-type test is a fascinating occupation, which can be done in odd moments throughout the year ; and the marking is simply a routine matter which involves no mental strain. By contrast, the marking of large numbers of essay-type scripts in psychology is the most trying work that he ever has to do.

The Guessing Factor.—Next we must admit that examinees may obtain a certain number of correct answers (in a recognition-type test) by pure chance guessing. If they filled in answers at random they would, on the average, achieve half-marks on the questions where two responses are provided (such as the true-false type), and quarter-marks on the questions where four responses are provided. This fact disturbs the teacher far more than it does the psychologist. For the latter realizes that every examinee has the same chance of scoring, let us say, 35%, by random guessing; he therefore regards 35% as the effective zero point and only gives credit to scores above this level. An alternative procedure, which comes to much the same thing, but is fairer in that it does not penalize the examinee who omits questions rather than guess them, is to subtract the total wrong responses in true-false questions from the total right ones; to subtract half the total wrong in three-response questions, one-third in four-response questions, and so on. That is to say, an examinee's score corrected for guessing $= R - \dfrac{W}{n-1}$, where R is the total right, W the total wrong, and n is the number of alternative responses provided in each question. In general practice the correction is omitted in four- or more response questions, since it is so small.

But the problem of guessing is a complex one which cannot be entirely settled by this mechanical correction. It has aroused widespread controversy, and a long discussion of it may be found in Ruch (1929). Although the above correction will compensate for the effects of guessing in the *average* examinee, yet it will not do so in all cases, since some will be luckier than others, in accordance with the principles of probability. Suppose that a large group of persons guesses the responses to ten true-false items; the average person will get 5 of them right, and one-half the group will get either 4, 5, or 6 right.[1] Only about one person in a thousand will be so lucky as to get 10 right,

---

[1] The situation is effectively the same as getting the persons each to toss a penny ten times, and counting up how many of them obtain 0, 1, 2, . . ., 9, 10, heads.

r so unlucky as to hit on none of the right answers. If he guessing correction is applied, the scores corresponding o 10, 6, 5, 4, and 0 right will be + 10, + 2, 0, — 2, and — 10 respectively. In a longer test the range of chance cores which may arise from guessing will be still greater, lthough their average (when corrected) will still be zero. Jndoubtedly, then, we must expect true-false tests to be omewhat unreliable, but the effect will be less marked in ests composed of three- or four-response items. Experimental evidence does indeed show true-false tests to be less eliable than multiple-choice tests ; and the latter are less eliable than tests made up of recall items. But the differnce between them is not large, and it may easily be offset y the fact that a true-false test can contain more items han a multiple-choice test which occupies the same length f time, since true-false items can be answered more quickly.

Now, though we must allow that a considerable error nay occur among the scores of a small proportion of xaminees on account of guessing, in actual practice ntirely random guessing (which was assumed in the previous paragraph) will very seldom occur. The examinee s more likely to possess an incomplete knowledge of certain items, sufficient, however, to make his guesses right ones. Teachers may regard it as unfair that such an xaminee will obtain the same marks on those items as vill the more able examinee who really knows the right answers. But a brief study of recognition-type questions, uch as those given above, will show that the examinee's haky knowledge may not always be to his advantage. For the alternative (wrong) answers are usually worded ufficiently plausibly to deceive the weak student. Hence ais ' semi-guesses ' will in practice be very frequently vrong. For this reason experimental researches indicate hat the guessing correction fully compensates, or even ver-compensates, for any advantages which the weak tudent might gain by guessing. Other investigations rove that the amount of guessing may be greatly reduced,

and the reliability and validity of the test slightly in
creased, by instructing examinees not to guess, and by
warning them that wrong guesses will be penalized.

To sum up : random guessing may considerably distor
the marks on a recognition-type test, especially when the
questions provide only two alternative answers.   It does
not actually do so to any great extent, partly because
guessing scarcely ever is random, partly because it can be
reduced by appropriate instructions, and partly because
such tests can include large numbers of items which make
for increased reliability.   If the recognition-type of item
is to be condemned, it must be primarily on account of
some of the other reasons discussed below.

Suggestive Effects of Wrong Responses.—Another common
criticism which we can refute is that the presentation of
false statements and wrong answers to the suggestible
minds of pupils is pedagogically unsound.   It is alleged
that they may absorb such statements and later on believe
them to be correct.   This theory is an *a priori* one, and
experiments which have been devised to try it out have
always failed to provide confirmation.   Probably the fact
that examinees know that about half the true-false state
ments, and more of the multiple-choice responses, are
wrong is sufficient to offset the effects of suggestion
Many teachers find that there is considerable pedagogica
value in getting pupils and students to correct their own
papers shortly after the test, so letting them see which
responses are wrong (cf. Ballard, 1923).

The Elementaristic Tendency in New-type Tests.—We
come now to the most obvious and most frequent objection
to new-type tests.   It is said that they measure only the
most trivial aspects of ability, such as details of informa
tion and fragments of knowledge.   Such tests may indeed
analyse complex mental operations into elements which can
be objectively marked, but they cannot put the elements
together again, and in the process of analysis they omit
many of the most important aspects of ability.   They
cannot, as can the essay-type of examination, show the

examinees' general understanding of the subject, nor his interpretation of facts, his capacity for organizing and formulating his knowledge, nor his initiative and originality. Far from reducing the tendency of examinees to cram mechanically, they may increase the amount of rote memorization and discourage any desire to achieve a general grasp of the field. Investigation has, indeed, shown that students revise their work in a different manner when they know they are to sit a new-type examination, and that they concentrate on acquiring such bits of knowledge as are most likely to appear in the test questions.

Such criticisms embody a number of half-truths, and may be countered by a number of arguments. The retort may first be made that even if the new-type test cannot measure ' understanding, originality, etc.,' the essay examination cannot do so either. For when examiners come to assess such qualities, they disagree widely with one another. The orthodox examination achieves a reasonable degree of reliability when it most close approximates to a new-type test, i.e. when it asks primarily for factual data, or when the examiners draw up a detailed analytic scheme of the points which they wish to mark. Secondly, it may be pointed out that examinees engaged on an essay examination do not usually shine in regard to organization of knowledge and original thinking. Rather they dash down all the ideas and facts which they can recall, many of them irrelevant. ' Thinking ' as contrasted with ' reproduction of items of information ' is at a minimum. The new-type test taps all the relevant knowledge, with much less waste of time, and prevents the candidate from producing irrelevant material.

Such recriminations are also, however, only partially justified. Though often true of present-day examinations, they would be less applicable if the recommendations made in Chap. XIV were put into effect. Much sounder is the argument which points to weaknesses in the critics' psychological analysis of the contrasted examinations. They commonly draw a sharp distinction between information and reproduction, on the one hand, and understanding and thinking, on the other hand. They assume, that is, that these mental processes are uncorrelated. In actual practice the two cannot be separated so readily. The acquisition and reproduction of information always involves a certain amount of thinking, and no thinking is possible unless a person possesses information to think about. Hence, experiments in which attempts have been made to measure these faculties separately have usually shown them to be highly inter-correlated. It follows, therefore, that even when a new-type test is apparently measuring nothing but information, it is at the same time providing a pretty good measure of other more complex types of ability. It cannot ask examinees to ' Discuss . . ., Compare . . ., etc.,' nor make any overt provision for independent thinking, yet it is certainly drawing to a considerable extent upon these ' higher ' mental processes which the orthodox examiner desires to assess. Conversely, a large proportion of the average essay-type answer consists of the sort of material which critics affect to despise when it is accurately measured by new-type tests.

The overlapping between the two kinds of mental processes is further demonstrated by the fact that a new-type response, or a sentence in an essay answer, may depend upon ' understanding ' in one examinee, but may result from ' facile reproduction ' in another examinee, according to the respective methods by which these examinees have studied the topic in question. Nevertheless, it seems legitimate to make a partial distinction between the two types, and to expect future experimental investigations to establish more precisely the nature of the difference. At least we can admit that examinees have more opportunity of displaying ' higher ' mental processes in essay-type than in most new-type examinations. And we must remember that, even if they do not usually write good English in their essay papers, yet they would probably never learn to write English at all if new-type examinations became the sole method of testing their abilities.

The reason why the criticisms of triviality and fragmentariness seem at first sight so justifiable and so serious is because many new-type tests are incompetently constructed. Questions which ask for bits of information are much the easiest to set, and, therefore, do only too frequently constitute the bulk of home-made examinations. But there is nothing inherent in new-type examining which makes better questions unattainable. And the writer would claim that at least half the questions in his own test, above, do demand not only the possession of information, but also the application of principles or the interpretation of information; that is to say, ' understanding.'

To conclude, then, the defect which we have been discussing is one which may occur in new-type tests, but need not do so to any great extent. Its effect upon the validity of the tests has been greatly exaggerated by critics owing to their faulty views of the nature and organization of mental abilities.

Defects Due to the New-type Medium of Expression.—Our next objection is of a different order. It does not try to point out something which new-type tests fail to measure, but rather to show that they measure a good deal over and above the abilities which we actually want to assess ; and that this extra factor, having little educational significance, seriously distorts and reduces the validity of all new-type test results. Some of the most ardent advocates of new-type testing, e.g. Ballard (1923), do not seem to have taken this criticism into account. An excellent account of it may be found in Hawkes and Lindquist (1937).

If the reader will analyse carefully the processes which take place in his own mind when answering the new-type questions above, he is likely to find a good deal going on besides the recollection and application of his knowledge of the subject. He must first study the instructions to discover what he has to do in each question, and then manipulate his knowledge in such a way as to fit it in with the requirements of the question. In a multiple-choice question he may arrive at the right response, not because he is certain that he knows it, but because he has eliminated the incorrect ones.   Sometimes a single word in the question or in the provided response will enable him to choose correctly, without his having to think out the full implications of all that is printed.   Some questions may, unknown to the author, contain clues to the correct responses which do not require any knowledge whatsoever of the subject. But if the reader is a sufficiently sophisticated new-type examinee, he will at once take advantage of such faults in construction.   Examples of these irrelevant clues are given in the next chapter.   Unfortunately, the questions which are most liable to contain such errors are those that aim to evoke ' understanding ' rather than ' reproduction.' Straightforward questions which ask primarily for factual information (e.g. Nos. 27–33 and 42–47) are generally free from them.   But more elaborate questions (e.g. Nos. 34–41, 48–54) involve a great deal of ' disentangling ' and complex inference.   The ability to do such questions may depend rather largely on the examinee's previous experience and practice with such tests, or upon some unknown group factor, and not solely on his knowledge of the subject being tested.

Such sources of unreliability and invalidity may be much reduced if the examiner is sufficiently skilled in anticipating all the diverse mental processes which examinees may employ, but they are likely to be eliminated only if he falls back on questions of the simple-recall type, and asks merely for scraps of information.   Actually no examiner can foresee all the possible weaknesses in his questions, for investigation shows that even tests constructed by experts may contain items whose validity is very low, or sometimes negative.   That is, these items are done no better, and sometimes worse, by good than by poor students.   A difficult multiple-choice item, for example, may contain wrong alternatives which are sufficiently plausible to deceive the majority of good students, but which are beyond the comprehension of the poor students, who consequently just guess, and often guess rightly.   Or the correct answer may contain some unsuspected ambiguity which is not noticed by mediocre students, who therefore choose it, but which is noticed by good students, who therefore reject it. Such faults in construction are still more likely to occur in tests devised by amateurs.

It was shown in the previous chapter that many of the defects of the orthodox examination derived from the fact that examinees have to formulate or express their knowledge and ability in a distorting medium, namely essays, and that examiners disagree in their interpretation and evaluation of these complex mental products. We see now that much the same is true of new-type examinations. Examinees have to express their knowledge and ability in a different but perhaps still more artificial medium. This 'roundaboutness,' and the complexity of the mental processes involved in arriving at their answers, undoubtedly reduce the validity of their marks.

The Subjectivity of New-type Tests.—A final defect in new-type tests, which has been entirely neglected by the majority of writers, is that they are, in a sense, just as subjective as essay-type examinations. Only the personal element enters, not in the marking, but in the setting of the questions. Pullias (1937) has recently demonstrated that when two or more examiners construct their own new-type test papers, intending to cover precisely the same field of knowledge and ability, and apply them to the same pupils or students, the average correlation between the two sets of marks is only of the order of $+ 0.50$. This figure may be unduly low because the examiners were teachers who may not have been highly skilled in test construction. Yet some thirty-five different teachers took part in the experiment, all of whom habitually employed new-type tests, and the results were very similar in different school subjects, and among pupils of various ages. Pullias further found that standardized educational tests, which were alleged to measure ability in the same school subjects, only yielded an average inter-correlation of $+ 0.68$. In some instances the coefficients were decidedly higher ($+ 0.8$ to $+ 0.9$), in others very much lower ($+ 0.2$ to $+ 0.3$).

How may we account for such results ? Actually the sources of unreliability described on pp. 224–33 apply here too. These were :

1. Actual changes in the examinees, or function fluctuation.

2. Inadequate sampling. As already mentioned (p 238), this should be much less prominent in new- than in essay-type examinations, especially if the instructions given at the beginning of the next chapter are followed. The trouble is not so much lack of thoroughness of the questions as the subjectivity of their selection.

3. Statistical defects. These can arise, not because different examiners adopt different scales of marks, but because the average level, and the range, of difficulty among their questions may differ. Such inconsistencies can, however, readily be eliminated, nor did they affect Pullias's correlations.

4. Subjectivity. The essay-examination is subjective because the examiner has to analyse the field of ability and decide which aspects are most important, and his personal opinion determines which characteristics of the examinees shall be assessed as good or bad. The new-type examination is subjective because the examiner has to perform a similar process of analysis in choosing questions, and in providing the good and bad answers between which the examinees are to discriminate. Again, the essay-examiner is unable to maintain objectivity because he must translate the answers presented to him, or ' penetrate through the medium of expression ' in order to discover the examinees' real merit. The new-type examiner carries out an equivalent translation when formulating his questions. Hence different examiners will formulate questions about a given topic differently, in just the same way that different essay-examiners will translate differently the answers to an essay-question on this topic.

Pullias points out that the main stages in examining—(a) constructing questions, (b) answering questions, (c) evaluating answers—in reality constitute a single whole.

The new-type examiner has, indeed, eliminated subjectivity from (c), but at the cost of greater subjectivity in (a). And his personal opinion has inserted itself into (b), since his questions embody a good deal of what, in essay-examinations, is normally carried out by the examinees.

Now that we recognize this subjectivity as the chief flaw in new-type tests, we should be able to control and reduce it more readily than in essay-examining. Nevertheless, we must certainly conclude that both types of examination are imperfect mental measuring instruments, and open to much the same objections. Conclusive evidence as to their relative validity is not easy to obtain, since usually it is only possible to compare their marks with the marks on subsequent, equally fallible, examinations. But by pooling the marks from several papers of both types, from class teachers' estimates, etc., a fairly good criterion may be achieved. And according to this, neither the essay-type nor the new-type is definitely superior (cf. Lee and Symonds, 1933). The evidence of the superior validity of new-type tests which Ballard (1923) puts forward is quite unconvincing. Certainly there is no proof that the application of new-type tests in university entrance or scholarship examinations would give appreciably better or poorer predictions of ultimate university success than at present. Since, however, the errors which reduce the validities of the two are different, it follows that they measure somewhat different aspects of ability. Hence by combining them the respective errors partially cancel one another out, and the total validity is definitely superior to that of either of the separate types. And as certain features of a scholastic subject may be more readily tested by the one, other features by the other, each should be employed in the spheres to which it is best adapted.

CHAPTER XIII

CONSTRUCTION OF NEW-TYPE EXAMINATIONS

THE first stage in the construction of a new-type examina
tion should be the preparation of a detailed statement of
what the examination is intended to measure. A list of
the topics which it is to cover should be written out, and
a rough assessment made of their relative importance, for
example on a 1 to 5 scale. Suppose that the sum of all
these assessments comes to 75, and that the examination
is to last two hours. Probably about 150 questions will
be needed. In that case each topic assessed as 1 in im
portance should eventually be covered by two questions,
each assessed as 5 by ten questions, and so on. Naturally
this distribution of questions need not be enforced mechani
cally ; but the principle of allotting most questions to the
most significant parts of the field *is* important. If the test
is designed simply to show the acquaintance of students
with a particular textbook, the questions dealing with each
topic may be proportioned to the number of pages on the
topic in the textbook.

We have already stressed the point that questions should
not deal with trivial details merely because these are the
easiest to set. It is very unwise also for teachers to take
sentences straight out of textbooks and turn them into
true-false or completion items. If this is done, the
examinees will assuredly begin to study their textbooks
with an eye to such sentences, and will try to learn them
off by rote rather than to understand them. Textbook
sentences may occasionally be adapted as *wrong* answers
in multiple-choice questions, since they may then trap the
parrot-learner.

When the teacher and the examiner are one and the same

258

person, suitable questions, or ideas for questions, are likely to occur to him while he is conducting the work of the class. These should be noted down and filed ; they will save him much time and effort when the examination has to be made up. No examiner should expect to be able to devise a complete test at one sitting, unless it is intended to last only about a quarter of an hour. He will soon discover for himself his speed of work, and will set aside sufficient hours, on a number of different days, to enable him to carry out the construction efficiently. The time needed will, of course, be much reduced if he can take over some of the questions from previous papers which he has set in the same subject. This is often possible since the papers are usually collected at the end of the examination, and not allowed to circulate freely round the school or university. Before he enters upon the final stage of construction, he should have in hand roughly double the number of questions he is likely to need. Many will have to be rejected for one reason or another, hence he requires plenty of spare ones.

The choice of questions must be governed by an entirely different conception of difficulty from that which prevails in traditional examinations. In accordance with the principles given in Chap. II, the test should be so arranged that the poorest examinees will obtain marks very little above 0%, the best ones very little below 100%, and so that the average will be as near as possible to 50%. (These figures may then later be converted into some more conventional scale.) A few questions, therefore, must be so easy that almost all (say 95%) can manage them, a few so difficult that scarcely any (say 5%) can manage them. Moreover, all intermediate grades of difficulty must be adequately represented. By contrast, all the questions in an ordinary examination are usually arranged to be roughly equivalent in difficulty. It follows that, in a new-type examination, several sections of the work may be omitted altogether if they are likely to be known so well that more than 95% of the students would answer ques-

tions on them correctly. It is a pure waste of time to
include items which everyone can do. Conversely section
of the work may have to be omitted if even the best 5%
are unlikely to be able to answer questions dealing with
them ; such questions would also be useless.

Thus the examiner's next step must be to grade each of
his tentative questions for difficulty, i.e. to assess what
proportions of examinees are likely to get each one right
The grading may be quite coarse, e.g. $A = 5$ to 20%
$B = 21$ to 40%, $C = 41$ to 60%, $D = 61$ to 80%,
$E = 81$ to 95%. These estimates are likely to be highly
inaccurate at first, and to diverge widely from similar
estimates made by other examiners. But if he takes the
trouble to check his predictions after each paper, and notes
how many examinees did actually pass each item, his
capacity will soon improve. The final version of the paper
should contain approximately equal numbers of A, B, C
D, and E items.

What particular form of new-type question to adopt
depends entirely upon the subject-matter. Some things
are more readily expressed in one form, some in another
No certain evidence of the superiority or inferiority of any
type is as yet available. Experiments on this matter have
been carried out ; but the skill of the authors of the items
has not been controlled. Suppose, for example, that
multiple-choice items are found to be more reliable and
valid than true-false ones, this may merely show that the
experimenter is himself better at compiling multiple
choice items. Nor can we definitely claim that different
types measure distinctive abilities. The correlation
between two multiple-choice tests, or two true-false tests
do not appear to be higher than those between a multiple
choice and a true-false test. This indicates that they both
measure the same thing.

There may, however, still be some advantage in probing
the mind by a variety of techniques. And several different
types may be employed in a long paper so as to reduce
monotony. In a short paper this is undesirable, since each

type needs to be prefaced by full instructions, and examinees may have to spend too large a proportion of time in reading the instructions, and in readjusting their 'mental set.' The following rule may be taken as a rough, though not a rigid, guide. If matching items are included, there should be at least five of them, each including 5 to 10 responses. If multiple-choice items are included, there should be at least ten of them. If true-false, simple recall, or completion items are included, there should be at least twenty of each. The numbers of other types of questions should be comparable to these figures.

When the questions have all been chosen they should be rearranged so that all those of any one type are grouped together. In each group the questions should be arranged in estimated order of difficulty, starting with the easiest. If this precaution is omitted, the poor and medium examinees may waste a lot of time attempting difficult items at the start, and fail to reach easier ones which they could do, and the reliability of their results will be reduced.

We will now consider each of the main types.

Simple Recall and Open-completion Type

A question or short problem is followed by a blank space where the answer is to be written. Alternatively certain words or short phrases are omitted from a sentence or paragraph, leaving blank spaces to be filled in. For example : [1]

1A. Who was the inventor of the steam engine ? . . . .
1B. The inventor of the steam engine was . . . .
2. If $y = 2x^3 + \dfrac{9}{x} + 3$, what is $\dfrac{dy}{dx}$? . . . .
3. Ohm's Law states that . . . . $\times$ Resistance = ...
4. When a salt is dissolved in water the molecules break up

[1] The author feels that an apology may be needed for the puerility of some of the illustrative questions in this chapter. They are intended to show the application of the technique to various school and university subjects, at varying levels of difficulty. Preferring to construct fresh ones rather than to quote from published tests, he is limited by the rustiness of his own education.

18

into .... A positive electric charge is carried by the ...., a negative charge by the .... A balanced action takes place whereby $XY \rightleftharpoons$ .... The .... theory provides an explanation of the .... of electricity by salt solutions.

5. A geography test may consist of a map on which numbers, but no names, are printed. Below is a column of these numbers and the examinee is instructed to write opposite each the town or river which it represents.

Each correct answer receives one mark; thus 6 marks may be scored on Question 4.

The advantages of this type of item are, first, its naturalness and its similarity to ordinary questioning; secondly, its freedom from the chance guessing effects which occur in closed or recognition items; and thirdly, the facility with which it may be constructed. This facility, however, is somewhat delusive, and unsuspected flaws are very likely to creep in. The chief disadvantage of the type is that its scope is practically limited to rote knowledge, or skill at simple arithmetical and scientific problems.

A number of hints on construction may be listed as follows.

(*a*) Try to ask only for important items of knowledge.

(*b*) Ensure as far as possible that there is only one right answer, and therefore confine the answers to single words or numbers, or to very short phrases. Some of the blanks in Question 4 violate this rule. The last one might be filled by 'conduction,' 'carriage,' or 'carrying.' If there is any likelihood of alternatives, the examiner should list them all beforehand, and decide which ones to allow as correct. In this instance he would have to decide whether to disallow 'passage.' Examiners may find it easier to conform to both these rules if they think of the answer first, and then build up the question or sentence around it, in such a way that the answer is completely delimited.

(*c*) Keep the questions and sentences as short and as unambiguous as possible, and in particular avoid over mutilation of a completion sentence by inserting too many blanks. A completion sentence should always be looked on as a form of question. See therefore that sufficient words are left to make it an intelligible question. For the same reason, do not put blanks near the beginning of a sentence, which can only be answered by consulting later clauses of the sentence, or later sentences in the paragraph. Most of the blanks should be at the end of the sentences.

(d) Study the whole content of a sentence or question to see that all of it is essential for the production of a correct response. In badly constructed items, it may be possible to deduce the response simply by the exercise of intelligence, without any knowledge of the subject-matter. In others the correct response may be given away somewhere in a later sentence ; or hints may be derived from the grammatical construction. For example, blank spaces should not be preceded by ' a ' or ' an.' An irrelevant clue is provided by the ' an ' in the following example :

6. A piece of land entirely surrounded by water is called an
. . . .

This difficulty could be overcome by wording the sentence as a question, or by printing ' a(n). . . . . '

(e) Never vary the length of the blank space according to the size of the answer expected. Do not even indicate by two or more lines that the answer contains two or more words. These practices would also supply irrelevant clues. See that the spaces are big enough for examinees with large writing.

(f) For purposes of easy marking, it is desirable to arrange for answers to be written in the right-hand margin. It is much more difficult for the eye to pick out answers scattered all over the page. Even the following is rather inconvenient :

Write down the author of each of these plays.
7. The Admirable Crichton . . . .
8. Candida . . . .

One solution is to number the blank spaces and to print

a separate column of numbers opposite which the answer are written, thus :

Write down the authors of each of these plays.
7. The Admirable Crichton   7. ....
8. Candida   8. ....

A paragraph-completion test, with scattered answers, ma be scored more efficiently by constructing a stencil of card board, with holes through which only the answers ar visible when the stencil is laid over the test paper. Unde each hole on the stencil is written the correct answer.

TRUE-FALSE TYPE

This generally consists of a set of statements, approxi mately half of which are true, the rest false. The examine has to indicate which is which. In a spelling test th ' statements ' may be reduced to single words, whos correctness or incorrectness is to be checked. For example

Write a + after each of the following words which is correctl spelled, and a — after each one wrongly spelled.
9. Medecine ....
10. Embarrassment ....
11. Accelerate ....
12. Sieze ....
13. Advertisement ....

A modification which is useful for tests of spelling grammar, and literary knowledge is to instruct th examinee to cross out, or underline, the one word in eac of a set of sentences which is ungrammatical, or wrongl spelled, or wrongly quoted. One example of each is given

14. I met him and she in the town.
15. The ruffian demolished all the aparatus in the laboratory
16. Rule, Britannia ! Britannia rules the waves.

The ordinary true-false type has been commonly use in tests of all subjects, because it is capable of samplin

---

[1] These should perhaps be classed as multiple-choice items, sinc the examinee has to pick out the incorrect word from about half dozen correct ones.

ery quickly a wide range of knowledge, and because xaminers find it easy to construct. But the uncertainties lue to guessing (cf. pp. 247–50) and, still more, its liability o unsuspected errors, have recently made it less popular. Some recommend that it should only be used when the multiple-choice type is ruled out for lack of plausible lternatives. Thus the following are justified since each nvolves only two possible answers :

17. Distance east or west of Greenwich is
known as longitude. True False
18. When summer time starts the clocks
are put back one hour. True False

There is no need to confine true-false items to rote in-ormation. Indeed, questions of general principle, of nterpretation and the like, can well be expressed in this orm. Great care is needed, however, to see that they do ot violate some of the following principles of construction.

(a) Statements should be simply worded, otherwise they re liable to contain sections which are true and sections vhich are false. In general it is best to use sentences vhich contain only a single clause, embodying only a ingle idea ; to word them positively ; and to refrain both rom negatives and from conjunctions such as ' because ' nd ' therefore.' The following examples are ambiguous, nd therefore unsatisfactory.

19. Napoleon lost the battle of Waterloo
ecause his army had insufficient ammunition. True False
20. Beethoven was a great composer who
rote many symphonies, operas, and sonatas. True False

The most crucial part of a statement, which renders it rue or false, should usually come near the end.

(b) It is not easy to construct difficult statements, nor o estimate their degree of difficulty beforehand. They eed to be sufficiently plausible to deceive the examinee vhose knowledge is incomplete, and therefore not too bviously true or false. And the true ones should be just s likely to appear false as the false ones true. At the ame time they must be clearly true or false to the able

examinee, and therefore must not contain 'tricks.
Good students look out for essentials, and so may be tripped
up if errors are introduced into minor details. The follow
ing example is bad for this reason.

21. Water boils at 212° and freezes at 32° C.   True   False

(c) It has been found that certain forms of wording are
much more apt to be used in true than in false statements
or vice versa. Examinees soon get to recognize these, and
so may answer correctly without any knowledge at all of
the subject-matter. The great majority of statements, in
amateur new-type tests, which contain the words : ' All,'
' Always,' ' Never,' ' Impossible,' are false. The majority
of those which contain ' Usually,' ' Often,' and the like
are true. Most very long statements also tend to be true
more often than false. There is no need to discard the
above words altogether, but they should be used with
caution, and, if possible, introduced as frequently into true
as into false statements.

(d) If the number of statements is less than, say, twenty
there should not be an exactly equal division betwen true
and false, else examinees will count up to make sure that
they have checked them half and half.

(e) The order in which the statements appear must, of
course, be entirely random. If the examiner never prints
more than two true or two false statements consecutively
examinees may again discover this and take advantage of
it. One way of arranging is to toss a coin. If it shows
heads, take the easiest of the true items as No. 1. If the
next four tosses are tails, take the four easiest false state
ments as Nos. 2 to 5 ; and so on.

(f) Various methods for recording the responses have
been used : underlining the words True or False, or Yes
or No, drawing a circle round the letters T or F, or writing
the letters T or F. One of the simplest and most satis
factory is to write a + or a − in a blank space at the end
of each statement. These spaces should all be aligned in
a straight column in the right- or left-hand margin.

(g) The correction for guessing, described on p. 248, should be applied, and examinees should be warned of this in the general instructions at the beginning of the test.

MULTIPLE-CHOICE TYPE, INCLUDING BEST REASON AND MATCHING ITEMS

A large number of variants of this type may be distinguished, examples of most of which are quoted below.

(i) The number of alternative responses is usually five, but it may range from seven to three, or even two, according to the number of possibilities implicit in the question. Six- or seven-response questions occupy rather a lot of space. Three- or two-response questions should usually be avoided because they require the application of guessing corrections. In any one new-type test there is no necessity to provide the same numbers of responses for all the questions.

(ii) When the responses consist of single words, they can be printed all on one line, consecutively. They should be enclosed in brackets, and preferably be printed in italics. The examinee is then instructed to underline the one word in each set of brackets which is correct. For example :

22. They (*was, were*) going (*to, too*) London (*too, to*) visit (*their, there*) aunt, (*who, what*) lived (*there, their*).

When, as in most of the remaining examples, the responses consist of several words or phrases, underlining is troublesome both for the examinee and for the marker. The responses may sometimes be printed consecutively and numbered, and the examinee writes the number of his choice in a blank space. For example :

23. What is the function of the sacral autonomic nervous system ? (1) To increase circulation and respiration. (2) To control posture and movements of the limbs. (3) To increase the activity of the reproductive organs. (4) To contract the sphincters of the excretory organs. (5) To inhibit the activity of the alimentary canal. ....3....

This type of question is, however, inconvenient to read, hence it is more usual, as in the examples below, to print the responses in a column.   The examinee indicates his choice by a cross in one of the blank spaces in the margin. Unfortunately this method tends to consume a lot of space.

(iii) The items may be stated in question or in completion form.   Thus Question 23 might equally well commence :

23. The function of the sacral autonomic nervous system is : (1) . . .

(iv) In the ' best reason ' type, the examinee is instructed to check the best of a set of reasons for a given statement. Occasionally a more suitable item may consist in finding the worst reason.   For example :

24. Many investigations indicate that children's intelligence is somewhat affected by environment and education.   Which of the following provides the *poorest* evidence for this conclusion ?
The correlation between the intelligence of orphans and their parents is lower than that between children and their parents who have reared them   .   .   .   .
The average difference between the I.Q.s of pairs of identical twins is higher among those reared apart than among those reared together   .   .   .   .
Children tested before placement in foster homes, and again after several years, show a greater increase in intelligence in the better than in the poorer homes .   .   .   .
Children of professional parents are on the average markedly superior in intelligence to children of unskilled labourers .   .   .   ...×...

(v) Two or three responses, instead of one, may be correct.   Occasionally none of them may be correct.   The instructions should make it absolutely clear to the examinees what is wanted.   For example :

25. Put a cross opposite *two* of the following English painters who are especially famous for their landscapes :

Constable   .. × ....   Reynolds   ....
Hogarth   ....   Romney   ....
Lawrence   ....   Turner   .. × ....

26. Put a cross opposite *one* answer only.

Sir Thomas Browne is best known as the author of :

Fiction   .   . ..
Plays .   .   . .
Poetry.   .   . ..
Works of travel   . ...
None of these   . .. × ....

(vi) The same set of responses may apply to several questions. For example :

Identify the following orchestral instruments by drawing a circle round S for strings, W for woodwind, B for brass, and P for percussion :

27. Clarinet   .   .   . S   Ⓦ   B   P
28. Triangle   .   .   . S   W   B   Ⓟ
29. Double bass   .   . Ⓢ   W   B   P
30. English horn   .   . S   Ⓦ   B   P
31. French horn   .   . S   W   Ⓑ   P

(vii) Matching tests are an extension of the previous category. A number of questions and a number of responses are listed in different order, and have to be fitted together. For example :

32. On the left is a list of Treaties or Peaces, on the right a list of historical developments which were associated with these Treaties. After each of these developments write the *letter* of the Treaty to which it corresponds. Note that some of these letters need not be used at all, and that some may be used twice.

Peace or Treaty of :   Historical Development :

(a) Berlin   Napoleonic empire broken up   ....g...
(b) Frankfort   League of Nations established   ....f...
(c) Paris   German annexation of Alsace-
(d) Tilsit   Lorraine   ....b...
(e) Utrecht   France regains Alsace-Lorraine   ....f...
(f) Versailles   Independence of Holland finally
(g) Vienna   recognized   ....h...
(h) Westphalia   Britain becomes supreme colonial
                       power   ....c...
                       Western powers set the stage for
                       Balkan wars   ....a...

Many matching tests have equal numbers of items in both columns, each item corresponding to one, and only one, in the other column.   Since, however, this makes possible the discovery of responses by a process of elimination, the above plan, with unequal numbers, is superior.   The numbers of items should usually be five to twelve in each column ;   a greater number involves waste of time in searching.   When possible the items in at least one column should be in alphabetical order, to facilitate the search. It may be noted that this type is more compact than ordinary multiple choice, and so saves considerable space.

The multiple-choice type of question is the most generally applicable in educational testing.   Not only factual information, but also quite elaborate reasoning and interpretation can be measured by it.   In the best-reason type, for example, the alternatives provided may be graded in reasonableness ;   but only one answer should be completely correct.   Again in matching tests, the examinees can be required to apply a series of principles to a series of problems.   Very great care, however, is needed in the construction, and the following hints may be useful.

(a) The multiple-choice type should not be used when simple-recall questions would be adequate, i.e. when there is only one definitely right answer to the question.   For example, it would be a waste of time to express arithmetical problems this way :

33. $$\frac{3}{7} \times \frac{28}{6} = \tfrac{1}{2}, 1, 1\tfrac{1}{2}, 2.$$

Indeed, most mathematical problems are better in open than in closed form, since the latter may enable the examinee to work backwards from each answer until he reaches the right question, which is a very different matter from working forwards from the question.

(b) All the responses provided must be sufficiently plausible to be selected by a fair proportion of the examinees.   Otherwise there is no object in including them. The incorrect alternatives can often be made up out of misconceptions and errors which are likely to be prevalent among the examinees. Sometimes, also, they will be selected by many of the poorer examinees if they contain several words or phrases identical with words or phrases in the question or introductory statement. Both correct and incorrect responses should, however, be homogeneous in their mode of expression, length, and other external characteristics. If the correct answer is always longer, or always shorter, than the incorrect ones, examinees may discover this and employ it to their advantage.

(c) Each response should be studied for possible irrelevant clues. For example, each one must be grammatically consistent with the question. This is especially necessary in matching tests. Some testers throw together such heterogeneous items that the examinees may be able to match them without any real knowledge of the subject. The following is an extreme (hypothetical) instance of a bad item which, although supposed to show knowledge of geographical terms, could be answered correctly by inference alone.

34. (a) A geographical line along which atmospheric pressures are equal   Watershed   ....

(b) Scottish lakes or sea inlets   Monsoons   ....

(c) Winds which blow at a certain season in the Indian Ocean   Isobar   ....

(d) A high piece of land from which rivers flow in two or more directions   Contour lines   ....

(e) Lines on a map showing heights above sea-level   Lochs   ....

' Contour lines ' must be (e), because ' lines ' are mentioned in (e). ' Monsoons ' and ' lochs ' must be either (b) or (c), since these are the only remaining plurals. It is unlikely that ' monsoons ' would be printed so nearly opposite its corresponding item, moreover ' lochs ' sounds like ' lakes,' hence ' lochs ' must be (b). (a) and (d) mention ' geographical line ' and ' rivers,' hence ' iso*bar* ' and ' *water*shed ' will probably fit them.

The examiner should remember that a matching test is an extended form of multiple-choice item, and should therefore see that for each item in one column there are at least three items, preferably four or more items, in the other column which constitute possible answers.

(*d*) Not infrequently a better item may be obtained by turning round a partly formulated question into an answer, and making the correct answer into a question. For example :

   35. Emphasis by means of an understatement is called :
           Meiosis   .   . ...×...
           Hyperbole .   . ..
           Euphemism .   . ..
           Metaphor .   . ..

This might be re-formulated as follows :

   36. Meiosis denotes :
       Emphasis by means of an understatement   . ...×...
       An exaggerated rhetorical expression   .   . ..
       Substitution of a pleasant for an offensive ex-
          pression .   .   .   .
       An imaginative simile .   .   .   .

Probably the second form (No. 36) requires a fuller understanding of the subject than does the first (No. 35). A third, perhaps still better form of the question, which would demand the application and not merely the possession of knowledge, would be a set of phrases from among which examinees would select the one showing meiosis. In general the examiner should study each item in an attempt to anticipate all the mental processes by means of which the correct answer may be reached. If any of these processes are not representative of the ability that he wishes to measure, then he should modify the item.

(*e*) It should hardly be necessary to point out that the position of the correct answer in the series must be chosen entirely at random. First and last places should be employed as often as any of the intermediate places.

REARRANGEMENT TYPE

A series of items which normally fall into a certain specific order is listed in disarranged order, and the examinee has to rearrange them. For example : [1]

37. Below is a list of waves or rays. Opposite No. 1 in the right-hand margin, write the *letter* (a, or b, or c, etc.) of the wave or ray with the longest wave-length. Opposite No. 2 write the letter of the wave or ray with the second longest wave-length, and so on down to No. 7.

(a)	Rays from a sodium vapour lamp	1.	....f...
(b)	Waves from a black kettle containing hot water	2.	....d...
(c)	Gamma rays	3.	....b...
(d)	Television transmission waves	4.	....a...
(e)	Rays from the green of the spectrum	5.	....e...
(f)	Wireless telephone waves	6.	....g...
(g)	X-rays	7.	....c...

The mental processes involved in answering this question will naturally depend on what has been taught. If the pupils have been provided with such a list, they may answer by rote recall ; if not, then they may have to perform an elaborate process of analysis and re-synthesis of their knowledge of various branches of physics.

By disarranging the order of phrases in sentences, Ballard (1923) provides a test which, he claims, measures knowledge of sentence structure and of the canons of English style. The time sequence of historical events, the sizes of geographical areas, the order of operations in some chemical or physical experiment, grammatical sequences in foreign languages, and the like, can readily be expressed in this type. It has not, however, been very widely used, probably because of the difficulty of devising a simple and just method of scoring (cf. Sims, 1937). Ballard's (1923) plan seems fairly satisfactory. Award one mark if the first

[1] The reader may wonder why the instructions are not simplified by requiring examinees to write 1 after the item that should come first, 2 after the next, and so on. The reason is that the scoring of such a response would be exceedingly time-consuming, unless the whole of it was correct.

item is correctly identified ; thereafter award one mark for each item which correctly follows the one preceding it. For instance, if an examinee answers Question 37 :

(f) (d) (a) (e) (g) (b) (c)   instead of   (f) (d) (b) (a) (e) (g) (c),

(f) is correctly placed first and scores one ; (d) correctly follows (f) and scores one ; (a) should not follow (d), but (e) and (g) are in correct sequence, and so score two ; (c) does not score, although it is correctly placed last, because it should not follow (b). The total score here is thus 4 marks.

Certain other minor types of question have been described by Ruch (1929), Rinsland (1938), and others. But these all appear to be variants of the simple-recall or completion, true-false, or multiple-choice types.

Final Stages in the Construction of a New-type Test.—The examiner should re-scrutinize every item, try to eliminate all ambiguities, and ensure that the whole of each item is going to function, i.e. that every word or phrase will be essential in arriving at a correct response, and that there is no possibility of obtaining correct responses through irrelevant clues (cf. Hawkes and Lindquist, 1937). This can be done much more effectively if the questions are submitted to other experienced examiners who may detect flaws which the author has not noticed.

Next it is essential to make up comprehensive instructions for each type of question, which will be appropriate to the mental level of the dullest examinees. Unless the examinees are fairly sophisticated to new-type testing, sample questions already answered should be included. In classroom work it is a good plan to provide three samples, one already answered, to read this through with the class and point out why the given answer is correct, and then to ask the class to suggest answers to the other samples, helping any individual members who still do not understand what is wanted.

Attention should then be directed to ease of scoring. If all the answers can be aligned in a column in the right-hand margin, a key can readily be prepared consisting of a sheet for each page of the test, down the left-hand edge of which are written the correct answers in the correct positions.

It might be supposed that as some questions are harder than others, they should be allotted more marks. But actually many experiments show that weighting is hardly worth the trouble. The unweighted total scores correlate almost perfectly with weighted totals. A very simple form of weighting such as the following may be used : award 1 mark to each correct simple-recall or completion response, also to each correct response in a matching item ; give 1 mark to each true-false or two-response multiple-choice item and apply the R–W correction ; give 1 mark to each three-response multiple-choice answer, but neglect the correction for guessing ; give 2 marks to each multiple-choice item where four or more responses are provided.

Although scoring is so rapid and fool-proof, slips do occur, particularly in adding up totals. Either then the marker should go through the papers twice, or else let the students or pupils re-mark their own papers and ask them to bring any errors to his notice.

Finally the examiner will certainly improve his future examining if he takes the trouble to study the difficulty and the diagnostic value of each item. A simple method is to sort the papers into four piles—the quarter with the highest totals, the quarters above and below the median, and the quarter with the lowest totals. The numbers of times each item is correctly answered by members of each group, and by the four groups combined, may be tabulated. The examiner may then compare the actual difficulties of the items with his estimates of difficulty made when setting the paper, and may note whether the proportions of passes for each item ascend regularly from the lowest to the highest group. If they fail to do so he should attempt to discern the flaw in the item which may be responsible for its poor validity.

CHAPTER XIV

IMPROVEMENTS IN EXAMINING

EXAMINATIONS have far too great a burden to bear. They
are supposed to indicate, as shown in Chap. XI, a large
number of only partially related traits and abilities. I
we could define more clearly what it is that we want to
measure, and use for each purpose the most appropriate
instrument, there is no doubt that we could effect a great
improvement in the efficiency of these instruments. Let
us consider first some of the substitutes for examinations
which have been recommended by educationists, and the
functions which they may serve.

Oral Examinations, Viva Voces, and Interviews.—Oral
examinations are, of course, much older methods of educational measurement than written examinations. Their
main defects were pointed out when written examinations
began to take their place, about one hundred years ago
It was recognized that the situation to which successive
candidates are subjected cannot be the same for all, so that
no sure basis exists for a comparison between different
candidates. The examiner's tone of voice, the wording of
his questions, his encouragement or criticism, etc., may
vary widely from one candidate to another. If, as in
school inspections, all the candidates are interviewed in
the presence of one another, the examiner has to pose a
series of *different* questions which are unlikely to be closely
comparable in difficulty. In any viva voce the amount of
time devoted to each candidate is usually so short that
reliable indications of his abilities can hardly be expected.
There is the further defect that the situation may cause
much greater emotional disturbance than does a written
examination. The interviewer may actually wish to take

qualities of temperament and character into account in his assessments, but the emotional qualities which are most prominent during the interview are probably not very typical of the candidate's usual behaviour, nor of any great significance for educational purposes. When care is taken to put the candidate at ease, skilful questioning may, indeed, reveal something of his interests, his attitude to work, and the like, which are educationally relevant. Oral examinations in foreign languages will bring out the candidate's goodness of pronunciation, but cannot be trusted to show his facility in conversation, because of the distorting effects of emotion. For the same reason, viva voces in other subjects cannot throw much light on the candidate's capacity for formulating his knowledge orally. Theoretically they should constitute a valuable supplement to written examinations, since they provide a fresh medium of expression for ability. But investigations have shown that judgments based on interviews tend to be still less reliable than those based on essay-examination answers.

Hartog and Rhodes's (1935) study of the Civil Service interview is particularly apposite. Sixteen candidates were interviewed in the ordinary way by two different boards, each composed of four or five experienced examiners. The members of each board consulted beforehand as to the questions they would ask (but the two boards did not inter-communicate), and had before them the candidates' educational records. During the quarter-to half-hour interviews the members attempted to assess a candidate's alertness, general intelligence, and the suitability of his personality for the Civil Service. After discussion they drew up a final mark. It was found that members of any one board did agree fairly closely in their judgments, but that the two boards had reached widely differing conclusions. The two final marks differed by 12% for the average candidate, in one case by as much as 31%, in another by as little as 1%. The correlation between the two sets of marks was only $+ 0.41 \pm 0.14$. Except for the small number of the candidates, there seems to be no

19

technical flaw in this experiment which would allow us to challenge its depressing results.

Another investigation, described by Hollingworth (1929), proved the complete inability of experienced business managers to agree, on the basis of independent interviews, as to the candidate who would be most suitable for a particular job. From such data one might conclude that the interview and oral questioning, though essential in education for purposes of teaching, are useless for purposes of assessing ability or the results of teaching. In the course of a school year a teacher can undoubtedly build up a fairly comprehensive and reliable picture of each of his pupils' abilities, which may be largely derived from oral work. But the conditions here are very different from those in a brief viva voce. The volume of questioning is far larger, the emotional atmosphere less strained, and the oral answers are supplemented by written work. In contrast to teachers' judgments of ability, their judgments of character are known to be decidedly unreliable, although by no means worthless (cf. Symonds, 1931 ; Vernon, 1938b).

Perhaps the best instance of the value of the interview is provided by the work of vocational psychologists. In advising a child on his career the psychologist applies several objective tests of aptitudes, and takes both medical and educational records into account. But his information as to the child's personality and interests is derived chiefly from an interview. This is conducted informally so as to put the child at ease, and though it follows no stereotyped plan of questioning, it has, in fact, been designed very carefully so as to elicit the child's main traits (cf. Oakley and Macrae, 1937). A further function of this interview is that it enables the psychologist to interpret the test results and other objective records, and to realize their significance in a synthetic view of the child as a whole. Guidance, which is based merely on the mechanical application of tests or examinations, is not successful. But there is ample proof that the guidance given by trained psychologists who adopt these test and interview methods does possess a high degree of predictive validity.   Similar methods are used in vocational selection, i.e. in choosing the best from a number of candidates for a given job.   They are known to work well in this field also, since the psychologist habitually checks his tests and the data for which he asks in the interview, and sees whether they really do enable him to select employees who turn out satisfactorily.

It would seem, then, that the interview, as at present employed in educational circles, is practically valueless, but that in skilled hands it may become a most useful tool. There is no reason other than expense and the scarcity of competent psychologists why the methods of vocational selection and guidance should not be applied in education, both for choosing pupils most likely to benefit from higher education, and for advising them as to the lines of study for which they are best fitted.   We would not claim that perfect predictions could be achieved thereby, but they would probably be greatly superior to those made on the basis of written examinations and ordinary viva voces.

Intelligence and Special Aptitude Tests.—Theoretically, intelligence tests should be able to fulfil one of the functions commonly assigned to examinations much better than examinations do at present, that is the selection of pupils or students with the greatest intellectual *promise*, as distinct from *achievement*.   Among the common definitions of intelligence are : ' learning capacity,' ' educability,' and ' innate ability apart from the effects of schooling.'   They should also be able to measure objectively the qualities which essay-type examinations are supposed to elicit, and which new-type tests are supposed to be incapable of eliciting, such as ' originality, power of thinking, grasp of general principles, etc.'   Experimental investigations indicate that they do have some value for such purposes, but that they need to be employed with caution.   Merely because they are given the name—intelligence tests—they do not necessarily predict very closely the same thing that secondary school or university authorities mean by intelligence. They seem to be most useful among younger children. The Stanford-Binet scale, applied at 6 or 7 years, correlates quite highly with educational achievement for the next few years. Coefficients of $+ 0.70$ or more may be expected. Group tests are applicable from about 9 years, but, as we have seen, are somewhat less trustworthy. Their validity for predicting secondary-school achievement is very moderate. Thomson's (1936) result, derived from large batches of pupils, may be quoted, though some investigators have reported better agreement. He obtained an average correlation of $+ 0.445$ between English and arithmetic special place examination marks and orders of merit supplied by head masters two years later, and a correlation of $+ 0.410$ between intelligence tests and this same criterion. At later ages the figures sink still lower, though American psychologists claim moderate correspondence when tests are applied to incomng freshmen and are compared with subsequent university work.[1] For three years the writer has applied different group tests to university graduate students entering on a one-year course for the training of teachers. In each year the correlation with final training college marks in all theoretical subjects was close to $+ 0.30 \pm 0.04$. Verbal tests generally correlated about equally with science and with arts subjects; non-verbal tests agreed distinctly better with the former than with the latter. Both types of test, however, gave coefficients of less than $+ 0.10$ with final marks for skill in teaching, i.e. with the marks which are chiefly taken to denote the student's merit *qua* teachers (cf. Vernon, 1939).

The reasons for this decline in the value of intelligence tests with age have been indicated in previous chapters. They include the greater degree of homogeneity, and higher standards of selection, among older pupils and students, and the apparent differentiation or specialization

---

[1] The median figure for some eighty such studies summarized by Boynton (1933) is $+ 0.425$. But the heterogeneity of students admitted to American colleges is usually so great that parallel results here would probably be distinctly lower.

of abilities in adolescence and adulthood.   Because of this latter development, attempts have been made to test special aptitudes, or group factors (mathematical, linguistic, etc.), rather than general intelligence, at the post-primary and later levels.   Prognostic tests are intermediate between intelligence and attainment tests.   They try to show, not how much mathematics or English the pupils have previously acquired, but how well they can apply their intelligence plus acquirements to fresh mathematical or linguistic problems.   Unfortunately, abilities have hardly differentiated sufficiently at 11 or 12 years (the age when secondary and technical school pupils are usually selected) for accurate predictions to be possible.   Nevertheless, Earle (1936) has obtained good results with his English and algebra tests.   A good deal of research along these lines at the university level has been carried out in America.   Thus, at Columbia University, the Thorndike Intelligence Examination—a three-hour test which includes educational material—is said to correlate over + 0·60 with first- and second-year marks.   This coefficient is decidedly better than those usually obtained either by ordinary intelligence tests or by entrance examinations. Many colleges apply ' placement examinations ' on entrance, consisting of general intelligence, English, mathematics, science, foreign language, and social studies tests, in order to determine the students' main aptitudes.   There is room for considerable development of such work in our own schools and universities.   So far very little has been published.

Meanwhile, group intelligence tests undoubtedly help at the change-over from primary to secondary education, and would still be quite useful in public school scholarship examinations at 13 or 14 +.   The Board of Education has already recommended their adoption in all special place examinations.   Even if Thomson's figures, quoted above, show them to be no better than the usual English and arithmetic examinations, yet they are measuring a somewhat different aspect of ability from the examinations, and

cover a different part of the ground which we wish to predict. It has often been claimed that selections based on
such tests would be fairer than selections based on examinations, since they eliminate the factors of coaching and cramming, and reveal the pupils' real abilities rather than their
schooling. Unfortunately, as shown above (pp. 191–2),
coaching for intelligence tests is only too easy and too
prevalent. Nevertheless, unpublished tests are available
which can usefully supplement, though hardly replace,
examinations. Beyond the age of 15 or so, the significance
of intelligence tests is so doubtful that they would probably
be better applied by no one except trained vocational and
educational psychologists.

Cumulative Record Cards.—The primary function of
many examinations is to provide a certificate of work done.
Ostensibly this is true of the School and Leaving Certificates, and of university degree examinations, though they
are also often interpreted prognostically. Now, in most
schools the teachers know quite well what work each pupil
has done. Hence there is every reason for making more
use of teachers' records of this work and less use of external
examinations. The former cover the whole ground, the
latter never more than a fraction of it. The former are
collected under everyday conditions, the latter when many
pupils are in an abnormal emotional state due to cramming
and fear of failure. The former are also less likely to produce the degrading effects upon teachers' and pupils'
educational values which are characteristic of public competitive examinations. Teachers' markings of school work
are, of course, just as liable as examiners' marks to
subjectivity and unreliability ; perhaps more so, because
of the prejudices they are likely to possess regarding each
pupil's character and ability, which may influence their
judgment of his written work. But if in the course of his
career a pupil is taught by several different persons, each
of whom records his achievements according to some
uniform system, the cumulative record should yield a fairly
reliable picture. Although, as stated above, the function

of such records should be to certify work done rather than to predict future promise, yet the investigation by the Scottish Council for Research in Education (1936) into the Leaving Certificate showed that teachers' marks did in fact correlate with subsequent university success just about as well as did the external examiners' marks. The many other uses to which cumulative records may be put, such as vocational and educational guidance, have been fully described by Hamley and his collaborators (1937).

The objection which will at once be raised to such schemes is—how are the standards of different schools to be compared ? The best pupil from one school might, in an open competitive examination, be found below the average pupils of certain other schools. Two solutions will at least partially meet this difficulty. Valentine (1938) proposes that at 11 + a general intelligence test should be applied to all the schools under one authority. From this may be deduced the average level and range of brightness in each primary school. The available places in secondary schools may then be apportioned to the primary schools, the greatest number being awarded to those schools known to possess the largest quantity of bright pupils. Finally, each head master may allot these places to the best pupils in his own schools, on the basis of their intelligence test results and their cumulative records of work. An alternative scheme would be for the secondary schools to tabulate for a considerable period the final marks which the pupils had received at their respective primary schools. They would also record the actual performance of these pupils during their secondary school careers. From these data it would soon be possible to determine the relative standards of all the primary schools from which the pupils were drawn. It would be known, say, that the pupil with 60% from school A was likely to be just as good as the pupil with 80% from school B. Hence the numbers of pupils worthy of selection from each school could be deduced. This method is already widely used at the university level in America.

Either of these methods would, of course, require a competent statistician to run it. They would not, as they stand, be appropriate as substitutes for the School or Leaving Certificates or Matriculation examinations. Yet in these instances, too, the relative levels of all schools which submitted fairly large numbers of candidates might be established by means of brief, scientifically conducted attainment and intelligence tests. On the basis of these results each school could be informed as to the number of certificates to which it was entitled. And the respective head masters would be left to decide, from school records, which pupils should be given these certificates.

IMPROVEMENTS IN ORDINARY EXAMINATIONS

Since external examinations will for a long time play a large, though we hope diminishing, part in education, and since even in an ideal system teachers must apply internal examinations, and mark their pupils' work, we must consider carefully the improvements which might be made in the examination as it now is. From the investigations we have described, and from the discussion in previous chapters, the following principles may be deduced.

1. The teacher or examiner should formulate as precisely as possible what it is that he wants to measure. This implies first a clear conception of the objectives or aims to which, in his view, education should be directed. At the primary school level he may be content with the view that education consists in implanting certain traditional knowledge in children's minds, such as the way to work out sums and to parse sentences. This may be one objective in the secondary school and university also, though surely not one of the most important. History, science, foreign languages, and the like do involve the acquisition of a certain body of facts—dates, chemical formulæ, meanings of words, etc.; but they are supposed to possess many additional values. Taste for literature, interest in foreign peoples, scientific habits of mind, ability to apply knowledge to the interpretation of present-day events, are but a

few of the things which we hope to inculcate. In making such an analysis, the teacher must be careful to take into account the facts which psychologists have established in regard to transfer of training, namely that general faculties, like observation, memory, and reasoning, will not be developed merely by the study of some particular school subject, and that indeed these faculties have little real existence. For example, a rational and scientific approach to contemporary problems can be developed by studying typical problems rationally, by conducting discussions and projects, by showing how irrationalities of thinking arise, and so on ; but *not* by the carrying out of stock experiments in physics, nor by memorizing the rules of grammar or logic. A Behavioristic formulation should be helpful : instead of talking in terms of vague mental qualities, we should ask—what can the educated pupil or student *do* in each specific field of study, or in the world at large, which the uneducated one cannot do ; and what are the precise elements of our teaching which are supposed to confer upon him these capacities ?

Having formulated as candidly as possible our general philosophy of education, we can ask which of these objectives are to be examined. We may decide that desirable moral conduct and social adjustment cannot be expressed in written work.[1] But each objective should be considered from the point of view—what can the educated pupil write, or what problems can he solve, which the uneducated one cannot.

The external examiner, who has not been responsible for teaching the examinees, should adopt a similar procedure in deciding what his examination is meant to measure. He needs, however, to be especially careful to emphasize ' can ' rather than ' ought ' in his analysis. It is merely futile for him to complain that teachers are not doing their work properly, and to insist that examinees must conform

---

[1] Teachers should, however, attempt to assess these qualities and record them on the pupils' cumulative records cards (cf. Hamley, *et al.*, 1937).

to intellectual standards which may be current among persons like himself, but which are quite unattainable by children or immature students. His job is to set tasks which will differentiate the better pupils who exist in real, not ideal, schools, from poorer ones. If he is supposed to pick out, say, the best 30%, but formulates objectives which even the best 1% can hardly achieve, then he is not doing his work efficiently and is creating unnecessary difficulties for himself when the time for marking arrives.

A group of persons, such as a head master and his staff, or a board of examiners, should be able to carry out such analyses much more logically and thoroughly than can any one person, however clearheaded he may be, since they can criticize one another's ideas.

Finally, the conclusions of this analysis should be communicated by the examiners to their prospective examinees, or by the teachers to their pupils. At the present time examining frequently degenerates into a battle between the examiners who try to catch out their victims, and examinees who try to find out what their examiners really want, and what are their personal prejudices, by conning the papers they have set in the past. All this is a stupid waste of everybody's time.

2. Having decided upon the abilities that he wishes to measure, the teacher or examiner should consider the form of examination which will be most appropriate for each of them. French conversation, qualitative chemical analysis, and other capacities obviously require special types. But in most instances the important point to be settled is whether the examination should be new-type, essay-type, or a mixture. Two pertinent considerations in this connection are the number of examinees, and the examiner's own skill in constructing new-type questions. If the numbers are very small, he may be justified in shirking the extra expenditure of time required by objective examining. And he should know from past experience that he is more successful in devising new-type measures of some things than of others.

Generally speaking, any kind of factual information, or straightforward skills, such as the carrying out of arithmetical operations or grammatical analyses, should be examined in new-type form, instead of being left to the vagaries of subjective marking.   This need not mean that only trivial and unrelated items of knowledge or skill should be included.   Good questions, as we have seen, can bring out the examinees' ability to interpret the significance of facts, grasp of general principles, and application of such principles to specific new problems.   True, there are many dangers in these more elaborate items, but they are hardly as serious as the dangers of trying to discover *all* the underlying abilities of the examinees from their answers to essay questions.

We admit, however, that many important aspects of ability may be displayed more clearly in essay-type answers or (with subjects such as mathematics and physics) in the working out of long and complex problems.   Literary style of composition, imaginative qualities and originality, evidence of the examinee's interest in the subject and of his own thinking about it, are some of the things which the examiner may wish to elicit, even if he can never hope to measure them perfectly reliably.   If the examination is designed primarily to bring out qualities such as these, then the examinees should be told so, and should be informed that amount and accuracy of information will not, in this instance, be taken into consideration.   Frank directions about what is wanted are particularly desirable when the same examination includes some new-type and some essay-type questions.

3. If, for one reason or another, essay-type questions have to be maids-of-all-work, then the examiner should ask himself which parts of the total field to be examined are the most important.   Knowing that his questions can sample only a fraction of it, he should avoid the less essential parts, even at the risk of his questions being easily ' spotted ' beforehand.   Overlapping among the questions is obviously undesirable also, since it is wasteful to cover

any one part twice over. With each question, the length
of time needed for a reasonable answer should be considered, so that the examinees shall not be set too much,
nor too little, to do in the period allowed. Finally,
although it may not be possible to increase the total
examination time, or the number of papers, yet the
examiner should keep in mind the unrepresentativeness of
single papers, and the desirability of improving reliability
by such increases.

4. Perhaps the most important quality in a good examiner is his ability to foresee the sort of answers he will
get, both through his insight into the minds of pupils or
students, and through his experience of their answers in
the past. If in formulating each question he possesses a
clear conception of the probable answers—good, average,
and bad—the following advantages are likely to accrue.
The questions will be simply worded, free from ambiguities,
and they will not be interpreted in such divers ways that
the answers are too heterogeneous to be compared, or
marked consistently. The questions will also be appropriate in difficulty, not, that is to say, the type of questions
which no one but the examiner himself could answer
adequately. Most important of all, the production of
answers to these questions will really bring into play the
abilities which the examination is aiming to measure.
When, later on, the examiner reads and marks the answers,
he should continually be trying to improve this 'faculty,'
by noting how far his expectations are fulfilled. Every
question may be regarded as an experiment in forecasting
which, although never likely to be completely successful,
may become progressively more so with practice.

In this, as in all other branches of examining, two
opinions are likely to be better than one, three than two.
A board of four or five will perhaps be the most efficient.

5. When essay-type questions call for answers of a
largely factual nature, a detailed scheme of marking should
be drawn up. This is especially necessary when several
different examiners each mark a certain proportion of the

papers. Experiments indicate that it will reduce their variability by roughly one-half. But a single examiner will also greatly improve his consistency if he decides beforehand just what points to look for, and marks these objectively.

In assessing the more general qualities which essay answers are supposed to bring out, the quality scale method cf. p. 40) should be adopted. The examiner should always be on the alert to ensure that he is judging the scripts solely on the basis of the criteria which he has previously formulated, that he is not being biased by bad handwriting or spelling, by some trick of style which jars on him, or by some personal predilection regarding the subject-matter. All marking which cannot be done objectively should consist largely in introspection : " Why does this strike me as good or bad ? Are these the qualities which I am supposed to be judging, and are they the qualities which I took into account when I selected my standard specimens ? "

Many questions may advantageously be marked both by the qualitative and by the objective (count) systems, the figures then being combined in due proportion. If two or more examiners mark the same, or even a few of the same, scripts, it will be particularly valuable to analyse the reasons for any discrepancies in marks, so as to clarify still further their criteria of good and bad.

One other source of prejudice often arises in marking if the examiner is personally acquainted with some, or all, of the examinees. Either he should carefully avoid looking at the names on the papers, or, if he cannot help recognizing their writing or style, should do his best to disregard any previous impressions he may have formed about them.

6. With the statistical aspects of marking we have already dealt in Chaps. II–IV. But the following main points in subjective marking (as distinct from count scoring) may be recalled. Marking is first and foremost the arranging of scripts in order of merit, or grouping them into categories of merit. It is not an attempt to give an

absolute judgment of the value of each script. All th
answers to one question should be classified into suc
categories before starting on another question. The cate
gories should be, approximately, evenly spaced, and shoul
not exceed ten in number. The frequency distribution o
marks for each question should tend to the normal shape
and the average mark should be very close to 5 (assumin
the middle category of merit to have been labelled 5). Th
dispersion of the distribution should also be approximately
constant for all questions, unless it is desired to weight som
more heavily than others. The final total scores for th
scripts may be converted into an appropriate distributio
of percentage marks by any of the three methods given i
Chap. IV. All decisions as to standards of passing an
failing should be postponed until the process of markin
has been completed.

Finally, we would register a plea for the elimination
whenever feasible, of the harsh system of expressing
examination results in only two, three, or four categorie
(Pass or Fail; First, Second, Third Class, etc.). Many mor
degrees of merit in the total marks can and should be recog
nized. If the system must be retained, then all thos
scripts which fall within, say, 5% above and below eac
borderline should be read a second time, preferably by
more than one examiner, so as to ensure that the fina
decision shall attain the utmost reliability of which human
fallibility is capable.

ANSWERS TO THE EXAMINATION ON PP. 240–6

1. 12.
2. 6.
3. 150.
4. 105 (104 or 106 may also count).
5. 80.
6. 21.
7. 32 (or 31).

8. 17 (or 15–16).
9. positive (or plus).
10. faculties.
11. Spearman.
12. *g*.
13. specific.
14. *g*.
15. group (or common).

16. *F* (or *k*).
17. +.   (In Nos. 17–25,
18. +.   subtract one mark
19. —.   for each incorrect
20. +.   answer. No guess-
21. —.   ing correction need
22. —.   be applied in sub-
23. —.   sequent questions.)
24. +.
25. —.
26. C.
27. C.
28. None.
29. A.
30. B.
31. 69 or 62.
32. — 4 or — 3.
33. C.
34. D.
35. B.

36. D.
37. B.
38. C.
39. A.
40. None.
41. D.
42. E.   (In Nos. 42–47 one
43. D.   point is scored by
44. CF. each   answer   in
45. A.   which one or both
46. CA. letters are given
47. EC. correctly.   Noth-
48. D.   ing is scored by
49. B.   any answer which
50. G.   also includes an
51. A.   incorrect letter.)
52. E.   (For scoring of Nos.
53. F.   48–54, see p. 273.)
54. C.

BIBLIOGRAPHY

* Books or articles recommended for further reading are marked with an asterisk. The prices of books which contain test material are included.

ALEXANDER, W. P. (1932), "A New Performance Test of Intelligence," *Brit. J. Psychol.*, XXIII, 52–63.

*ALEXANDER, W. P. (1935), "Intelligence, Concrete and Abstract," *Brit. J. Psychol.*, *Monog. Suppl.*, No. XIX. Pp. 177.

ALEXANDER, W. P. (1938), "Intelligence, Concrete and Abstract : Note," *Brit. J. Psychol.*, XXIX, 74.

ANASTASI, A. (1936), "The Influence of Specific Experience upon Mental Organization," *Genet. Psychol. Monog.*, XVIII, 245–353.

ARTHUR, G. (1930), *A Point Scale of Performance Tests.* New York : Commonwealth Fund, Vol. I. Pp. 82. Price 7*s*.

*BALLARD, P. B. (1920), *Mental Tests.* University of London Press. Pp. 235. Price 4*s*.

*BALLARD, P. B. (1922), *Group Tests of Intelligence.* University of London Press. Pp. 252. Price 4*s*.

*BALLARD, P. B. (1923), *The New Examiner.* University of London Press. Pp. 269. Price 4*s*.

BLACKBURN, J. M. (1936), "The Acquisition of Skill : An Analysis of Learning Curves," *Industr. Health Res. Board Rep.*, No. 73. Pp. 84.

BLACKBURN, J. M. (1939), "Intelligence Tests," *The Study of Society* (ed. F. C. Bartlett and E. J. Lindgren). London : Kegan Paul. Pp. 154–183.

*BOYD, W. (1924), *Measuring Devices in Composition, Spelling, and Arithmetic.* London : Harrap. Pp. 187. Price 4*s*. 6*d*.

BOYNTON, P. L. (1933), *Intelligence : Its Manifestations and Measurement.* New York : Appleton.

BUEHLER, C. (1938), "The Ball and Field Test as a Help in the Diagnosis of Emotional Difficulties," *Charact. & Pers.*, VI, 257–273.

*BURT, C. (1917), *The Distribution and Relations of Educational Abilities.* London : King. Pp. 93.

*BURT, C. (1921), *Mental and Scholastic Tests.* London : King. Pp. 432. Price 18*s*.

BURT, C. (1923), *Handbook of Tests for Use in Schools*. London : King. Pp. 106. Price 3s. 6d.

*BURT, C. (1935), *The Subnormal Mind*. Oxford University Press. Pp. 368.

*BURT, C. (1937), *The Backward Child*. University of London Press. Pp. 694. Price 20s.

BURT, C. (1938), " Factor Analysis by Sub-matrices," *J. Psychol.*, VI, 339–375.

BURT, C. (1939a), " The Relations of Educational Abilities," *Brit. J. Educ. Psychol.*, IX, 45–71.

*BURT, C. (1939b), " The Latest Revision of the Binet Intelligence Tests," *Eugen. Rev.*, XXX, 255–260.

CATTELL, R. B. (1934), " Occupational Norms of Intelligence, and the Standardization of an Adult Intelligence Test," *Brit. J. Psychol.*, XXV, 1–28.

CATTELL, R. B. (1936), *A Guide to Mental Testing*. University of London Press. Pp. 312. Price 10s. 6d.

*CATTELL, R. B. (1937), " Measurement Versus Intuition in Applied Psychology," *Charact. & Pers.*, VI, 114–131.

COLLINS, M. (1937), " Tests in Common Use for the Diagnosis of Colour Defect," *Rep. 107th Annual Meeting Brit. Assoc. Adv. Sci.*, 207–226.

COX, J. W. (1934), *Manual Skill*. Cambridge University Press. Pp. 247.

*DAVIES, J. B. T., and JONES, G. A. (1936), *The Selection of Children for Secondary School Education*. London : Harrap. Pp. 181.

*DAWSON, S. (1933), *An Introduction to the Computation of Statistics*. University of London Press. Pp. 192.

DREVER, J., and COLLINS, M. (1936), *Performance Tests of Intelligence* (2nd ed.). Edinburgh : Oliver & Boyd. Pp. 56. Price 5s.

*EARL, C. J. C. (1939), " Some Methods of Assessing Temperament and Personality," *The Study of Society* (ed. F. C. Bartlett and E. J. Lindgren). London : Kegan Paul. Pp. 230–256.

EARLE, F. M. (1936), *Tests of Ability for Secondary School Courses*. University of London Press. Pp. 138. Price 5s.

EL KOUSSY, A. A. H. (1935), " Investigation into Factors in Tests Involving the Visual Perception of Space," *Brit. J. Psychol.*, *Monog. Suppl.*, No. XX. Pp. 89.

FARMER, E. (1933), " The Reliability of the Criteria used for Assessing the Value of Vocational Tests," *Brit. J. Psychol.*, XXIV, 109–119.

20

FISHER, R. A. (1930), *Statistical Methods for Research Workers.* Edinburgh : Oliver & Boyd. Pp. 239.

FRASER ROBERTS, J. A., NORMAN, R. M., and GRIFFITHS, R. (1935), " Studies on a Child Population : I," *Annals of Eugen.,* VI, 319–338.

*GARRETT, H. E. (1937), *Statistics in Psychology and Education.* London : Longmans, Green. Pp. 493.

GAW, F. (1925), " Performance Tests of Intelligence," *Industr. Fat. Res. Board Rep.,* No. 31. Pp. 45. Price 2s. 6d.

GOODENOUGH, F. L. (1926), *Measurement of Intelligence by Drawings.* London : Harrap. Pp. 192. Price 7s. 6d.

*GREENE, H. A., and JORGENSON, A. N. (1936), *The Use and Interpretation of High School Tests.* London : Longmans, Green. Pp. 614.

*GUILFORD, J. P. (1936), *Psychometric Methods.* New York : McGraw-Hill. Pp. 566.

*HAMILTON, E. R. (1929), *The Art of Interrogation.* London : Kegan Paul. Pp. 174.

*HAMLEY, H. R., et al. (1937), *The Educational Guidance of the School Child.* London : Evans. Pp. 122. Price 3s. 6d.

HARDING, D. W. (1933), " Psychological Defects of the Examination System," *The Human Factor,* VII, 291–299.

*HARTOG, P., and RHODES, E. C. (1935), *An Examination of Examinations.* London : Macmillan. Pp. 81.

*HAWKES, H. E., and LINDQUIST, E. F., et al. (1937), *The Construction and Use of Achievement Examinations.* London : Harrap. Pp. 497.

*HOLLINGWORTH, H. L. (1929), *Vocational Psychology and Character Analysis.* New York : Appleton. Pp. 409.

HOLZINGER, K. J. (1934), *Preliminary Report on Spearman-Holzinger Unitary Trait Study.* Chicago : Statist. Lab., Dept. Educ., Univ. Chic.

HOLZINGER, K. J. (1937), *Student Manual of Factor Analysis.* Chicago : Statist. Lab., Dept. Educ., Univ. Chic. Pp. 101.

*HUNT, E. P. A., and SMITH, P. (1935), *Teacher's Guide to Intelligence and Other Psychological Testing.* London : Evans. Pp. 94.

*KANDEL, I. L. (1936), " Examinations and their Substitutes in the United States," *Carnegie Foundation Bull.,* No. XXVIII. Pp. 183.

KELLEY, T. L. (1924), *Statistical Method.* New York : Macmillan. Pp. 390.

KENDALL, M. G., KENDALL, S. F. H., and BABINGTON SMITH, B. (1938), " The Distribution of Spearman's Coefficient of

Rank Correlation in a Universe in which All Rankings occur an Equal Number of Times," *Biometrika*, XXX, 251–271.

*KENT, G. H. (1937), " Suggestions for the Next Revision of the Binet Scale," *Psychol. Record*, I, 407–434.

*KNIGHT, R. (1933), *Intelligence and Intelligence Tests*. London : Methuen. Pp. 98.

*LEE, J. M., and SYMONDS, P. M. (1933), " New-type or Objective Tests," *J. Educ. Psychol.*, XXIV, 21–38.

MACDONALD, A. (1938), " A Scheme of Vocational Guidance for Use in an Education Area," *Occup. Psychol.*, XII, 291–301.

McGREGOR, G. (1934), *Achievement Tests in the Primary School*. University of London Press. Pp. 136.

MACMEEKEN, A. M. (1939), *The Intelligence of a Representative Group of Scottish Children*. University of London Press. Pp. 144.

MOWAT, A. S. (1938), *City and Rural Schools*. University of London Press. Pp. 79.

MURRAY, J. (1933), " Arithmetic in Scottish Schools," *Suppl. to Scot. Educ. J.*, No. X. Pp. 7.

NADEL, S. F. (1939), " The Application of Intelligence Tests in the Anthropological Field," *The Study of Society* (ed. F. C. Bartlett and E. J. Lindgren). London : Kegan Paul. Pp. 184–198.

OAKLEY, C. A. (1935), " A New Formboard," *The Human Factor*, IX, 105–108.

*OAKLEY, C. A., and MACRAE, A. (1937), *Handbook of Vocational Guidance*. University of London Press. Pp. 337.

OLDHAM, H. W. (1937–8), " A Psychological Study of Mathematical Ability," *Brit. J. Educ. Psychol.*, VII, 269–286 ; VIII, 16–28.

*PULLIAS, E. V. (1937), " Variability in Results from New-type Achievement Tests," *Duke Univ. Res. Stud. in Educ.*, No. II. Pp. 100.

RAVEN, J. C. (1939), "The R.E.C.I. Series of Perceptual Tests: An Experimental Survey," *Brit. J. Med. Psychol.*, XVIII, 16–34.

*RINSLAND, H. D. (1938), *Constructing Tests and Grading*. London : Harrap. Pp. 323.

*RUCH, G. M. (1929), *The Objective or New-type Examination*. Chicago : Scott, Freeman. Pp. 478.

SCHONELL, F. J. (1932), *Essentials in Teaching and Testing Spelling*. London : Macmillan. Pp. 96. Price 1s. 6d.

*SCHONELL, F. J. (1935), " Diagnostic Tests for Specific Disabilities in School Subjects," *The Testing of Intelligence* (ed. H. R. Hamley). London : Evans. Pp. 80–113.

*SCHONELL, F. J. (1937), *Diagnosis of Individual Difficulties in*

Arithmetic. Edinburgh : Oliver & Boyd. Pp. 115. Price 2s. 6d.

SCOTTISH COUNCIL FOR RESEARCH IN EDUCATION (1933), *The Intelligence of Scottish Children.* University of London Press. Pp. 160.

SCOTTISH COUNCIL FOR RESEARCH IN EDUCATION (1936), *The Prognostic Value of University Entrance Examinations in Scotland.* University of London Press. Pp. 197.

SIMS, V. M. (1937), " A Note on Scoring the Re-arrangement Test," *J. Educ. Psychol.,* XXVIII, 302–304.

*SPEARMAN, C. (1927), *The Abilities of Man.* London : Macmillan. Pp. 415.

SPEARMAN, C. (1939), " Thurstone's Work Re-worked," *J. Educ. Psychol.,* XXX, 1–16.

STARCH, D., and ELLIOT, R. C. (1913), " Reliability of Grading Work in Mathematics," *School Rev.,* XXI, 254–259.

STEEL, J. H., and TALMAN, J. (1936), *The Marking of English Compositions.* London : Nisbet. Pp. 55.

STUTSMAN, R. (1931), *Mental Measurement of Pre-school Children.* London : Harrap. Pp. 368. Price 11s. 6d.

*SUTCLIFFE, A., and CANHAM, J. W. (1937), *Experiments in Homework and Physical Education.* London : Murray. Pp. 194.

*SYMONDS, P. M. (1931), *Diagnosing Personality and Conduct.* London : Appleton-Century. Pp. 602.

*TERMAN, L. M., and MERRILL, M. A. (1937), *Measuring Intelligence.* London : Harrap. Pp. 461. Price 10s. 6d.

THOMSON, G. H. (1932), " The Standardization of Group Tests and the Scatter of Intelligence Quotients," *Brit. J. Educ. Psychol.,* II, 92–112, 125–138.

THOMSON, G. H. (1935), " On Complete Families of Correlation Coefficients and their Tendency to Zero Tetrad Differences," *Brit. J. Psychol.,* XXVI, 63–92.

THOMSON, G. H. (1936), " The Value of Intelligence Tests in an Examination for Selecting Pupils for Secondary Education," *Brit. J. Educ. Psychol.,* VI, 174–179.

*THOMSON, G. H. (1939), *The Factorial Analysis of Human Ability.* University of London Press. Pp. 326.

*THOULESS, R. H. (1930), *Straight and Crooked Thinking.* London : Hodder & Stoughton. Pp. 284.

THOULESS, R. H. (1936), " Test Unreliability and Function Fluctuation," *Brit. J. Psychol.,* XXV, 325–343.

THOULESS, R. H. (1937), " Review of Mr. Whately Carrington's Work on Trance Personalities," *Proc. Soc. Psychical Res.,* XLIV, 223–275.

THOULESS, R. H. (1939a), " The Effects of Errors of Measurement on Correlation Coefficients," *Brit. J. Psychol.*, XXIX, 383–403.

*THOULESS, R. H. (1939b), Scientific Method and the Use of Statistics," *The Study of Society* (ed. F. C. Bartlett and E. J. Lindgren). London : Kegan Paul. Pp. 125–153.

THURSTONE, L. L. (1931), " A Multiple Factor Study of Vocational Interests," *Pers. J.*, X, 198–205.

THURSTONE, L. L. (1938), *Primary Mental Abilities.* University of Chicago Press. Pp. 121.

TULCHIN, S. H. (1934), " Clinical Studies of Mental Tests," *Amer. J. Psychiat.*, XIV, 1237–1248.

*VALENTINE, C. W. (1938), *Examinations and the Examinee.* The Birmingham Printers. Pp. 39.

*VALENTINE, C. W., and EMMETT, W. G. (1932), *The Reliability of Examinations.* University of London Press. Pp. 196.

VERNON, H. M. (1936), *Accidents and their Prevention.* Cambridge University Press. Pp. 336.

*VERNON, P. E. (1935a), " Tests of Temperament and Character," *The Testing of Intelligence* (ed. H. R. Hamley). London : Evans. Pp. 114–132.

VERNON, P. E. (1935b), " Tests in Æsthetics," *The Testing of Intelligence* (ed. H. R. Hamley). London : Evans. Pp. 133–141.

VERNON, P. E. (1935c), " The Significance of the Rorschach Test," *Brit. J. Psychol.*, XV, 199–217.

VERNON, P. E. (1936), " The Matching Method Applied to Investigations of Personality," *Psychol. Bull.*, XXXIII, 149–177.

VERNON, P. E. (1937a), " A Study of the Norms and Validity of Certain Mental Tests at a Child Guidance Clinic," *Brit. J. Educ. Psychol.*, VII, 72–88, 115–137.

VERNON, P. E. (1937b), " The Stanford-Binet Test as a Psychometric Method," *Charact. & Pers.*, VI, 99–113.

VERNON, P. E. (1938a), *The Standardization of a Graded Word Reading Test.* University of London Press. Pp. 43. Price 1s.

*VERNON, P. E. (1938b), " The Assessment of Psychological Qualities by Verbal Methods," *Industr. Health Res. Board Rep.*, No. 83. Pp. 124.

VERNON, P. E. (1938c), " Intelligence Test Sophistication," *Brit. J. Educ. Psychol.*, VIII, 237–244.

VERNON, P. E. (1939), " Educational Abilities of Training College Students," *Brit. J. Educ. Psychol.*, X.

WALTERS, E. (1935), " Retentivity in the Special Senses," *Ability and Knowledge* (by F. C. Thomas). London : Macmillan. Pp. 312–315.

WALTERS, E. H., and THOMAS, F. C. (1929), " Some Notes on the Standardization of Professor Spearman's ' Measure of Intelligence for Use in Schools,' " *J. Exper. Ped.*, VII, 35–42.

WELLMAN, B. L. (1938), " Our Changing Concept of Intelligence," *J. Consulting Psychol.*, II, 97–107.

WHIPPLE, G. M. (1919), *Manual of Mental and Physical Tests*, Vols. I and II. Baltimore : Warwick & York. Pp. 365, 336. Price 21s.

WOOD, B. P. (1921), " Measurement of College Work," *Educ. Adminis. & Supervis.*, VII, 301–304.

INDEX OF NAMES (INCLUDING NAMES OF TESTS)

INDEX OF SUBJECTS